Woman's Book of Baking

EDITED BY Diane Harris

Simon and Schuster / New York

Published by Simon and Schuster
A Division of Gulf & Western Corporation
Simon & Schuster Building
Rockefeller Center
1230 Avenue of the Americas
New York, New York 10020

Designed by Irving Perkins
Manufactured in the United States of America
1   2   3   4   5   6   7   8   9   10

Library of Congress Cataloging in Publication Data

Main entry under title:
Woman's day book of baking.

   Includes index.
   1. Baking. I. Harris, Diane. II. Woman's
day.
TX763.W65   641.7′1   77–22663
ISBN 0-671-22506-5

Contents

The Joys of Baking

BAKING is one of the most rewarding of all the activities in the kitchen, and in recent years more and more people have discovered the pleasures of home baking. They have found that there is something deeply satisfying, almost magical, in transforming simple ingredients into golden brown loaves of bread, flavorful cakes, tender muffins, flaky pies and mouthwatering cookies. And sharing these good things to eat with family and friends makes the satisfaction complete.

The Woman's Day name has long been associated with the best in cooking and baking, and *The Woman's Day Book of Baking* offers a delightfully varied collection of the very finest recipes for yeast breads, coffee cakes, quick breads, pies, cakes and cookies. Chosen with both beginners and experienced bakers in mind, the recipes strike a happy balance between old-time favorites and appealing new treats, between the very easy to make and the more challenging, between simple everyday fare and food for festive occasions. All have been tested time and again in the Woman's Day kitchens and all are precise and easy to follow.

Home-baked breads, both yeast-risen and quick breads, are a great pleasure to make and to eat. There is almost nothing quite as satisfying as a slice of freshly baked homemade bread. In our bread sections, we have included breads of every variety—delectable white loaves, hearty whole-grain favorites, fruit-laden holiday breads, golden egg breads, nut breads, and a variety of light and crusty rolls. You will find Old World favorites and brand-new breads that are unusually rich in protein and bran. And the collection of muffin recipes is the most tempting we have seen anywhere. Because muffins are so quick to mix and quick to bake, you might want to start with an especially appealing muffin recipe. That would be a great introduction to baking.

If you love the taste of home-baked pies, but you think of them as difficult to make, you will be delighted by our section on pies. We offer a number of super-easy pie crust recipes, which even a beginner can make with assurance, as well as many quick-to-make fillings of all kinds. And when a recipe does require more time and care, you will find that the results are well worth it.

Many people say that the smell of a cake baking in the oven is as good as the taste. Our own feeling is that great as home-made cakes smell, they taste even better. In choosing the cake recipes for this collection, we have stressed variety and exceptional flavor. We think you will agree that these are some of the best cakes ever. There are outstanding gold cakes, white cakes, chocolate cakes, spice cakes, pound cakes, fruitcakes, cheesecakes and cupcakes. And in every category, we offer both simple recipes that are quick to make and festive ones for special occasions.

Woman's Day is famous for its cookie recipes and we have chosen a truly delightful collection of cookies for this book. Naturally we have included such all-time favorites as Crisp Chocoate-Chip, Oatmeal-Raisin, Sugar Cookies, Brownies and Hermits, but we have also selected some very popular newer cookies to add to your pleasure. And for Christmastime eating, giving and tree-trimming, we offer some of the best-loved Christmas cookie recipes from around the world. To celebrate any holiday you can transform almost any cookies into holiday cookies by decorating them with colored sugars, icings, sprinkles, raisins and other suitable decorations. That is part of what makes cookie baking creative and so much fun.

All in all, we think you will find *The Woman's Day Book of Baking* a superlative collection of recipes for good things to eat. With so many wonderful recipes to choose from, we feel sure that you will recapture old pleasures, discover new favorites and come to savor the joys of baking.

Baking Basics

YOUR OVEN

Success in baking depends on accurate oven temperatures. If you are new to baking or if you bake only occasionally, the temperature control on your oven can be inaccurate by many degrees and you can be unaware of it. It is wise to check the accuracy of your temperature control before you start baking by using a portable oven thermometer. Put the thermometer in the oven and turn the control to the desired temperature. After 10 to 15 minutes, check to see whether the temperature registered by the oven thermometer matches the setting of the control. If not, you should have the control fixed. Of course, if you want to bake on the day you make the test, you can simply change the temperature setting. But in the long

15

run, it is more convenient to have the control fixed than to continually have to set it higher or lower to compensate for the error.

THE RIGHT PANS

In most forms of cooking, the size of the pan you choose does not have much effect on the result—unless you choose one much too large or much too small. In baking, if you use the wrong size pan, you can change the results of the recipe. Woman's Day baking recipes always specify the size of the pan required. Using that size is important, particularly in cake recipes. Sometimes a bread that is baked in the wrong size pan will simply have a misshapen appearance but will taste fine. With cakes, the wrong pan can lead to a thoroughly unsatisfactory result. When you are baking cookies, if you have a high-sided roasting pan rather than a cookie sheet, turn the pan over and bake the cookies on the bottom of the roasting pan. Using it right side up is undesirable because the high sides interfere with the flow of heat.

EXPERIMENTING WITH RECIPES

Since baking is a much more exact process than other forms of cooking, adding a pinch of this and teaspoon of that is not recommended. You can add a small amount (½ cup) of toasted wheat germ, nuts or candied fruits to a bread recipe or the same amount of nuts or raisins to a cookie recipe without altering the results, but other changes in recipes, unless you are a very experienced baker, can ruin the end product.

A WORD ABOUT INGREDIENTS

EGGS

Large eggs should be used in all the recipes. Eggs are easier to separate when they are cold, but egg whites can be beaten to greater volume when they are at room temperature.

FLOUR

White flour, both all-purpose and cake flour, is available at supermarkets. Whole wheat flour, cracked wheat, rye flour and other unusual flours are often not stocked by supermarkets. You can usually buy them in health food stores.

HONEY

Measuring Honey

When baking with honey, measure the shortening first and then measure the honey in the same cup. The honey will slide out more easily.

Storing Honey

Store honey in a dry place, because it absorbs and retains moisture. Do not refrigerate. Refrigeration or freezing won't harm the color or flavor, but it may hasten granulation. If granulation, or solidification, does occur, put the container in a bowl of warm water (no warmer than the hand can bear), until the crystals melt and the honey liquefies. Mild-flavored clover honey should be used in baking. The moisture content varies in the less common types of honey, such as tupelo, sage, orange-blossom, buckwheat and many others, and this may unbalance the recipe. Serve these stronger types as spreads in order to appreciate more fully their unusual flavors.

DRIED FRUITS

To Snip Dates and Raisins

When cutting up dates and raisins for use in baking, use a scissors. Oil scissors or rinse in hot water before using.

To Plump Prunes

Put fruit in a jar or bowl and cover with cold water, allowing 1 quart water to 1 pound prunes. Cover and soak 24 hours. Refrigerate and use as needed.

To Store Dried Fruits

Store fruits tightly covered in cool, dry, well-ventilated place; in hot weather, in refrigerator.

COCONUT

Buying Fresh Coconuts

Fresh coconuts are available year-round but are at their peak during the early winter months. Select coconuts heavy for their size that sound full of liquid when shaken. Avoid those with wet or moldy eyes.

Storing Fresh Coconuts

Store unopened coconuts at room temperature. Grated coconut and unused pieces should be kept tightly covered in refrigerator or freezer.

Preparing Fresh Coconuts

Pierce eyes in end of coconut and drain off liquid; reserve if needed in individual recipe. Put coconut in shallow pan in moderate oven (350°F.) 20 minutes, or until shell cracks in several places. Remove from oven and pound with hammer or mallet to crack shell open. Remove coconut meat and cut off black outer shell. Coconut pieces can then be eaten like any nut. Or for use in recipes, grate meat on grater or whirl a few small pieces at a time in blender until finely grated or shredded.

Packaged Coconut

Sweetened coconut, in cans or bags, comes flaked, grated (cookie coconut) and shredded. Length of shreds and moisture content vary. Frozen unsweetened coconut and coconut syrup, honey and chips are also available. Coconut syrup is made by adding sugar to the emulsion obtained by pressing coconut and cooking it to form a syrup. It is used for milk shakes and as a sauce. Coconut honey is similar but the cooking time is longer and the brown skin on the coconut meat is not removed. The honey is used as a spread. Coconut chips are thin chips of toasted coconut, salted and used as a snack.

Yeast Breads and Rolls

IN RECENT YEARS there has been a great surge of interest in baking yeast breads at home. If you have already baked bread, you know the reasons for the enthusiasm. If not, you have a richly satisfying experience to look forward to. Every step in the process—from mixing the dough to removing the crusty brown loaves from the oven—has its own special pleasure. Some people say that making bread cheers them up when they are down and makes them feel even better when they are up. However, there are other people who still think that baking yeast breads is something only the very brave should attempt. They talk about yeast with awe and mistrust, as though it were the villain of a science fiction movie. In fact, yeast is quite easy to work with, and anyone can learn the simple rules of bread baking. We think a great place to begin would be with any of the wonderful recipes in the collection we have assembled here. We have included a variety of white breads, hearty whole-wheat breads, oatmeal loaves, light and dark ryes, golden cornmeal breads and a moist, flavorful potato bread. There are fruit breads, nut breads and cinnamon breads. And some of the best dinner rolls you have ever tasted.

Because of the various steps involved in making yeast bread—mixing the dough, kneading it, letting it rise (sometimes twice), and baking the loaves—you have to plan your schedule on the day or night that you bake. You don't have to stand by in attendance, but you do have to be around to punch down the risen dough, to shape the loaves, and to check near the end of the baking time to make sure the loaves come out at just the right moment. So read through the recipe you intend to make before you begin and write out a little schedule. You can sandwich in a number of other activities if you plan ahead. And the joy of producing golden brown, soul-satisfying loaves of bread is worth the effort.

TIPS FOR MAKING YEAST BREADS

YEAST

Yeast is a living plant that needs air, food and moisture to grow. It will grow best in a warm environment. A temperature that is a little too high can cause yeast to grow too fast or if it is a lot too high, it kills the yeast. Chilling or freezing yeast simply retards its growth. Yeast is sold in both dry and compressed cake form but the dry form is more widely available and we have listed that kind in our recipes. However, the two kinds can be used interchangeably —substitute a ¾-ounce cake of compressed yeast for every ¼-ounce package dry yeast. Make sure you use water at the ideal temperature for each. Dry yeast calls for warm water (105°F. to 115°F.), whereas compressed yeast requires lukewarm water (80°F. to 90°F.). At first you may want to use a candy thermometer to test the temperature, but after a few ventures in bread baking, you will be able to gauge the correct temperature of the water simply by testing it with your fingers. Also note that any liquid you add to the yeast-water mixture should be at the same temperature as the mixture.

Before you add yeast to water in a mixing bowl, rinse out the bowl with warm water to assure that water added to the yeast stays at the proper temperature.

FLOUR

You do not have to sift before measuring flour. Simply spoon flour into a measuring cup and level off. Measure out into a bowl, or onto a sheet of waxed paper or aluminum foil, the largest amount of flour called for in the recipe. Flours vary in the amount of moisture they will absorb and this means that you may not need the full amount. Also remember you should save out about ½ cup of the flour to sprinkle over the bread board and to flour your hands. Mix in flour until you have a dough similar in consistency to biscuit dough, or follow the advice given in the individual recipe.

QUICK METHOD

In recent years a new somewhat quicker method for mixing yeast breads has been developed. If you like you can convert most yeast bread recipes to use this method. In the large bowl of an electric mixer, add dry yeast, approximately 2 cups of the flour and all the other dry ingredients. Heat liquid to 120°F. to 130°F. and add butter or other shortening. When shortening has melted add liquid mixture to dry ingredients and mix at medium speed for about 2 minutes. Add more flour, a cup at a time, until half the flour called for in the recipe has been used. After that you gradually beat in the remaining flour with a wooden spoon or your hand until the dough is the consistency called for in the recipe.

KNEADING

Use a board lightly sprinkled with flour. Rub a little flour on your hands. Shape the dough in a round ball and fold it toward you. Using heels of hands, push dough away with rolling motion. Turn one quarter-turn around. Repeat until dough is smooth and elastic.

Some heavy-duty mixers come equipped with a dough hook for kneading bread.

If you are using a dough hook to knead the dough, be careful to follow manufacturer's directions. Knead for 3 to 4 minutes at low speed on the mixer.

RISING

Doughs need an even temperature of 80°F. to 85°F. for rising. There are several ways to provide a warm place.

Always cover bowl or loaves with a slightly damp kitchen towel.

1. Set bowl on rack in an unheated oven with large pan of hot water on another rack beneath it.

2. Warm bowl with hot water and dry before greasing it for dough.

3. Fill a large pan two-thirds full with hot water, put a wire rack on top and set bowl on it.

4. Set bowl in a deep pan of warm, not hot, water.

5. Put bowl in draft-free place near, not on, range or radiator.

TESTING FOR DOUBLED IN BULK

Press tips of two fingers lightly and quickly ½″ into dough. If dent remains, dough is doubled.

BAKING

When baking bread in glass loaf pans, use an oven temperature 25° less than specified in recipes. This prevents formation of a thick crust (undesirable to some). Baked bread, unless otherwise noted, should sound hollow when bottom and sides are tapped with fingers.

COOLING

Remove from baking sheet or pans and put on wire racks. Cover with towel for a soft crust; leave uncovered for crisp crust. For extra good flavor, brush hot bread and rolls with soft butter.

STORING

Yeast bread kept at room temperature gets dry in 2 to 3 days; it keeps better (at least a week) if refrigerated. But for best flavor serve at room temperature or toasted.

FREEZING

After bread or rolls are thoroughly cooled, wrap in foil, freezer paper, heavy-duty plastic wrap or airtight plastic bags. Press out all air by smoothing wrap close to bread; seal tightly. Properly frozen bread will retain its freshness for 3 months.

THAWING

Thaw in original wrapper and unwrap just before serving.

Batter White Bread
MAKES 2 LOAVES.

> 2 packages active dry yeast
> 6½ cups all-purpose flour
> 3 tablespoons sugar
> 3 teaspoons salt
> 2 tablespoons soft shortening

In large bowl of electric mixer, sprinkle yeast into 2¾ cups warm water; let stand a few minutes, then stir until dissolved. Add 3¼ cups flour, the sugar, salt and shortening. Blend at low speed, then beat 2 minutes at medium speed (or beat by hand). Beat in remaining flour by hand. Cover and let rise until doubled (about 45 minutes). Stir batter, beating hard ½ minute. Spread in 2 greased 9″ x 5″ x 3″ loaf pans. Let rise until doubled (about 20 minutes). Bake in moderate oven (375°F.) 40 to 50 minutes.

Basic White Bread
MAKES 2 LOAVES.

Following mixing, kneading and first-rising techniques of this basic recipe for a variety of breads, substituting amount and kind of flour, shaping of loaves and/or baking as specified in each variation.

> 1¼ cups water
> 1 cup milk
> ¼ cup butter or margarine
> About 6 cups all-purpose flour
> 3 tablespoons sugar
> 2 teaspoons salt
> 1 envelope active dry yeast

In saucepan heat water, milk and butter until very warm (120° to 130°). Butter will not be melted completely. In large bowl of mixer combine 2 cups flour, the sugar, salt and yeast. Add liquid mixture, beating at low speed, then heat at high speed 3 minutes. Add 1 cup flour and beat 5 minutes longer. Stir in 2½ cups flour or enough so that dough comes away from sides of bowl. Turn out on lightly floured surface. Knead, adding up to ½ cup flour, 8 to 10 minutes or until dough is smooth, elastic and appears blistered beneath surface. Place in large greased bowl, turning to grease top. Cover with plastic and dish towel. Let rise in warm (85°) draft-free place about 1 hour or until doubled. Punch down and knead until smooth. Cut in half, cover with plastic and towel and let rest 15 minutes. To shape, roll out each half in 12″ x 9″ rectangle. If dough sticks, lightly flour surface and rolling pin.

Starting at narrow edge, roll as for jelly roll. Seal ends and seam by pinching with fingers. Place each roll, seam side down, in greased 8 x 4 x 3-inch loaf pan. Cover with plastic and towel and let rise in warm draft-free place until doubled, about 45 minutes. Bake in 400° oven 25 to 30 minutes or until loaves sound hollow when tapped on bottom. (If using glass pans, lower temperature to 375°.) Remove from pans and cool on racks.

Note Bread may be baked in 9 x 5 x 3-inch loaf pans, but loaves will be slightly smaller.

BREADSTICKS

Prepare Basic White Bread dough. To shape breadsticks divide dough in fourths, then roll out each in 12" x 7" rectangle and cut in twelve 7" x 1" strips. With fingertips roll each strip in 8" to 10" rope. Place about 2" apart on greased cookie sheets. Cover and let rise. Brush with mixture of 1 egg yolk and 1 tablespoon water. If desired, sprinkle with sesame, poppy or caraway seed or coarse salt. Bake in 400° oven 15 to 20 minutes or until golden. Makes 48 sticks.

CRESCENT ROLLS

Prepare Basic White Bread dough. To shape crescents divide dough in fourths, then roll out each in a 12" circle. Brush lightly with melted butter or margarine. Cut circle in 12 wedges. Starting at wide end of each wedge, roll up. Place point down slightly curved about 3" apart on greased cookie sheets. Cover and let rise. Brush with mixture of 1 egg yolk and 1 table-spoon water. If desired, sprinkle with sesame, poppy or caraway seed or coarse salt. Bake in 400° oven 15 to 20 minutes or until golden. Makes 48 rolls.

Old-Fashioned White Bread
MAKES 2 LOAVES.

1 package active dry yeast
¼ cup warm water
2 cups milk, scalded
¼ cup butter or margarine
2 tablespoons sugar
2 teaspoons salt
6 cups all-purpose flour

Sprinkle dry yeast into the warm water. Let stand a few minutes; then stir until dissolved. Pour hot milk over butter, sugar and salt. Cool to lukewarm and add yeast and 3 cups of flour. Beat well. Add remaining flour and mix well. Turn out onto floured board and knead until smooth and satiny. Put into a greased bowl; turn once, cover with plastic wrap or a damp kitchen towel and let rise until doubled in bulk (about 1½ hours). Punch down dough. Shape dough into 2 loaves and put in greased 9″ x 5″ x 3″ pans. Let rise again until doubled (about 45 minutes). Bake in a pre-heated 400°F. oven for about 35 minutes, or until done.

Butter Braid
A rich-tasting golden-white bread that is especially good for buffets and parties. It looks as good as it tastes.
MAKES 1 BRAID.

1 cup milk
½ cup butter or margarine
⅓ cup sugar
2 teaspoons salt
2 packages active dry yeast
¼ cup very warm water
3 eggs, beaten
6 to 7 cups all-purpose flour
Poppy or sesame seeds
1 egg white

Scald milk and pour it over butter, sugar and salt. Sprinkle yeast into water. Let stand a few minutes, then stir until dissolved. Stir into the cooled milk mixture. Add beaten eggs and 3 cups of flour. Beat until smooth. Stir in rest of the flour to make a stiff dough. Turn onto lightly floured board and knead well. Put into a greased bowl. Cover and let rise until double in bulk. Punch down and turn onto board. Divide in half. Cut one half of dough in 3 equal pieces and roll out into strips about 18″ long. Braid. Place on greased cookie sheet. Divide two-thirds of the remaining dough into 3 equal pieces, roll into strips a little shorter than first braid, and braid. Place this shorter braid over the first. Form remaining dough into braid and lay over the first two. Brush with melted butter or margarine and sprinkle with poppy or sesame seeds. Let rise until double. Brush with a mixture of egg white and 1 tablespoon water. Bake in preheated moderate oven for 30 to 35 minutes, or until done. Brush twice with egg white-and-water mixture while baking.

Buttermilk Bread
MAKES 2 LOAVES.

    1   package active dry yeast
    ¼   cup warm water
    1½ cups buttermilk
    ½   cup butter or margarine
    1½ teaspoons salt
    ⅓   cup sugar
    2   eggs
    5½ to 6 cups all-purpose flour

Sprinkle yeast into the warm water and let stand 5 minutes, then stir until dissolved. Scald buttermilk in top part of double boiler over simmering water. In a large bowl, pour hot buttermilk over butter, salt, sugar and soda. Stir until butter is dissolved. Cool to lukewarm, then stir in eggs, yeast mixture and about 2 cups of flour. Beat vigorously until blended. Gradually add more flour to make a soft but firm dough. Turn out on a floured board and knead until smooth and elastic. Put in greased bowl and turn dough over to grease top. Cover and let stand in warm place 1½ hours, or until doubled in bulk. Punch down and shape into 2 loaves. Put in 2 greased 9″ x 5″ x 3″ loaf pans. Let rise again 1 hour, or until doubled. Then bake in a 350° F. oven 45 minutes, or until done.

French Bread
MAKES 2 LOAVES.

>   1 package active dry yeast
> ¼ cup warm water
>   1 tablespoon solid vegetable shortening
>   2 teaspoons salt
>   1 tablespoon sugar
>   6 cups (about) all-purpose flour
>   1 egg white

Sprinkle yeast on ¼ cup warm water. Let stand a few minutes, then stir until dissolved. Pour 1 cup boiling water over the shortening, salt and sugar in large mixing bowl. Add ¾ cup cold water and cool to lukewarm. Add yeast and gradually beat in enough flour to form a stiff dough. Turn out on floured pastry cloth or board and knead until smooth and satiny. Put in greased bowl, turn once, cover and let rise 1½ hours, or until doubled. Shape in 2 oblong loaves about 14″ long. Put on greased baking sheets. Let rise 1 hour, or until doubled. Brush with beaten egg white and, with knife, make 3 slashes across top. Bake in preheated 425°F. oven 30 minutes. Reduce heat to 350°F. and bake 20 minutes.

Raisin Bread

MAKES 2 LOAVES.

2 packages active dry yeast
½ cup warm water
½ cup sugar
¼ cup butter or margarine
1½ teaspoons salt
1 cup milk, scalded
1 egg
4½ cups all-purpose flour
1 cup raisins

Sprinkle yeast into the warm water in a small bowl. When softened, stir until dissolved. Put sugar, butter and salt in large bowl; add hot milk and mix well. Let stand until lukewarm, then stir in yeast. Add egg and 3 cups flour and beat with electric mixer or wooden spoon until smooth. Stir in remaining flour by hand. Cover tightly with sheet of plastic wrap and let rise in warm place 1 hour, or until doubled in bulk. Cover raisins with hot water and let stand 10 minutes to plump; drain. Stir down batter and add raisins. Mix well and put in two 1-quart casseroles well greased with solid vegetable shortening. Smooth tops of loaves with floured hands and let rise 30 minutes, or until light. Bake in preheated 350°F. oven about 40 minutes. Turn out on racks.

Vienna Loaf

MAKES 1 LONG LOAF.

1 package active dry yeast
¼ cup warm water
2 tablespoons sugar
1 cup milk
4 tablespoons butter or margarine
1 teaspoon salt
4 cups all-purpose flour
1 egg white
Poppy seeds

In a large bowl sprinkle yeast into water and add sugar. Let stand a few minutes and stir until dissolved. In a small saucepan scald milk; add butter and salt. Cool to lukewarm; combine with yeast mixture. Add half the flour; beat until smooth. Gradually add remaining flour to make a stiff dough. Turn out on a lightly floured board and knead until satiny, about 10 minutes. Cover. Let rise in a warm place until doubled in bulk, about 1 hour. Punch down; shape in long sausage shape. Place on greased baking sheet and cut diagonal slashes across top of loaf. Cover and let rise again until doubled, about 45 minutes. Bake at 400° for 50 minutes. Remove from oven, brush with beaten egg white, sprinkle with poppy seeds. Return to oven for 10 minutes longer or until done.

Coriander Raisin Bread

This unusual bread, flavored with coriander and brown sugar, is delicious toasted for breakfast. Try it with a little butter or margarine and honey.
MAKES 3 LOAVES.

         1 cup warm water
         2 packages active dry yeast
         2 cups boiling water
         2 cups seedless raisins
        ½ cup butter or margarine, softened
        ¼ cup firmly packed brown sugar
         2 eggs
         2 tablespoons ground coriander
         3 teaspoons salt
        ¼ cup wheat germ
         1 cup nonfat dry milk
        9½ cups all-purpose flour

Use very warm water (105°F. to 115°F.). Sprinkle yeast into the warm water in large bowl. Let stand for a few minutes, then stir until dissolved. Pour boiling water over raisins and let stand until lukewarm. Add raisins and remaining ingredients except 5 cups flour to yeast; mix well. Add 5 cups flour; mix well and turn out on floured pastry cloth or board. Knead until smooth and satiny. Put in greased bowl; turn once, cover, and let rise until doubled in bulk (about 1 hour). Punch down and let rise for 30 minutes. Shape into 3 loaves and put in greased loaf pans (9″ x 5″ x 3″). Let rise until doubled (about 45 minutes). Bake in preheated moderate oven (350°F.) for about 50 minutes.

Coffee-Can Bread

This is a tender cakelike bread, wonderful for sandwiches.
MAKES 2 LOAVES.

    4   cups all-purpose flour
    1   package active dry yeast
    ½   cup water
    ½   cup milk
    ½   cup vegetable oil
    ¼   cup sugar
    1   teaspoon salt
    2   eggs

Measure 1½ cups flour into large mixing bowl. Stir in yeast. Put the water, milk, oil, sugar and salt in saucepan. Heat only until warm. Add to flour and yeast and beat until smooth. Stir in eggs. Add remaining flour and beat with spoon until smooth and elastic. Spoon into 2 well-greased 1-pound coffee cans. Cover with plastic lids and let rise in warm place about 35 minutes. (Dough should rise almost to top of cans.) Remove lids and bake in preheated moderate oven (375°F.) 35 minutes, or until well browned. Set on wire rack and let stand 10 minutes before removing from cans. Cool before slicing.

Buttermilk Cheese Bread

MAKES 2 LOAVES.

          1 cup buttermilk
        1/3 cup butter
          1 cup water
        1/4 cup sugar
       2 1/2 teaspoons salt
          1 package active dry yeast
        1/2 teaspoon baking soda
       1 1/2 cups shredded sharp Cheddar cheese
       5 to 5 1/2 cups all-purpose flour

Heat buttermilk, butter and the water until butter melts. Stir in sugar and salt and cool to about 120°F. In large bowl of electric mixer, combine yeast, baking soda and cheese with half the flour. Add butter mixture and beat at low speed 30 seconds, then beat at medium-high speed 3 minutes. With wooden spoon, stir in more flour to make a soft but firm dough and turn out on floured board. Knead 7 to 10 minutes, or until smooth and elastic. Put in greased bowl and turn greased side up. Cover and let rise in warm place 1 hour, or until doubled in bulk. Punch down and shape in 2 loaves. Put in greased 9″ x 5″ x 3″ loaf pans and let rise 30 to 40 minutes, or until doubled. Bake in preheated hot oven (400°F.) 30 to 40 minutes. Turn out on wire racks; cool before cutting.

Potato Bread

MAKES 3 LOAVES.

          2 packages active dry yeast
          1 cup warm potato water (water used to boil potatoes)
          1 cup fresh mashed potato
          2 tablespoons sugar
          2 cups milk, scalded and cooled
          3 tablespoons vegetable oil
       2 1/2 teaspoons salt
          8 cups all-purpose flour

Sprinkle dry yeast into potato water. Let stand a few minutes; then stir until dissolved. Add mashed potato, sugar, milk, oil, salt and half the flour. Beat until smooth. Add enough of remaining flour to make a stiff dough that leaves sides of bowl. Turn out onto floured board; knead until smooth and satiny. Put in greased bowl; turn once, cover and let rise until doubled in bulk (about 1 hour). Shape in 3 loaves; put in greased 9″ x 5″ x 3″ loaf pans. Let rise until doubled. Bake in preheated 350°F. oven about 40 minutes.

Sour Cream Dill Bread
MAKES 2 SMALL LOAVES.

    1 package active dry yeast
    ¼ cup warm water
    ½ teaspoon salt
    1 tablespoon margarine, softened
    1 cup dairy sour cream
    1 small onion, minced
    2 teaspoons dillweed
    2 tablespoons sugar
    ½ teaspoon baking soda
    1 egg, slightly beaten
    2¾ to 3 cups all-purpose flour
    Melted margarine
    Salt

Soften yeast in the warm water in large mixing bowl. Stir in ½ teaspoon salt, 1 tablespoon softened margarine, sour cream, minced onion, dillweed, sugar, baking soda and beaten egg. Then add half the flour and beat well with wooden spoon. Add enough of remaining flour to make a stiff dough. Turn out on lightly floured board and knead 5 to 10 turns. Put back in bowl, cover and let rise in warm place 50 minutes, or until doubled in bulk. Turn out on board and shape in 2 small loaves. Put each in greased 9″ x 5″ x 3″ loaf pan and let rise 30 to 40 minutes. Then bake in preheated moderate oven (350°F.) 40 minutes, or until golden brown. Brush with melted margarine and sprinkle lightly with salt.

Cinnamon Swirl Loaf
MAKES ONE 9″ x 5″ x 3″ LOAF.

> 1 package active dry yeast
> 3 cups all-purpose flour
> ½ cup granulated sugar
> ½ teaspoon salt
> ½ cup margarine
> ⅔ cup milk
> 2 eggs, slightly beaten
> 1½ teaspoons cinnamon
>   Melted butter or margarine

In large bowl of electric mixer, combine undissolved yeast with 1 cup flour, ¼ cup granulated sugar and the salt and mix thoroughly. Heat ¼ cup of the margarine with the milk over low heat until lukewarm (margarine need not melt). Add to dry ingredients. Beat at medium speed, scraping bowl occasionally, 2 minutes. Add ½ cup flour, or enough to make a thick batter. Add eggs and beat at high speed, scraping bowl occasionally, 2 minutes. Stir in remaining flour. Turn dough out on lightly floured board and knead until smooth and elastic. Put in greased bowl, turn to grease top, cover and let rise in warm place free from drafts 1 hour, or until doubled in bulk. Punch down and knead lightly. Roll out on lightly floured board to 18″ x 9″ rectangle. Spread with remaining ¼ cup margarine, softened, and sprinkle with combined remaining sugar and the cinnamon. Roll up tightly, starting from narrow end, and put, seam side down, in greased 9″ x 5″ x 3″ loaf pan. Brush with 2 tablespoons melted butter or margarine and let rise until doubled (about 45 minutes). Bake in preheated 350°F. oven about 30 minutes. Cool.

Wheat-Germ Batter Bread

MAKES 2 LOAVES.

1½ cups boiling water
6 tablespoons shortening, softened
½ cup honey
2 teaspoons salt
2 packages active dry yeast
½ cup warm water
2 eggs
1 cup wheat germ
5½ cups all-purpose flour
Melted butter or margarine

Pour the boiling water over shortening, honey and salt and stir until shortening melts. Cool to lukewarm. Dissolve yeast in the warm water. Add to honey mixture with eggs, wheat germ and 3 cups flour. Beat 2 minutes at medium speed with electric mixer or give 300 vigorous strokes with spoon. Blend in remaining flour with spoon. (Dough will be sticky.) Spread evenly in 2 well-greased 9″ x 5″ x 3″ loaf pans. Smooth tops by patting with floured hand. Let rise in warm place 1 hour, or until 1″ from tops of pans. Bake in preheated moderate oven (375°F.) 45 to 50 minutes. Turn out on racks and brush with butter.

Oatmeal Bread

MAKES 2 LOAVES.

1 cup quick-cooking rolled oats (not instant)
2 cups milk, scalded
1 package active dry yeast
½ cup warm water
½ cup old-fashioned molasses
2 teaspoons salt
¼ teaspoon ground ginger
4½ cups all-purpose flour

Put oats in large bowl and cover with hot milk. Stir and let stand until lukewarm. Soften yeast in the warm water and stir to dissolve. Add with molasses, salt and ginger to oat mixture. Stir in flour. Cover with sheet of plastic wrap and let rise in warm place 1 hour, or until doubled in bulk. Knead down on well-floured board, divide in half and put in 2 greased 9″ x 5″ x 3″ loaf pans. Cover and let rise about 45 minutes. Bake in preheated 350°F. oven 45 to 50 minutes.

Bran Bread
MAKES 2 LOAVES.

          7 to 8 cups all-purpose flour
          3 cups whole-bran cereal
          3 tablespoons sugar
          1 tablespoon salt
          3 packages active dry yeast
       1½ cups milk
        ¾ cup water
          3 tablespoons honey
        ½ cup butter or margarine
          3 eggs, at room temperature
             Melted butter or margarine

In large bowl of electric mixer, stir together thoroughly 1½ cups flour, the cereal, sugar, salt and yeast. Combine milk, water, honey and ½ cup butter in saucepan. Put over low heat until very warm (120°F. to 130°F.). Gradually add to dry ingredients and beat with electric mixer at medium speed, scraping bowl occasionally, 2 minutes. Add eggs and ½ cup flour. Beat at high speed, scraping bowl occasionally, 2 minutes. Stir in enough flour to make a stiff dough, then turn out on lightly floured board and knead 10 minutes, or until smooth and elastic. Put in greased bowl, turning to grease top. Cover and let rise in warm place free from drafts 1 hour, or until doubled in bulk. Punch down and divide in half. Roll each half to a 14″ x 9″ rectangle. Shape in loaves and put in

2 greased 9″ x 5″ x 3″ loaf pans. Cover and let rise in warm place free from drafts 1 hour, or until doubled in bulk. Bake on lowest rack of preheated 375°F. oven about 40 minutes. Remove from pans and cool on wire racks. Brush tops with melted butter.

Whole-Wheat Wheat-Germ Bread
MAKES 2 LOAVES.

```
¼   cup warm water
2   packages active dry yeast
1¼  cups water
3   tablespoons sugar
2½  teaspoons salt
⅓   cup butter or other shortening
⅓   cup molasses
¾   cup milk, scalded
1   cup wheat germ
4   cups unsifted whole-wheat flour
2   cups all-purpose white flour
    Melted butter or other shortening
```

Measure ¼ cup warm water (105°F. to 115°F.) into large bowl. Sprinkle dry yeast into water. Let stand a few minutes; then stir until dissolved. In saucepan mix the 1¼ cups water, sugar, salt, ⅓ cup butter, and molasses. Heat until butter melts. Cool to lukewarm. Pour scalded milk over wheat germ. Let stand until liquid is absorbed and mixture is lukewarm. Stir the lukewarm molasses mixture and the lukewarm wheat-germ mixture into the yeast. Mix whole-wheat and white flours. Add half to yeast mixture and beat until smooth. Stir in the remaining flour mixture. Turn the dough out on a lightly floured board. Knead quickly and lightly until smooth and elastic. Place in a greased bowl and brush the top lightly with melted butter or shortening. Cover with a clean damp towel. Let rise in a warm place, free from drafts, until doubled in bulk (about 1½ hours); punch down and divide into 2 equal portions. Shape into loaves and place in 2 greased loaf pans (9″ x 5″

x 3″). Cover with a clean damp towel. Let rise in a warm place, free from drafts, for about 1¼ hours, or until doubled in bulk. Bake in preheated hot oven (400°F.) for about 50 minutes.

Whole-Wheat Cinnamon Bread
MAKES 2 LOAVES.

1¼ cups water
1 cup milk
¼ cup butter or margarine
About 3½ cups all-purpose flour
3 tablespoons sugar
2 teaspoons salt
1 envelope active dry yeast
3 cups whole-wheat flour
6 tablespoons dark brown sugar
1 teaspoon cinnamon
⅔ cup raisins

In saucepan heat water, milk and butter until very warm (120° to 130°F.). Butter will not be melted completely. In large bowl of mixer combine 2 cups all-purpose flour, the sugar, salt and yeast. Add liquid mixture, beating at low speed, then beat at high speed 3 minutes. Add 1 cup all-purpose flour and beat 5 minutes longer. Stir in 3 cups whole-wheat flour or enough so that dough comes away from sides of bowl. Turn out on a lightly floured surface (use all-purpose flour to flour surface). Knead, adding up to ½ cup all-purpose flour, 8 to 10 minutes or until dough is smooth, elastic and appears blistered beneath surface. Place in a large greased bowl, turning to grease top. Cover with plastic and dish towel. Let rise in warm (85°F.) draft-free place about 1 hour or until doubled. Punch down and knead until smooth. Cut in half, cover with plastic wrap and towel and let rest 15 minutes. To shape, roll out each half in 12″ x 9″ rectangle. Sprinkle each with 3 tablespoons dark brown sugar, ½ teaspoon cinnamon and ⅓ cup raisins. Roll up tightly; seal seam and ends by pressing. Place each roll, seam side down, in greased 8″ x 4″ x 3″ loaf pan. Cover and let rise. Bake in preheated 400° oven 25 to 30 minutes or until loaves sound hollow when tapped on bottom. Remove from pans and cool on racks.

Cranberry Whole-Wheat Bread
MAKES 2 LOAVES.

> 9 cups whole-wheat flour
> 1 package active dry yeast
> 3 cups water
> 2 tablespoons butter or margarine
> 3 tablespoons honey
> ½ cup sugar
> 2 teaspoons salt
> ¼ cup nonfat dry milk
> ¾ cup chopped nuts
> 2 cups fresh or frozen cranberries, coarsely chopped

Mix 3 cups flour with the yeast in large bowl of electric mixer. Put the water, butter, honey, sugar, salt and dry milk in saucepan over low heat until very warm (120°F. to 130°F.). Pour over flour mixture and beat at medium speed, scraping bowl occasionally, 3 minutes. Stir in remaining flour, nuts and berries. Turn out on floured board and knead 8 to 10 minutes. Put in greased bowl and turn to grease top. Cover bowl with damp kitchen towel. Let rise in warm place 1¼ hours, or until doubled in bulk. Punch down and divide in half. Roll each half to a 14″ x 9″ rectangle. Roll up, starting at short end, and shape in a loaf. Seal ends and put each loaf in a greased 9″ x 5″ x 3″ pan. Cover and let rise in warm place 1 hour, or until doubled in bulk. Bake in preheated 375°F. oven 45 to 50 minutes. Cool on wire rack.

Cracked-Wheat Flat Bread

MAKES 3 LOAVES.

>   1 cup cracked wheat
>   1 cup water
>   1 cup milk
>   2 tablespoons sugar
>   2 tablespoons butter or margarine
>   2 teaspoons salt
>   2 cups whole-wheat flour
>   1 package active dry yeast
>   ½ cup raisins
>   2 to 2½ cups all-purpose flour
>   Vegetable oil

Combine cracked wheat and the water in saucepan. Bring to boil and remove from heat. Stir in milk, sugar, butter and salt and cool to very warm (120°F. to 130°F.). In large bowl of electric mixer, stir together whole-wheat flour and yeast. Add liquid mixture and beat at medium speed of electric mixer, scraping bowl occasionally, 3 minutes, or until smooth. Stir in raisins and enough all-purpose flour to make a moderately stiff dough. Turn out on lightly floured board and knead 10 to 12 minutes. Shape in ball and put in lightly greased bowl, turning to grease top. Cover and let rise in warm place 1¼ hours, or until doubled in bulk. Punch down, divide in thirds, then shape in balls. Let rest 10 minutes, then roll each ball to a circle 7" in diameter and ½" thick. Brush with oil. Put on greased baking sheets and let rise in warm place 45 minutes, or until doubled. Bake in preheated 400°F. oven 12 to 15 minutes, or until done. Remove from baking sheet and cool on wire rack. Split and toast.

Granola Bread

MAKES 2 LOAVES.

    2 cups water
    2 tablespoons butter or margarine
    ¼ cup molasses
    ½ cup orange marmalade
    1 cup granola
    2 cups whole-wheat flour
    ½ cup wheat germ
    2 teaspoons salt
    2 packages active dry yeast
    4 cups all-purpose flour

Put the water, butter, molasses and marmalade in saucepan over low heat until very warm (120°F. to 130°F.). Stir together in large bowl of electric mixer granola, whole-wheat flour, wheat germ, salt, dry yeast and 1 cup all-purpose flour. Pour heated liquid over flour mixture and beat at medium speed, scraping sides of bowl occasionally, 3 minutes. Stir in enough flour to make a moderately stiff dough. Turn out on floured board and knead, adding more flour as needed, 8 minutes, or until smooth and elastic. Put in greased bowl and turn to grease top. Cover and let rise in warm place, free from drafts 1¼ hours, or until doubled in bulk. Punch down and divide in 2 equal parts. Roll each to a rectangle about 14″ x 9″. Shape in 2 loaves by rolling up dough from short end. Seal ends and put each loaf in a greased 9″ x 5″ x 3″ pan. Cover and let rise in warm place 1½ hours, or until doubled in bulk. Bake in preheated 375°F. oven 40 minutes. Cool on wire racks.

Graham Raisin-Nut Bread
MAKES 2 LOAVES.

> 4 to 5 cups all-purpose flour
> 2 cups whole-wheat flour
> ¼ cup sugar
> 2 packages active dry yeast
> 1 tablespoon salt
> 1¾ cups milk
> ¼ cup butter or margarine
> 2 eggs
> ⅓ cup molasses
> 1 cup raisins
> 1 cup chopped nuts

Stir together flours. In large bowl of electric mixer stir together 2 cups mixed flours, the sugar, yeast and salt. In saucepan heat milk and butter over low heat until very warm (120°F. to 130°F.); gradually stir into flour-yeast mixture and beat at medium speed 2 minutes, scraping bowl occasionally. Add eggs, molasses and 1 cup of the mixed flours; beat at high speed 2 minutes. Stir in raisins and nuts. Stir in enough of the remaining mixed flours to make a soft dough. Turn out on lightly floured board and knead 8 to 10 minutes, or until dough is smooth and elastic. Shape into ball and put in greased bowl, turning to grease top. Cover with plastic wrap and let rise in warm place free from drafts 1½ hours, or until doubled in bulk. Punch down, cover with damp towel and let rest 10 minutes. Divide dough in half and with rolling pin lightly roll out each half to a 14″ x 9″ rectangle. Beginning at narrow end, roll up each as for jelly roll. Tuck ends under and put each, seam side down, in greased 9″ x 5″ x 3″ pan. Cover tightly with plastic wrap and let rise in warm place free from drafts 1½ hours, or until doubled in bulk. Bake in preheated 375°F. oven 35 to 40 minutes, or until loaves sound hollow when lightly tapped with fingers. Cool in pans 10 minutes, then turn loaves out on rack to cool.

Oatmeal Pull-Apart Loaves
MAKES 2 LOAVES.

1¼ cups water
1 cup milk
¼ cup butter or margarine
About 5 cups all-purpose flour
3 tablespoons sugar
2 teaspoons salt
1 envelope active dry yeast
1 cup rolled oats
1 egg yolk

In a saucepan heat water, milk, and butter until very warm (120° to 130°F.). Butter will not be melted completely. In large bowl of mixer combine 2 cups flour, the sugar, salt and yeast. Add liquid mixture, beating at low speed, then beat at high speed for 3 minutes. Add 1 cup oats and beat 5 minutes longer. Stir in 2½ cups flour or enough so that dough comes away from sides of bowl. Turn out on lightly floured surface. Knead, adding up to ½ cup flour, 8 to 10 minutes or until dough is smooth, elastic and appears blistered beneath surface. Place in large greased bowl, turning to grease top. Cover with plastic and dish towel. Let rise in warm (85°F.) draft-free place about 1 hour or until doubled. Punch down and knead until smooth. Pinch off 32 pieces of dough and shape in 1½-inch balls. Arrange balls in 2 greased 9″ round cake pans. Cover and let rise. Brush with mixture of 1 egg yolk and 1 tablespoon water. Bake in 400° oven 25 to 30 minutes or until golden brown. Remove from pans and cool on racks.

Apple-Oatmeal Bread

MAKES ONE 9" x 5" x 3" LOAF.

> 1 cup quick-cooking rolled oats (not instant)
> ¼ cup packed brown sugar
> 2 tablespoons butter or margarine
> 1½ teaspoons salt
> ¼ teaspoon nutmeg
> 1½ cups apple juice
> 1 package active dry yeast
> 3½ cups (about) all-purpose flour
> Melted butter or margarine (optional)

Combine oats, sugar, butter, salt and nutmeg in large bowl. Bring juice to boil, pour over oat mixture, stir well and cool to lukewarm (about 20 minutes). Sprinkle with yeast and mix well. Let stand about 1 minute, then stir in ½ cup flour. Mix well, then stir in 1 cup flour. Cover tightly with plastic wrap and let stand in warm place 1 hour, or until doubled in bulk. Stir down, add 2 cups remaining flour or enough to make firm dough that leaves sides of bowl. Turn out on lightly floured surface and knead 5 minutes or until smooth and elastic. Shape in loaf and place in greased 9" x 5" x 3" loaf pan. Cover loosely and let rise 1 hour, or until dough comes to top of pan. Bake in preheated 350°F. oven 50 minutes or until top is quite brown (it will *not* sound hollow when tapped). Turn out on rack and brush with melted butter. Store in cool dry place; will keep about 1 week. Can be frozen.

Oatmeal-Date-Nut Bread

MAKES 2 LOAVES.

> 4¾ cups all-purpose flour
> 2 packages active dry yeast
> ¾ cup water
> ¾ cup milk
> 2 tablespoons butter or margarine

    2 tablespoons molasses
    2 teaspoons salt
    1 egg, at room temperature
    1 cup quick-cooking rolled oats (not instant)
    ¼ cup chopped dates
    ½ cup chopped walnuts or pecans

Measure 1¾ cups flour into large bowl of electric mixer. Add yeast and mix well. Put water, milk, butter, molasses and salt in saucepan. Put over low heat until very warm (120°F. to 130°F.). Pour into flour-yeast mixture. Add egg and beat at low speed until blended, then at high speed, scraping bowl as needed, 3 minutes. Stir in oats, dates and nuts. Add enough flour to form a soft dough. Turn out on lightly floured board and knead 8 to 10 minutes. Put in greased large bowl, turn to grease top, cover and let rise in warm place free from drafts 45 minutes, or until doubled in bulk. Punch down and divide in half. Roll each half to a rectangle about 14″ x 7″. Roll up from short end to form a loaf and seal ends. Put in 2 greased 9″ x 5″ x 3″ loaf pans. Let rise in warm place 45 minutes to 1 hour, or until doubled in bulk. Bake in preheated 375°F. oven about 40 minutes. Cool on wire rack.

Honey-Oatmeal Bread (Refrigerator Method)
MAKES 2 LOAVES.

       1 cup boiling water
    1½ cups quick-cooking rolled oats (not instant)
      ⅓ cup honey
      ¼ cup butter or margarine
       1 tablespoon salt
       1 cup dairy sour cream
       2 packages active dry yeast
      ½ cup warm water
       2 eggs
    4½ to 5 cups all-purpose flour
         Honey butter (optional)

Combine the boiling water, oats, honey, butter and salt, and stir until butter is melted. Add sour cream and cool to lukewarm. Soften yeast in the warm water. Add yeast, eggs and 2 cups flour to oat mixture and beat until smooth. Add enough more flour to make a stiff dough. Turn out onto lightly floured board and knead until elastic. Cover dough on board with damp towel or bowl and let rest 20 minutes. Then divide in 2 equal portions and shape in 2 loaves. Put each in a greased 9″ x 5″ x 3″ loaf pan. Cover pans loosely with plastic wrap and refrigerate 12 to 24 hours. When ready to bake, remove from refrigerator and let stand at room temperature 10 minutes while oven is heating. Bake in preheated moderate oven (375°F.) 50 minutes, or until done. Remove from pans at once and cool on rack. Slice when cold and serve with honey butter (equal parts honey and butter), if desired.

Golden Cornmeal Yeast Bread

This is a mildly sweet bread with a slightly crunchy texture. It is ideal for breakfast and brunch or as an accompaniment to split pea or Yankee bean soup for supper.
MAKES 2 LOAVES.

    1 package active dry yeast
   ¼ cup warm water
   ⅓ cup sugar
   ⅓ cup butter or margarine
   3 teaspoons salt
   2 cups milk
   7 cups (about) all-purpose flour
   2 eggs, well beaten
   1 cup yellow cornmeal

Dissolve yeast in the warm water. Put sugar, butter and salt in large mixing bowl. Scald milk, pour over ingredients in bowl and mix well. Let stand until lukewarm, then add 4 cups flour, the eggs and cornmeal and beat with wooden spoon until smooth. Stir in enough more flour to make a soft but firm dough. Turn out on floured board and knead 5 minutes, or until smooth and dough doesn't stick to board. Grease bowl and add dough, turning greased side up. Cover and let rise in warm place 1 hour, or until doubled in bulk. Punch down and let rise 10 minutes longer. Shape in 2 loaves and put in well-greased 9″ x 5″ x 3″ loaf pans. Let rise 35 minutes, or until light. Bake in preheated moderate oven (350°F.) 50 minutes, or until loaves sound hollow when tapped with knuckle. Turn out on wire racks and let stand until cold.

Anadama Bread
MAKES 2 LOAVES.

2½ cups milk
½ cup yellow cornmeal
2 teaspoons salt
⅓ cup molasses
3 tablespoons butter or margarine
2 packages active dry yeast
⅓ cup lukewarm water
5 cups sifted all-purpose flour

Combine milk, cornmeal and salt in top part of double boiler. Cook over boiling water for at least 5 minutes, stirring constantly. Add molasses and butter and cool to lukewarm. Pour into mixing bowl. Sprinkle yeast into warm water (105°F. to 115°F.). Let stand for a few minutes, then stir until dissolved. Add dissolved yeast to cornmeal mixture. Add 2 cups flour. Beat thoroughly. Add remaining flour and beat thoroughly. Turn out onto board, adding more flour if necessary, and knead for 10 minutes. Put in greased bowl, cover with damp towel and let rise until doubled in bulk. Knead and shape into 2 loaves; put loaves in greased 9″ x 5″ x 3″ loaf pans. Bake in preheated 375°F. oven for 50 minutes.

Dark Rye Bread

MAKES 4 LOAVES.

1 cup dark molasses
4 cups warm water
2 packages active dry yeast
Cooking oil (about ⅔ cup)
2 tablespoons salt
4 egg yolks
2 cups riced hot cooked potato
2 cups nonfat dry milk
2 cups rye meal or rye flour
7 cups dark rye flour
3½ to 4½ cups all-purpose flour

Add molasses to warm water (105°F. to 115°F.). Sprinkle yeast over this and let stand for 10 minutes. Beat ½ cup oil, the salt, egg yolks and potato together and add to yeast mixture. Mix in dry ingredients, adding enough all-purpose flour to make a stiff dough that pulls from the spoon after it has been beaten. Brush top of dough lightly with oil, cover with damp towel and allow to rise until doubled in bulk. Punch down and let rise again. Shape into 4 round loaves and put in well-greased 2-quart heatproof glass casseroles. Let rise until doubled in size. Bake in preheated hot oven (400°F.) for 15 minutes. Reduce heat to moderate (350°F.) and bake for about 40 minutes more.

Note Recipe can be halved, if desired. Or, if four 2-quart casseroles are not available, bread can be baked in loaf pans (9″ x 5″ x 3″).

Round Rye Bread

MAKES 2 LOAVES.

1¼ cups water
1 cup milk
¼ cup butter or margarine
About 4½ cups all-purpose flour

   1½ cups rye flour
    3 tablespoons sugar
    2 teaspoons salt
    1 envelope active dry yeast

In saucepan heat water, milk and butter until very warm (120° to 130°). Butter will not be melted completely. In large bowl of mixer combine 2 cups all-purpose flour, the sugar, salt and yeast. Add liquid mixture, beating at low speed, then beat at high speed 3 minutes. Add 1 cup all-purpose flour and beat 5 minutes longer. Stir in 2½ cups combined flours or enough so that dough comes away from sides of bowl. Turn out on lightly floured surface. Knead, adding up to ½ cup flour, 8 to 10 minutes or until dough is smooth, elastic and appears blistered beneath surface. Place in large greased bowl, turning to grease top. Cover with plastic and dish towel. Let rise in warm (85°) draft-free place about 1 hour or until doubled. Punch down and knead until smooth. Cut in half, cover with plastic and towel and let rest 15 minutes.

Shape dough in 2 round slightly flattened loaves. Place on greased cookie sheets. Cover and let rise. Brush with mixture of 1 egg yolk and 1 tablespoon water.

Bake in 400° oven 25 to 30 minutes or until loaves sound hollow when tapped on bottom. (If using glass pans, lower temperature to 375°.) Cool on racks.

Sour Rye Bread

This is a coarse bread with fermented flavor; dough stands overnight.
MAKES 3 LOAVES.

   3½ cups warm water
    2 envelopes active dry yeast
    8 cups whole-rye flour
    ¼ cup molasses
    1 tablespoon salt
    1 tablespoon cumin seed, lightly crushed
   3½ to 4 cups all-purpose flour

Late in evening of first day pour 3½ cups warm water (115° to 120°F.) into large mixing bowl. Sprinkle yeast into water, let soften and stir to dissolve. Gradually stir in rye flour. Cover dough with a wet clean towel (to prevent skin from forming) and let rise at room temperature overnight. Early next morning punch down dough, add molasses, salt, cumin seed and about 1 cup all-purpose flour and mix well. Gradually stir in more flour until a stiff dough is formed. Turn out on floured board and knead until smooth and elastic and dough no longer sticks to hands or board. Divide in 3 equal pieces and shape each in a smooth loaf about 12″ long. Put on greased large baking sheet and let rise in warm place free from drafts 35 to 40 minutes, or until a few cracks develop in tops of loaves. Bake in preheated 350°F. oven 1 hour, or until bread is done. Brush loaves with hot water, once toward end of baking time and again just before putting on rack to cool; then cover with several towels. Can be frozen.

Caraway Casserole Rye Bread

MAKES 1 ROUND LOAF.

  4 cups all-purpose flour
1½ cups rye flour
    Caraway seeds
  ⅓ cup packed dark-brown sugar
  2 teaspoons salt
  2 packages active dry yeast
  1 cup milk
  1 cup water
  2 tablespoons butter or margarine
    Vegetable oil

Combine flours. In large bowl of electric mixer, stir together thoroughly 1½ cups mixed flours, 1½ teaspoons caraway seed, the brown sugar, salt and dry yeast. Combine milk, water and butter in saucepan. Put over low heat until very warm (120°F. to 130°F.). Gradually add to dry ingredients and beat at medium speed of electric mixer, scraping bowl occasionally, 2 minutes. Add ¾ cup flour mixture. Beat at high speed, scraping bowl occasionally, 2 minutes. Stir in enough flour to make a stiff dough. Cover and let rise in warm place free from drafts 40 minutes, or until doubled in bulk. Stir down and turn into well-greased 1½-quart casserole. Let rise again for 40 minutes until doubled in bulk. Brush lightly with oil and sprinkle with caraway seeds. Bake in preheated 400°F. oven 35 to 40 minutes. Remove from casserole and cool on wire rack.

Swedish Limpa Bread
MAKES 2 LOAVES.

> 1 package active dry yeast
> ½ cup warm water
> 1½ cups cold water
> ¼ cup firmly packed brown sugar
> 2 teaspoons caraway seeds
> 1 tablespoon grated orange rind (optional)
> 2 tablespoons shortening
> 2 teaspoons salt
> 4 cups all-purpose flour
> 2 cups (about) rye flour

Sprinkle dry yeast into ½ cup warm water. Let stand a few minutes; then stir until dissolved. In saucepan mix ½ cup cold water, the sugar, caraway, orange rind, shortening and salt. Bring to a boil and simmer for 5 minutes. Pour into large mixing bowl and add 1 cup cold water. Stir in 2 cups all-purpose flour. Add yeast and mix well. Stir in remaining all-purpose flour. Add 1½ cups rye flour and mix well. Sprinkle ¼ cup rye flour on bread board. Turn dough out and knead until smooth and satiny, using more rye flour as necessary. Put in greased bowl; turn once, cover, and let rise until doubled in bulk (about 1½ hours). Punch down. Divide in half. Shape each half into a ball. Put on greased baking sheet. Make 3 cuts, ½" deep, in tops. Let rise until doubled. Bake in preheated 400°F. oven for 35 minutes.

Swedish Sabina Loaf
MAKES ONE 9" x 5" x 3" LOAF.

> 2 packages active dry yeast
> ½ cup warm water
> 2 tablespoons shortening
> 1 cup milk
> Grated rind of 1 orange
> 1 teaspoon salt
> 2 tablespoons white vinegar
> ¾ cup molasses
> 4 cups whole-rye flour
> 1½ cups all-purpose flour

In mixing bowl, dissolve yeast in the warm water (105°F. to 115°F.). Melt shortening in small saucepan, add milk and heat to warm (105°F. to 115°F.). Add to yeast with orange rind, salt, vinegar, molasses and whole-rye flour. Stir to blend. Gradually add all-purpose flour. Turn dough out onto floured board and knead until smooth and elastic, adding more flour if necessary. Shape in a loaf and put in greased 9" x 5" x 3" loaf pan. Cover and let rise in warm place 45 minutes, or until almost doubled. Bake in preheated 300°F. oven 1½ hours, or until done. Turn out on rack and cool, well wrapped in a towel. Serve in thin slices.

Pumpernickel
MAKES 3 LOAVES

> 1½ cups cold water
> ¾ cup yellow cornmeal
> 1½ cups boiling water
> 1½ teaspoons salt
> 2 tablespoons sugar
> 2 tablespoons shortening
> 1 tablespoon caraway seeds
> 2 packages active dry yeast

¼ cup warm water
2 cups mashed potato
4 cups rye flour
4 cups whole-wheat flour

Stir the cold water into cornmeal in a saucepan, add the boiling water, and cook, stirring constantly, until thick. Add salt, sugar, shortening and caraway seeds and let stand until lukewarm. Sprinkle dry yeast into the ¼ cup warm water (105°F. to 115°F.). Let stand for a few minutes; then stir until dissolved. Add yeast and mashed potato to the cornmeal; mix well. Stir in flours. Turn out on floured pastry cloth or board and knead until smooth and satiny. Put in greased bowl; turn once, cover, and let rise until doubled in bulk. Divide dough into 3 portions, form into balls, and let rest for a few minutes. Roll each loaf twice as long and twice as wide as the pan in which it is to be baked. Fold ends in to center and overlap slightly; press at sides to seal. Then fold sides over in similar fashion to fit pan. Put each loaf in a greased pan with seam side down. Let rise until doubled. Bake in preheated moderate oven (375°F.) for about 1 hour.

Raisin Pumpernickel
MAKES 2 LOAVES.

¾ cup yellow cornmeal
2¼ cups cold water
2 teaspoons salt
½ cup old-fashioned molasses
2 tablespoons butter or margarine
2 packages active dry yeast
¼ cup warm water
1 teaspoon sugar
3 to 3½ cups whole-wheat flour
3 to 3½ cups rye flour
1 cup raisins
Butter or margarine

Put cornmeal in large saucepan with 2¼ cups cold water. Bring to boil and cook, stirring, until thickened. Remove from heat and stir in salt, molasses and butter; cool to lukewarm. Soften yeast in the warm water. Add sugar and stir until dissolved. Add to cornmeal mixture with enough flour (about 2½ cups of each) to make a firm dough. Turn out on board and use remaining flour for kneading. Knead dough 10 minutes. Then knead in raisins, shape dough in a ball and put in greased large bowl, turning to grease top. Cover with plastic wrap and let rise in warm place 1½ hours, or until doubled in bulk. Punch down and divide in half. Shape each half in a well-rounded ball and put on greased baking sheet. Cover and let rise 45 minutes, or until doubled. Bake in preheated 375°F. oven 45 minutes, or until done. Remove from oven to rack and rub with butter. Cool before cutting.

Cumin Rye Rings
MAKES ABOUT 1 DOZEN.

     3 packages active dry yeast
    1½ cups whole-rye flour
    1½ cups all-purpose flour
     2 teaspoons cumin seed
    1½ teaspoons aniseed
     ½ teaspoon salt
     3 tablespoons butter or margarine
     1 cup milk
     2 tablespoons dark corn syrup

Combine dry yeast, rye and all-purpose flours, cumin seed, aniseed and salt in mixing bowl. Melt 2 tablespoons butter in small saucepan over low heat; add the milk and syrup and heat until lukewarm. Pour over dry ingredients. With wooden spoon, beat until dough is smooth and leaves sides of bowl. Turn out on floured board and knead until smooth and elastic. Put in greased bowl, turning to grease top. Cover with plastic wrap or put bowl into large plastic bag. Let rise in warm place free from drafts 20 minutes, or until doubled in bulk. Punch down, turn out on lightly floured board and knead until smooth. Roll or pat dough to ½″ thickness and prick with fork. Cut out 2½″ rounds and, with thimble, cut ¾″ hole just off center of each round. Reroll scraps and cut. Put on greased baking sheet and let rise 10 minutes. Bake in preheated hot oven (425°F.) 10 minutes, or until well browned and light. Move to wire rack and brush with a mixture of 2 tablespoons hot water and 1 tablespoon butter. Cover with towel. When cool, split rings with fork and serve with butter.

Note The large amount of yeast causes dough to rise quickly. Don't let it over-rise, especially during second rising, or dough will fall flat.

Buttery Dinner Rolls
MAKES SIXTEEN 2½″ ROLLS.

> 1 package active dry yeast
> ¼ cup lukewarm water
> ½ cup milk
> ¼ cup butter
> 1 tablespoon sugar
> 1 teaspoon salt
> 2 eggs
> 2 cups all-purpose flour
> Melted butter

Soften yeast in water; let stand 5 minutes. Scald milk; stir in ¼ cup butter, the sugar and salt; cool to lukewarm. Add unbeaten eggs, yeast and flour. Beat vigorously; cover, and let rise in warm place (80° to 85°F.) about 1 hour. Stir well, and spoon into greased muffin-pan cups, filling them about half full. Let rise in warm place until doubled in bulk (about 30 minutes). Pour ½ teaspoon melted butter over each roll; bake in preheated moderate oven (375°F.) 20 minutes. Can be frozen.

Parkerhouse Rolls

No kneading or second rising is required in making these tender rolls.

MAKES ABOUT 3 DOZEN.

    1 package active dry yeast
    ½ cup warm water
    ½ cup butter or margarine
    ¼ cup sugar
    ½ cup boiling water
    1 egg, beaten
    3 cups unsifted all-purpose flour
    1 teaspoon salt
    Melted butter or margarine

Sprinkle dry yeast into warm water. Let stand a few minutes; then stir until dissolved. Put ½ cup butter, the sugar and boiling water in bowl and stir until butter is melted. Cool to lukewarm; then add yeast and egg. Add flour and salt; mix well, cover and put in refrigerator at least 24 hours. Roll on lightly floured board to ¼″ thickness and cut with floured 2½″ cutter. With handle of wooden spoon, make a crease in each circle to one side of center; flatten smaller half of round slightly by rolling handle of spoon toward edge. Brush with melted butter; fold thicker half over thinner half; press edges together. Put on baking sheets and brush again with butter. Bake in preheated hot oven (400°F.) 12 to 15 minutes.

Butter Horns

MAKES 2 DOZEN.

    1 package active dry yeast
    ½ cup warm water
    ½ cup milk, scalded
    ½ cup butter
    ⅓ cup sugar

¾ teaspoon salt
1 egg, beaten
4 cups (about) all-purpose flour

Sprinkle yeast into the water. Let stand a few minutes, then stir until dissolved. Pour hot milk over butter, sugar and salt. Cool to lukewarm. Add yeast, egg and 2 cups flour. Beat well. Add enough of remaining flour to make a dough that will not stick to bowl. Turn out on floured pastry cloth or board and knead lightly. Put in greased bowl, cover and let rise until doubled in bulk (about 1 hour). Divide dough in half. Roll each half out on floured board to form a circle 12″ in diameter. Cut each circle like a pie, into 12 wedges. Roll up each wedge from wide end and put, pointed side down, on greased baking sheets. Let rise until doubled (about 30 minutes). Bake in preheated hot oven (400°F.) 15 minutes.

Note Unraised dough can be refrigerated overnight. Let stand at room temperature to soften enough to roll, then proceed as directed.

PEANUT-BUTTER CRESCENTS

Follow recipe for Butter Horns. Before rolling wedges, spread with mixture of ⅔ cup peanut butter, ⅔ cup honey, ¼ teaspoon salt, 1 teaspoon cinnamon and ½ teaspoon allspice. Proceed as directed.

CLOVERLEAF ROLLS

Follow recipe for Butter Horns. After first rising, cut dough in 24 pieces. Cut each piece in thirds and roll in a ball. Put 3 balls in each of 24 greased 2¼″ muffin cups. Proceed as directed.

SEEDED BUTTER HORNS

Follow recipe for Butter Horns. Before second rising, brush rolls with melted butter and sprinkle with seed such as poppy, sesame or celery. Proceed as directed.

Best-Ever Rolls
MAKES 3½ DOZEN MEDIUM ROLLS.

>   ¾ cup water
>   1¼ cups milk
>   ¼ cup instant mashed-potato granules
>   ⅔ cup margarine
>   ½ cup sugar
>   1½ teaspoons salt
>   1 package active dry yeast
>   ½ cup warm water
>   2 eggs, well beaten
>   6 to 7 cups all-purpose flour
>   Melted margarine

Bring ¾ cup water and ¼ cup milk to boil and pour into large mixing bowl. Add potato granules and beat with whisk or fork until blended. Heat remaining milk in same saucepan and pour over potato granules, ⅔ cup margarine, the sugar and salt. Cool to lukewarm. Soften yeast in the warm water and add to first mixture with eggs and 3 cups flour. Beat with wooden spoon or electric mixer until smooth and light. Stir in enough of remaining flour by hand to make a dough firm enough to knead. Turn out on floured board and knead 10 minutes, or until elastic. Put in greased bowl and turn greased side up. Cover with plastic wrap and refrigerate until needed. When ready to bake, shape as many rolls as desired in preferred form. Brush with melted margarine and let rise in warm place 1 hour, or until light. Bake in preheated hot oven (400°F.) 15 to 20 minutes.

Note Rolls can be shaped without refrigerating, if preferred. Rising time may be slightly less.

Pumpkin-Raisin Rolls
MAKES ABOUT 2 DOZEN.

>   1¼ teaspoons salt
>   ½ cup sugar

¼ cup margarine
1 cup hot water
1 package active dry yeast
¼ cup warm water
1 cup canned pumpkin
1 cup golden or dark raisins
4½ cups (about) all-purpose flour

Put salt, sugar and margarine in large bowl and add the hot water. Stir until margarine is melted. If necessary, cool to luke-warm. Dissolve yeast in the warm water and stir into margarine mixture with pumpkin and raisins. Add half the flour and beat well with wooden spoon. Then stir in enough more flour to make a soft but firm dough. Turn out on floured board and knead 5 min-utes, or until dough is elastic. Put in greased bowl and turn greased side up. Cover and let rise in warm place 1 hour, or until doubled in bulk. Punch down and shape in balls about 2″ in diameter. Put in greased large muffin-pan cups or arrange side by side in greased baking pan. Let rise 30 minutes, or until doubled in bulk. Bake in preheated 375°F. oven about 20 minutes. Serve at once.

Cracked-Wheat Batter Rolls
MAKES ABOUT 2 DOZEN.

1½ cups water
¾ cup cracked-wheat cereal or cracked wheat
¼ cup butter or margarine
1 cup milk
3¼ cups all-purpose flour
¼ cup sugar
1 tablespoon salt
1 package active dry yeast
2 eggs

Bring water and cereal to boil. Reduce heat and simmer 2 minutes. Remove from heat and stir in butter until melted; add milk and cool until very warm (120°F. to 130°F.). In large mixing bowl combine 2 cups flour, the sugar, salt and yeast. Beating at low speed, add cereal mixture. Add eggs and beat at high speed 5 minutes. Stir in 1¼ cups flour. Cover and let rise in same bowl in warm (85°F.) draft-free place until doubled in bulk (about 1 hour. Mixture should be like a thick batter; no kneading is necessary.) Stir down batter and spoon into about 24 greased 2⅝" muffin cups, filling each just over half full. Let rise 30 to 35 minutes, until batter bulges over tops of cups. Bake in preheated 375°F. oven 18 to 22 minutes, or until nicely browned.

WHOLE-WHEAT BATTER ROLLS

Reduce all-purpose flour to 1¼ cups and add 2 cups whole-wheat flour. Prepare as directed above.

Corn Rolls
MAKES 2 DOZEN.

> About 4¼ cups all-purpose flour
> 3 tablespoons sugar
> 2¼ teaspoons salt
> 1 package active dry yeast
> 1½ cups buttermilk
> ¼ cup butter or margarine
> 2 eggs
> 1 cup cornmeal

In large bowl of electric mixer, combine 1 cup flour, the sugar, salt and yeast. Heat buttermilk and butter until very warm (120°F. to 130°F.). Milk may curdle, which will not affect results. Butter does not need to melt. Gradually beat buttermilk mixture into flour mixture, then beat 4 minutes at high speed. Add eggs and ¾ cup flour and beat 4 minutes longer. Stir in 2¼ cups flour and the cornmeal. Turn dough out onto floured surface and knead until smooth and elastic. (Do not knead in too much flour; dough should be soft and a bit sticky.) Shape in ball. Put in greased bowl, turn to grease top and let rise in warm (85°F.) draft-free place until doubled in bulk (about 1½ hours). Punch down and divide in 24 pieces. Shape in smooth balls and place in greased 2⅝″ muffin cups. Cover and let rise 1 hour, or until doubled. Bake in preheated 375°F. oven 20 minutes, or until browned.

Whole-Wheat English Muffins
MAKES ABOUT 1½ DOZEN.

> 1 cup milk
> 2 tablespoons sugar
> 1 teaspoon salt
> 3 tablespoons margarine
> 1 cup warm water
> 1 package active dry yeast
> 1½ cups whole-wheat flour
> 3½ cups (about) all-purpose flour
>   Cornmeal

Scald milk and stir in sugar, salt and margarine; cool to warm (105°F. to 115°F.). Measure 1 cup warm water (105°F. to 115°F.) into large warm bowl. Sprinkle in yeast, let soften; then stir until dissolved. Stir in milk mixture, then stir in whole-wheat flour and 1½ cups all-purpose flour and beat with spoon until smooth. Add enough of the remaining flour to make a stiff dough. Turn out onto floured board and knead 2 to 3 minutes, or until dough can be formed into ball (dough may be slightly sticky). Put in greased bowl, turning to grease top. Cover and let rise in warm place 1 hour, or until doubled in bulk. Punch dough down with lightly floured fingertips. Divide dough in half. On board heavily sprinkled with cornmeal, pat each half to ½″ thickness. Cut with floured 3″ cookie cutter and put about 2″ apart on un-greased baking sheets. Let rise in warm place ½ hour, or until doubled. Cook on lightly greased medium-hot griddle or skillet until well browned on both sides—about 10 minutes on each side. Cool on racks. To serve, split muffins and toast.

Georgia Raised Biscuits

These are light and fluffy double-decker biscuits, with melted butter between the two layers.

MAKES ABOUT 3 DOZEN.

>   1 package active dry yeast
> 1½ cups warm water
> 4½ cups unsifted all-purpose flour
>   2 teaspoons salt
>   1 tablespoon sugar
>   ½ cup butter, softened
>   Melted butter
>   1 egg yolk
>   1 tablespoon water

Soften yeast in the 1½ cups warm water; let stand 5 minutes. Sift dry ingredients into large bowl. Cut in the ½ cup soft butter. Add yeast and mix well. Roll about ¼″ thick on floured board. Cut with floured 2″ cutter and put half the biscuits on baking sheets. Brush with melted butter. Top with remaining biscuits. Beat egg yolk and 1 tablespoon water together. Brush on biscuits. Let rise in warm place about 1 hour. Bake in preheated hot oven (425°F.) 10 minutes.

Holiday Breads, Yeast Coffee Cakes and Sweet Rolls

AT HOLIDAY TIMES and on other festive occasions there is something especially gratifying about baking and serving traditional sweet breads, fruit-laden coffee cakes and delectable sweet rolls. Rich in eggs, spices, fruits and nuts, these breads were created to express joyous celebration. And because they are usually shaped into braids, wreaths and other special forms, they are as delightful to look at as they are to eat. In this collection we have included many of the best-loved traditional sweet breads as well as several new favorites. Once you have tried such treats as Babka, Saffron Bread, Panettone, our Holiday Coffee Wreaths and Glazed Almond Knots, we think you will find yourself inventing special occasions so that you can serve them again and again.

In many homes, baking sweet yeast breads to serve during holiday seasons has become a family tradition. The pleasures involved in making these breads add to the joy and good fellowship at festive times of the year. In addition, such special baked goods make very appealing and practical gifts. When you give a bread as a gift, it is always thoughtful to give the recipe with it. You could write it in red ink on a pale green index card at Christmas and in green on a yellow card at Easter.

For the beginning baker, we recommend starting with such simple recipes as Babka, Pannetone or Hot Cross Buns. The more complicated filled breads are not very hard to make, but you might find a little prior experience with sweet yeast dough is helpful.

Make all these breads a day or two in advance of when you want to serve them—or even earlier if you have freezer space. If you do freeze them, it is best to frost and decorate them after they thaw.

For tips on making yeast breads see pp. 24–27.

Babka
This is Polish Easter bread that derives its name from the word meaning "old woman."

  4 cups all-purpose flour, spooned into cup
  1 package active dry yeast
 ½ cup sugar
  1 teaspoon salt
 ½ teaspoon cinnamon
 ½ cup butter or margarine
 1¼ cups milk
  5 egg yolks, 1 kept separate
  1 cup golden raisins
   Grated rind of 1 lemon
 ¼ cup sliced blanched almonds

Measure flour onto piece of waxed paper. Combine 2 cups flour, the dry yeast, sugar, salt and cinnamon in large bowl of electric mixer. Stir well. Melt butter and add milk. (Mixture should be lukewarm.) Gradually add milk mixture to dry ingredients and beat at low speed, scraping sides of bowl occasionally, 2 minutes. Add 4 egg yolks and 1 cup flour. Beat at medium speed, scraping sides of bowl occasionally, 2 minutes, or until thick and elastic. With wooden spoon, gradually stir in remaining flour to make a soft dough. Cover and let rise in warm place free from drafts until doubled in bulk. Stir in raisins and lemon rind. Put in well-greased 3-quart fluted tube pan or heavy bundt pan. Brush with mixture of egg yolk, slightly beaten, and 2 tablespoons water. Sprinkle with almonds and let rise, uncovered, 1 hour. Bake in preheated moderate oven (350°F.) 30 to 40 minutes. Turn out of pan and turn right side up. Cool on rack.

Bohemian Ring

This raisin and pecan coffeecake is decorated with candied fruit.

> 2 packages active dry yeast
> ½ cup warm water
> 1½ cups scalded milk, cooled to lukewarm
> ½ cup sugar
> 2 teaspoons salt
> 2 eggs, slightly beaten
> ½ cup butter or margarine, softened
> 2 teaspoons grated lemon rind
> ¼ teaspoon mace
> 1 cup raisins
> 1 cup chopped pecans
> 7 to 7½ cups all-purpose flour
> 2 tablespoons cold water
> 1 egg yolk
>   Mixed candied fruit

In mixing bowl, soften yeast in the warm water. Add milk, sugar, salt, 2 beaten eggs, butter, lemon rind, mace, raisins, pecans and half of the flour. Mix well with spoon. Add enough remaining flour to handle easily, mixing with hand. Turn onto lightly floured board and knead 5 minutes, or until smooth and elastic. Turn once in a greased bowl, bringing greased side up. Cover with damp cloth and let rise in warm place until doubled in bulk (about 1½ hours). Punch down; let rise again until almost doubled (about 30 minutes). Punch down again, cut off one-third of dough and reserve. Divide larger portion in 3 equal 26″ strands. Put on lightly greased baking sheet. Braid loosely, fastening strands at one end, then tucking under. Divide reserved portion of dough in 3 parts and shape into 3 strands each 24″ long. Make another braid and arrange on top of large braid. Cover and let rise until doubled (45 to 60 minutes). Brush with mixture of the cold water and egg yolk. Bake in preheated moderate oven (350°F.) 30 to 40 minutes. When cool, decorate top with candied fruits.

Challah
Sabbath or holiday braided bread.
MAKES 1 VERY LARGE LOAF, OR 2 SMALLER LOAVES.

    1 package active dry yeast
    2 tablespoons sugar
1½ cups warm water
    5 cups (about) all-purpose flour
    2 teaspoons salt
    2 eggs
    2 tablespoons oil
    1 egg yolk, slightly beaten
    2 tablespoons poppy seed

Combine yeast, sugar and ¼ cup warm water. Let stand 5 minutes. Sift 4½ cups flour and the salt into large bowl. Make a well in center and drop in eggs, oil, remaining 1¼ cups warm water and yeast mixture. Work liquids into flour. Knead on floured board until dough is smooth and elastic, kneading in enough of remaining flour to make a manageable dough. Place in bowl, brush top with oil, cover with damp towel and let stand in warm place to rise

1 hour. Punch down, cover and let rise until doubled in bulk. Divide dough in 3 equal parts. Between lightly floured hands roll dough into 3 strips of equal length. Braid these and place on greased baking sheet. Cover and let rise until doubled. Brush with egg yolk and sprinkle with poppy seed. Bake in preheated 375°F. oven 45 to 50 minutes, or until golden brown.

Note This recipe can be used for a pan loaf or for rolls instead of for braided bread.

Finnish Cardamom Braids
MAKES 2 BRAIDS.

> 6 to 6½ cups all-purpose flour, spooned into cup
> 2 packages active dry yeast
> 2 cups warm water
> 1 teaspoon crushed cardamom seed
> 2 eggs, at room temperature
> ⅓ cup sugar
> 1 teaspoon salt
> ½ cup butter or margarine, softened
> 1 tablespoon milk
> Granulated sugar

Measure flour onto piece of waxed paper. Sprinkle yeast into the warm water in large mixing bowl. Let stand 3 to 5 minutes; stir. Stir in cardamom seed, 1 egg, the sugar, salt, butter and about half the flour. Beat with wooden spoon until smooth and elastic. Gradually add enough remaining flour to make a soft dough. Turn out onto lightly floured board and knead 5 to 10 minutes, or until smooth and elastic. Put in greased bowl, turning to grease top. Cover and let rise in warm place free from drafts 1 hour, or until doubled in bulk. Punch down, turn out onto lightly floured board and knead until smooth and free from air bubbles. Cut in 6 equal pieces and shape in even ropes 1″ wide. Using 3 at a time, make 2 braids. Put on lightly greased large baking sheet, leaving 2″ space between braids. Cover and let rise in warm place free from drafts about 30 minutes. Then brush with mixture of remaining egg, slightly beaten, and the milk. Sprinkle generously with granulated sugar and bake in preheated moderate oven (375°F.) 20 to 25 minutes, or until well browned and done. Remove to rack and cover with soft cloth. Cool before slicing.

Christmas Coffee Ring

   ¾ cup butter or margarine, softened
   ½ cup sugar
    1 teaspoon grated lemon rind
   ½ cup ground almonds
    3 cups all-purpose flour
    1 teaspoon salt
    1 package active dry yeast
   ½ cup warm water
    1 egg
   ½ cup milk
    1 cup chopped mixed candied fruits
     Thin Confectioners'-Sugar Frosting (see below)
     Red candied cherries
     Pecan halves
     Sliced green candied pineapple

Cream ¼ cup each butter and sugar, then add lemon rind and almonds and mix well; set aside. In large bowl, mix remaining sugar, the flour and salt. Add remaining ½ cup butter and work in with fingers or pastry blender as for piecrust. Soften yeast in the warm water and add to flour mixture. Beat egg with the milk and add to mixture. Beat well with wooden spoon and turn into lightly greased bowl. Cover tightly with sheet of plastic wrap and refrigerate at least 4 hours or overnight. Punch down, then roll dough on lightly floured board to a 14″ x 10″ rectangle. Sprinkle butter-sugar mixture evenly over dough; then spread evenly with chopped mixed candied fruits. Roll up from long side as for jelly roll and seal edges by pinching together. Put, sealed edge down, in ring on lightly greased baking sheet. Seal ends together firmly. With scissors or sharp knife, cut through ring from edge to center about three quarters of the way, making a cut every 3″. Set a greased custard cup in center. Cover and let rise in warm place about 45 minutes. Bake in preheated 350°F. oven about 30 minutes. Cool on wire rack. Then put on serving plate and decorate with frosting, candied cherries, pecan halves and candied pineapple. If desired, set a nondrip candle in center of ring.

Thin Confectioners'-Sugar Frosting

Add 1 to 2 tablespoons hot milk a little at a time to 1 cup confectioners' sugar, stirring to blend thoroughly, until mixture is of thin spreading consistency. Add ½ teaspoon vanilla extract and mix well.

Holiday Breads
MAKES 2 BREADS.

   4 to 4¼ cups all-purpose flour
  ¼ cup sugar
1½ teaspoons salt
  2 packages active dry yeast
  ½ cup butter or margarine
1⅓ cups milk
  1 egg, slightly beaten
  1 tablespoon sesame seed
18 unblanched almonds
  1 tablespoon raisins

In large bowl of electric mixer thoroughly blend 2 cups flour, the sugar, salt and yeast. Melt butter in saucepan; add milk and heat until very warm (120°F. to 130°F.). Gradually add to dry ingredients and beat at medium speed 2 minutes, scraping bowl occasionally. Add 1 cup flour and beat at medium speed 2 minutes. Stir in enough of remaining flour to make a soft dough. Turn out on lightly floured surface and knead until smooth and elastic (about 10 minutes). Place in greased bowl, turning to grease top. Cover and let rise in warm place free from drafts until doubled in bulk (about 1½ hours). Punch down and knead on lightly floured surface until smooth and elastic. Divide in half and pat or roll one half to a 7½" circle. Put on greased baking sheet. Divide remaining half in 3 equal pieces. Shape each into ¾" rope; braid ropes, then shape in circle, pinching ends together. Put on greased baking sheet. Let breads rise in warm place until light (about 30 minutes). Brush both with egg and sprinkle braid with sesame seed. On round bread, press almonds and raisins firmly into dough in any desired pattern, then brush again with egg. Bake both in preheated 350°F. oven 15 to 20 minutes, or until golden. Remove to racks to cool. Best served freshly baked, or store airtight in cool place about 1 week. Can be frozen up to 3 months.

Holiday Coffeecake

> 2 packages active dry yeast
> 1 cup warm water
> 4 cups all-purpose flour
> 8 eggs
> ½ cup sugar
> 2 teaspoons grated lemon rind
> 1 teaspoon salt
> 1 cup butter or margarine, softened
>   Vanilla Frosting (see below)
>   Red candied cherries
>   Thin strips of angelica

Sprinkle yeast into water; let stand a few minutes. Then stir until dissolved. Add 1 cup flour and beat until smooth with rotary or electric beater. Add eggs, one at a time, beating thoroughly with spoon after each addition. Beat in remaining flour, the sugar, lemon rind and salt. Cover and let rise in a warm place 45 minutes. Add butter a small amount at a time, beating after each addition until blended. Pour into well-greased 3-quart bundt pan and let stand 10 minutes. Bake in preheated moderate oven (375°F.) 35 to 40 minutes. Let stand 5 minutes. Then turn out on rack to cool. When cold, spread with frosting and decorate with cherries and strips of angelica.

Vanilla Frosting Cream ¼ cup soft butter or margarine, ¼ teaspoon salt and 1 teaspoon vanilla extract. Add 3 cups sifted confectioners' sugar alternately with 1 unbeaten egg white, beating after each addition. Add enough milk to make frosting of spreading consistency.

Holiday Coffee Wreaths
MAKES 2 WREATHS.

> Filling (see below)
> 6 cups all-purpose flour, lightly spooned into cup
> ½ cup granulated sugar
> 1 teaspoon salt
> 3 packages active dry yeast
> ½ cup butter or margarine, softened
> 1 cup hot water
> 4 eggs, 3 at room temperature
> Confectioners' sugar
> Red or green candied pineapple and cherries

Prepare Filling and set aside while making dough. To make dough, measure flour onto a piece of waxed paper. In large bowl of electric mixer, combine 2 cups of the flour, the granulated sugar, salt, yeast and butter. Gradually add the hot water (120°F. to 130°F.) and beat, scraping bowl occasionally, 2 minutes. Add 3 eggs and ½ cup flour. Beat at high speed, scraping bowl occasionally, 2 minutes. Stir in enough of remaining flour to make a soft dough. Turn out on lightly floured board and knead 5 minutes, or until smooth and elastic. Divide dough in half and shape each half in a round ball. Roll one ball to a 16″ circle. With pastry wheel or sharp knife, cut circle in 12 triangles. Using half the filling, put about 1 teaspoonful on each triangle. Roll up to form crescents, starting at base of triangle. Bring two ends of each crescent toward each other and pinch. Repeat with remaining half of dough. When ready to bake, arrange each 12 crescents with sides touching on baking sheet in shape of wreath. Cover lightly, (thaw, if frozen) and let rise in warm place free from drafts 2 hours, or until doubled. Brush with remaining egg, beaten, and bake in preheated moderate oven (375°F.) 20 to 25 minutes. Loosen with spatula and remove to racks to cool. Sift confectioners' sugar over top and decorate with fruits as desired.

Note May be frozen as follows. Arrange crescents side by side on baking sheet, cover loosely with foil and freeze until firm. Remove from sheet, divide into 2 freezer bags and store in freezer for up to 4 weeks. When desired, remove from freezer and follow directions to form wreaths and bake; or remove one bag of pastries from freezer early in morning, arrange on baking sheets, thaw and proceed as directed. Bake remaining pastries later as desired.

Filling Cream ¼ cup softened butter or margarine. Add ¾ cup confectioners' sugar, 2 teaspoons grated orange rind and ¾ cup finely chopped pecans, walnuts, filberts or almonds. Mix well.

Kugelhopf
In Vienna, they serve this lemon-scented cake on Christmas morning—and as a special treat other times, too.

    1 package active dry yeast
    ¼ cup warm water
    ¾ cup milk, scalded and cooled
    4 cups all-purpose flour
    1 cup butter or margarine, softened
    ¾ cup sugar
    5 eggs

> 1 teaspoon salt
> Grated rind of 1 lemon
> 1 cup seedless raisins
> ½ cup chopped blanched almonds

Sprinkle dry yeast into the water. Let stand a few minutes, then stir until dissolved. Add milk and beat in 1 cup flour. Cover and let rise 1½ hours. Cream butter and sugar until light. Beat in eggs, one at a time. Add yeast mixture, remaining flour and salt. Beat well. Stir in lemon rind, raisins and ¼ cup nuts. Grease a 10″ tube pan and sprinkle with remaining ¼ cup nuts. Pour in batter and let rise until light (about 45 minutes). Bake in preheated moderate oven (350°F.) 1 hour.

Kulich

This Russian Easter bread is usually served with paska, *a molded cheese dish.*

> 4½ cups all-purpose flour, spooned into cup
> 2 packages active dry yeast
> ½ cup sugar
> 1 teaspoon salt
> ¼ teaspoon powdered saffron
> ½ cup margarine
> 1 cup milk
> 2 eggs, at room temperature
> ½ cup chopped blanched almonds
> 1 teaspoon grated lemon rind
> 1 cup raisins
> Confectioners'-Sugar Frosting (see below)
> Yellow food coloring
> Nuts, candied fruit

Measure flour onto piece of waxed paper. Combine 1½ cups flour, dry yeast, sugar, salt and saffron in large bowl of electric mixer. Stir well. Melt margarine and add milk. (Mixture should be lukewarm.) Gradually add to dry ingredients and beat at low speed, scraping sides of bowl occasionally, 2 minutes. Add eggs and 1 cup flour. Beat at medium speed, scraping sides of bowl occasionally, 2 minutes, or until thick and elastic. With wooden spoon, gradually stir in remaining flour to make a soft dough that leaves the sides of bowl. Turn out on lightly floured board, shape in a ball and knead 5 to 10 minutes, or until smooth and elastic. Put in greased bowl, turning to grease top. Cover with plastic wrap or put in plastic bag and let rise in warm place free from drafts 1 hour, or until doubled in bulk. Punch down and turn out onto lightly floured board. Knead in almonds, lemon rind and raisins. Shape in a smooth ball and press into well-greased 2-pound coffee can. Cover loosely and let rise 30 minutes. Bake on low rack in preheated moderate oven (350°F.) 35 to 40 minutes. If top gets too brown before baking is finished, cover with foil. Cool in can on rack, then loosen around edge with spatula, invert and shake loose. Tint frosting with a few drops of food coloring and spread on top of bread. Decorate with nuts and candied fruit. Serve in thin slices, starting from bottom.

Confectioners'-Sugar Frosting

Add 1 to 2 tablespoons hot milk a little at a time to 1 cup confectioners' sugar, stirring to blend thoroughly, until mixture is of spreading consistency. Add ½ teaspoon vanilla extract and mix well.

Norwegian Julekage

This is a festive Christmas bread, flavored with cardamom and citron.

MAKES 2 LOAVES.

> 2 packages active dry yeast
> ½ cup lukewarm water
> ½ cup sugar
> ¾ teaspoon ground cardamom
> 2 teaspoons salt
> 1 egg, beaten

1 cup milk, scalded
¼ cup butter
5 cups all-purpose flour
½ cup seedless raisins
½ cup diced citron
   Melted butter
   Confectioners'-Sugar Frosting (see below)
   Nuts, cherries, angelica

Combine yeast, warm water and 1 tablespoon of the sugar. Let stand about 5 minutes. Stir in remaining sugar, cardamom, salt and egg. To milk, add butter, stirring until melted; cool to lukewarm. Add to yeast mixture. Stir in 3 cups flour and beat until batter falls in sheets from spoon. Add raisins, citron and remaining flour. Mix well. Turn out onto floured board and knead until smooth and elastic. Put into large greased bowl, turning to grease top. Cover and let rise 1 hour, or until doubled in bulk. Divide in half; shape each half into a ball; place on board; cover and let rest 10 minutes. Punch down and divide each ball in 3 equal parts. Shape each into a roll 16″ long. Pinch ends of 3 rolls together and braid. Put each braid in greased 9″ x 5″ 3″ loaf pan. Repeat with remaining dough. Brush tops with melted butter. Cover and let rise in warm place until doubled in bulk (about 1 hour). Bake in preheated moderate oven (350°F.) 45 minutes, or until done. Remove from pans and cool. Frost with confectioners'-sugar frosting. Decorate with nuts, cherries and angelica.

Confectioners'-Sugar Frosting

Add 2 to 3 tablespoons hot milk gradually to 2 cups confectioners' sugar, stirring after each addition, until you have a frosting of spreading consistency. Add ½ teaspoon vanilla extract and mix well.

Panettone (Italian Coffeecake)
MAKES TWO 7" ROUND LOAVES.

    2 packages active dry yeast
    1 cup warm water
  4½ cups sifted all-purpose flour
    ½ cup sugar
    ½ cup butter or margarine
    2 or 3 eggs
    1 teaspoon salt
    2 teaspoons grated lemon rind
    2 tablespoons chopped citron
    ¼ cup golden raisins
    1 cup broken nuts
      Melted butter

Sprinkle yeast into the water in a bowl. Let stand for a few minutes, then stir until dissolved. Beat in 1 cup flour. Let stand covered until doubled in bulk. Cream sugar and butter until light and fluffy. Beat in eggs, one at a time. Add salt and lemon rind. Beat in yeast mixture. Gradually beat in 3½ cups flour. Beat for 5 minutes, until dough pulls cleanly from spoon when it is pulled out of the dough. Beat in fruits and nuts. Let stand covered until doubled in bulk. Stir dough and place in 2 greased 7" springform pans. Let rise in pans for 30 minutes. Brush tops of dough with melted butter. Bake in preheated moderate oven (350°F.) for 30 minutes, or until golden brown.

Moravian Sugar Cake

 3½ to 4 cups all-purpose flour
  ⅔ cup granulated sugar, divided
  2 packages active dry yeast
  1 teaspoon salt
  ¾ cup butter or margarine, divided
  ½ cup very warm (120° to 130°) water

  2 eggs
½ cup unseasoned mashed potatoes
⅓ cup packed light-brown sugar
  1 teaspoon cinnamon
    Confectioners'-Sugar Frosting (optional)

Measure flour onto waxed paper or into bowl. Combine 1 cup flour, ⅓ cup granulated sugar, the yeast and salt in large bowl of electric mixer. Stir well and add ½ cup softened butter and the water. Beat at low speed, scraping sides of bowl occasionally, 2 minutes. Add eggs, potatoes and 1 cup flour. Beat at medium speed, scraping sides of bowl occasionally, 2 minutes. With spoon, gradually stir in enough additional flour to make a soft dough that leaves sides of bowl. Turn out on lightly floured surface, shape in ball and knead 5 to 10 minutes, or until smooth and elastic. Put in greased bowl, turning to grease top. Cover with plastic wrap or plastic bag and let rise in warm place free from drafts 1 to 1½ hours, or until doubled. Punch down and let rest 10 minutes. Press dough into greased 13″ x 9″ x 2″ pan or divide equally between two greased 8″ square pans. With thumb, make holes about 2″ apart on top of dough. Drizzle with remaining butter, melted. Mix remaining granulated sugar, the brown sugar and cinnamon and sprinkle on dough. Cover and let rise 30 minutes. Bake in preheated 350° oven about 25 minutes. Cool on rack. Drizzle with frosting, if desired.

Confectioners'-Sugar Frosting Mix 1 cup confectioners' sugar, 1 tablespoon butter or margarine, melted, and 3 tablespoons milk or cream until smooth.

Raised Fruitcake

    2 packages active dry yeast
  ½ cup warm water
  ⅓ cup milk, scalded
  ½ cup sugar
  1 teaspoon salt
3½ cups all-purpose flour
  ½ cup butter
  2 eggs, beaten
1½ teaspoons grated orange rind
  1 cup raisins
  1 cup chopped walnuts
  1 cup chopped mixed candied fruit
  1 teaspoon cinnamon
  1 teaspoon ginger
  ½ teaspoon nutmeg
     Orange Glaze (see below)

Sprinkle dry yeast into water. Let stand a few minutes; then stir until dissolved. Pour hot milk over ¼ cup sugar and the salt. Cool to lukewarm. Add yeast mixture and 1 cup flour; beat until smooth. Cover and let rise in a warm place, free from drafts, until light, about 20 minutes. Cream butter until light and fluffy. When yeast mixture is light, beat in butter, remaining sugar, eggs and orange rind. Stir in remaining 2½ cups flour; beat hard. Add remaining ingredients, except glaze. Turn into a well-greased 3-quart bundt pan. Cover and let rise in a warm place, free from drafts, about 1½ hours. Bake in preheated moderate oven (375°F.) for 40 to 45 minutes. Cool and top with Orange Glaze.

Orange Glaze

Mix thoroughly 1 teaspoon grated orange rind, 2 tablespoons orange juice and 1 cup confectioners' sugar.

Saffron Bread

    5 to 5½ cups all-purpose flour
    2 packages active dry yeast
  ½ cup butter or margarine
1½ cups milk
  ½ cup sugar
    1 teaspoon salt
  ½ to 1 teaspoon saffron threads, crumbled
    1 egg
  ½ cup raisins
    1 egg yolk beaten with 1 tablespoon milk
    1 tablespoon sugar mixed with
    1 tablespoon chopped nuts

Combine 2 cups flour and the yeast in large bowl of electric mixer. Melt butter in small saucepan over low heat; stir in milk, sugar, salt and saffron and heat until warm (120°F.). Pour over flour mixture and beat 3 minutes at medium speed; add egg and 2 cups flour and beat 2 minutes at low speed. With spoon stir in raisins and enough flour to make soft dough. Turn out on lightly floured surface and knead until smooth and elastic; cover with mixing bowl and let rest 30 minutes. Punch down and knead until smooth. Divide dough in half. Pat or roll one half to make 10″ circle; place on lightly greased baking sheet. Divide remaining dough in thirds and roll each piece between hands to make ¾″-thick rope. Braid ropes and form a wreath; place on top of circle about 1″ from edge, pressing lightly. Let rise in warm place about 30 minutes. Brush with egg-yolk mixture and sprinkle with nut mixture. Bake in preheated 350°F. oven 25 to 30 minutes, or until lightly browned and done. Remove to rack, cover with towel and cool. Cut in wedges to serve.

Stollen

Although Dresden is the native city of this fruit-and-nut-filled coffee cake, it is served throughout Germany on Christmas morning and often at other times during the Christmas season.
MAKES 2.

¾ cup raisins
¼ cup chopped mixed candied fruit
2 tablespoons light rum
1 cup milk
¾ cup butter or margarine, softened
½ cup sugar
1 package active dry yeast
¼ cup warm water (115°F.)
4¾ cups all-purpose flour
2 eggs, well beaten
½ teaspoon salt
¼ teaspoon grated lemon rind
⅛ teaspoon nutmeg
¾ cup finely chopped blanched almonds
Melted butter or margarine
Granulated sugar

Combine raisins, candied fruit and rum and set aside. In small saucepan scald milk; add butter and, when melted, stir in ½ cup sugar until dissolved; cool to lukewarm (85°F.). Dissolve yeast in the warm water and stir into milk mixture; pour into large bowl. Stir in 1½ cups flour and beat well with wooden spoon until smooth. Let stand in warm place until bubbly (about 10 minutes). Combine eggs, salt, lemon rind and nutmeg and stir into batter; stir in 1 cup flour and mix with spoon until smooth. Stir in remaining 2¼ cups flour ½ cup at a time, mixing after each addition until smooth. Turn out on floured surface and knead until smooth and satiny (about 8 to 10 minutes). Knead rum-soaked fruits and the nuts into dough in 4 additions, kneading well after each to assure even distribution. Place dough in well-greased large bowl, brush with melted butter, cover and let rise in warm place until doubled in bulk (about 1 hour). Punch down and divide dough in half. Place on greased cookie sheets and pat each half into 10″ x 7″ oval. With side of hand, crease in center lengthwise and fold over; brush with melted butter. Let rise in warm place until doubled (about 1 hour). Bake in preheated 350°F. oven 45 minutes, or until lightly browned. If necessary, cover with foil to prevent excessive browning. Remove from oven and brush with melted butter; sprinkle with granulated sugar. Cool thoroughly on wire racks; store well wrapped.

Fruit-Filled Ring

    1 package active dry yeast
  ½ cup warm water
  ½ cup milk, scalded
  ¾ cup butter or margarine, softened
  ½ teaspoon salt
  ¼ cup granulated sugar
    2 eggs, beaten
    4 cups all-purpose flour
      Filling (see below)
    1 cup confectioners' sugar
    2 tablespoons orange juice
      Rind of 1 orange, finely grated

Sprinkle yeast into the water. Let stand a few minutes, then stir until dissolved. Pour hot milk on ¼ cup butter, the salt and sugar. Let stand until lukewarm. Add yeast, eggs and 3½ cups flour. Beat until smooth. Using remaining ½ cup flour, turn dough out on lightly floured board and knead until smooth and elastic (about 5 minutes). Put in lightly greased bowl, turn to grease top, cover and let rise in warm place until doubled in bulk (about 1 hour). Punch down, turn out on board and knead until gas bubbles disappear. Roll into an 18″ x 12″ rectangle ¼″ thick. Sprinkle with Filling. Dot with ½ cup butter and roll as for jelly roll. Put in a greased straight-sided 9″ loose-bottomed tube pan, bringing the ends together to form a ring. Punch down to make the top even. With scissors, make deep cuts every 2″. Twist each section slightly so that the cuts remain open. Cover and let rise about 1 hour. Bake in preheated moderate oven (350°F.) 25 to 30 minutes. While still warm, remove from pan and glaze top with confectioners' sugar mixed with orange juice. Sprinkle with grated orange rind. Cool, and store airtight. Can be frozen.

Filling Mix ½ cup each seedless golden raisins, seedless dark raisins, currants, finely chopped candied orange and lemon peel, chopped pecans, packed light-brown sugar, and 1 teaspoon cinnamon.

Hungarian Coffee Cake

       1 package active dry yeast
      ¼ cup very warm water
      ¾ cup milk, scalded and cooled
       1 cup sugar
       1 teaspoon salt
       1 egg
      ¾ cup butter or margarine, softened
    3½ cups (about) all-purpose flour
       1 teaspoon cinnamon
      ¾ cup finely chopped nuts
       4 tablespoons raisins

Sprinkle yeast into water. Let stand a few minutes, then stir until dissolved. Add milk, ¼ cup sugar, the salt, egg, ¼ cup softened butter and half the flour. Beat with spoon until smooth. Gradually add enough more flour to make a stiff dough. Turn out on lightly floured board and knead 5 minutes, or until smooth and elastic. Put in greased bowl and turn greased side up. Cover and let rise in warm place 1½ hours, or until doubled in bulk. Punch down and let rise 30 minutes, or until almost doubled. Cut dough in pieces the size of walnuts and shape in balls. Roll balls in remaining butter, melted, then roll in mixture of remaining sugar, the cinnamon and nuts. Put a layer of balls barely touching in well-greased 9″ or 10″ tube pan (if bottom is removable, line with foil). Sprinkle with 2 tablespoons raisins. Add another layer of balls and sprinkle with remaining raisins, pressing in slightly. Let rise about 45 minutes. If any cinnamon mixture remains, sprinkle on top. Bake in preheated moderate oven (350°F.) 35 to 40 minutes. Loosen from pan and invert so butter-sugar mixture runs down over cake. To serve, break apart with 2 forks and serve warm or cool.

Poppy-Seed Coffee Cake

> 1 package active dry yeast
> 2 tablespoons warm water (115°F.)
> 1 cup milk
> 4 cups (about) all-purpose flour
> 3 egg yolks
> ½ cup sugar
> ¼ teaspoon salt
> ¾ cup butter or margarine, melted and cooled
> 1 tablespoon grated lemon peel
> 3 tablespoons butter or margarine, softened
>   Poppy-Seed Filling (see below)
>   Confectioners' sugar

Sprinkle yeast into water, allow to soften, then stir to dissolve. Heat milk to warm (105°F. to 115°F.) and pour into large mixing bowl. Stir yeast mixture into milk until dissolved. Stir in 2½ cups flour. Cover dough with clean damp towel and let rise in warm place until almost doubled in bulk (about 1 hour). Beat together egg yolks, sugar and salt until thick and light yellow; stir into dough. Stir in melted butter and lemon peel. Gradually stir in 1½ cups flour. Let stand 20 minutes. Turn out on lightly floured board (dough should be barely firm enough to handle). Knead thoroughly, working in additional flour, until dough is just firm enough to cut without sticking (dough must be soft; add no more flour than necessary). Roll out in 20″ x 16″ rectangle. Spread with softened butter; sprinkle with Poppy-Seed Filling. Starting at long edge, roll up as for jelly roll. Carefully lift into greased and floured 3-quart fluted tube pan or 10″ tube pan. Gently press ends together to join. Cover with damp towel and let rise in warm place until almost doubled in bulk (about 1 hour). Bake in preheated 325°F. oven 1 hour 15 minutes (as soon as top is rich golden brown, cover loosely with foil). Cool in pan 5 minutes, then turn out onto wire rack. Sprinkle generously with confectioners' sugar stirred through strainer. Cool. Store airtight at room temperature up to 3 days or freeze up to 3 months. To serve, cut in thin slices.

Poppy-Seed Filling

Whirl poppy seed about ¼ cup at a time in blender to very coarse powder; measure 1¼ cups into saucepan. Add ½ cup milk, ⅓ cup sugar and 10 tablespoons golden raisins. Cook over low heat, stirring, until blended and thickened (about 10 minutes). Stir in 1 teaspoon vanilla extract and cool.

Sally Lunn

        4½ cups all-purpose flour
         ⅓ cup sugar
         1 teaspoon salt
         1 package active dry yeast
        1¼ cups milk
         ½ cup butter or margarine
         3 eggs, beaten

Measure flour onto waxed paper or into bowl. Combine 2 cups flour, the sugar, salt and yeast in large bowl of electric mixer. Stir well. Heat milk and butter until very warm (120° to 130°). Gradually add to dry ingredients and beat at low speed, scraping sides of bowl occasionally, 2 minutes. Add eggs and ½ cup flour. Beat at medium speed, scraping sides of bowl occasionally, 2 minutes. With spoon, gradually stir in remaining flour to make a soft dough. Cover and let rise 1 hour, or until doubled. Stir down and spoon into greased and floured 10″ tube pan. Cover and let rise 1 hour, or until doubled. Bake in preheated 400° oven about 30 minutes. Turn out and cool on rack. Serve warm with butter.

Sunday Breakfast Ring

 1 package active dry yeast
 ¼ cup warm water
 ¾ cup milk, scalded
 ½ cup sugar
 ½ cup butter or margarine
 1 teaspoon salt
 1 egg, beaten
 3 cups (about) all-purpose flour
 1 teaspoon cinnamon
 ¼ cup raisins
 ¼ cup chopped nuts
 6 maraschino cherries, thinly sliced
  Frosting (optional, see below)

Sprinkle yeast into the water. Let stand a few minutes, then stir until dissolved. Pour hot milk over ¼ cup each sugar and butter and the salt. Cool to lukewarm and add yeast, egg and about half the flour. Beat well. Add enough more flour to form a dough that will not stick to bowl. Turn out on floured pastry cloth or board and knead until smooth and satiny. Put in greased bowl, cover and let rise until doubled in bulk (about 1 hour). Punch down and let rise again. Roll out on floured board to form a rectangle 15″ x 9″. Spread with remaining butter and sprinkle with mixture of remaining sugar, the cinnamon, raisins, nuts and cherries. Roll up from 15″ side and shape in a ring on greased baking sheet. Seal ends by pinching together. Cut two thirds of the way through ring at 1″ intervals. Turn each section slightly on side to hold cuts open. Let rise until light (about 30 minutes). Bake in preheated moderate oven (375°F.) 30 minutes, or until done. Serve warm or cold and frost, if desired.

Frosting Mix 1 cup confectioners' sugar with milk until of spreading consistency.

Almond Fruit Braid

    1 package active dry yeast
    ¼ cup warm water
    ¾ cup milk, scalded
    3 tablespoons granulated sugar
    1 teaspoon salt
    3 cups all-purpose flour
    1 egg
    1 egg, separated
    ¼ cup butter or margarine, softened
    ½ cup blanched, chopped almonds
    ¼ cup sliced almonds
    ½ cup chopped mixed candied fruit

Sprinkle yeast into warm water (110°F. to 115°F.). Let stand a few minutes; then stir until dissolved. Pour hot milk over granulated sugar and the salt. Cool to lukewarm. Add yeast, 2½ cups flour, beaten egg and yolk and the butter. Beat until well blended. Cover and let rise in warm place until doubled in bulk (about 45 minutes). Add remaining ½ cup flour, chopped nuts and fruit, mixing to a stiff dough. Turn out on floured board and knead lightly. Divide in 3 equal parts. Roll each to form a 12″ rope. Braid loosely and press and fold ends under slightly to seal. Put in greased 9″ x 5″ x 3″ loaf pan. Let rise until even with top of pan (about 1 hour). Bake in preheated moderate oven (375°F.) about 30 minutes. Brush braid with beaten egg white and sprinkle with sliced almonds. If desired, return braid to oven for 5 minutes to brown nuts slightly.

Little Brioches

MAKES 2 DOZEN.

    2 packages active dry yeast
    ¼ cup very warm water
    ¾ cup milk, scalded
    1 cup butter or margarine

½ cup sugar
2 teaspoons salt
6½ cups all-purpose flour
5 eggs

Sprinkle yeast into the warm water. Let stand a few minutes, then stir until dissolved. Pour hot milk over butter, sugar and salt. Cool to lukewarm. Add 2 cups flour and beat well. Add yeast and beat. Cover and let rise until bubbly; stir down. Add 4 eggs and beat well. Add enough flour to make a soft dough. Turn out on lightly floured board and knead until smooth and satiny. Put in greased bowl, turn to grease top, cover and let rise 1½ hours, or until doubled in bulk. Punch down and divide in 24 pieces. From each piece, cut a small piece. Shape large pieces in balls and put in well-greased 2¾″ muffin cups. Shape small pieces in balls. Make indentation in center of each large ball by pressing with thumb. Press small balls into indentations. Let rise 45 minutes, or until doubled. Mix remaining egg and 1 tablespoon water. Brush on rolls. Bake in preheated moderate oven (375°F.) about 15 minutes.

Cinnamon Raisin Buns
MAKES 2 DOZEN.

1 package active dry yeast
2 tablespoons warm water
1 cup milk, scalded
¼ cup butter
⅓ cup sugar
½ teaspoon salt
1 egg, beaten
3 to 3½ cups all-purpose flour
1 teaspoon cinnamon
¾ cup seedless raisins
Cinnamon Frosting (see below)

Soften yeast in water. Pour hot milk over butter, sugar and salt in bowl. Let stand until lukewarm; then stir in yeast. Stir in egg and half the flour sifted with cinnamon; beat smooth. Stir in raisins and enough of remaining flour to make a soft dough. Cover and let rise in warm place until doubled in bulk. Punch down and shape in balls the size of a walnut; let rise on baking sheet until doubled. Bake in preheated hot oven (425°F.) for 25 minutes. Cool slightly and frost.

Cinnamon Frosting Mix together 1 cup sifted confectioners' sugar, 1 tablespoon water and ¼ teaspoon cinnamon.

Cinnamon Rolls
MAKES ABOUT 28.

> ½ cup granulated sugar
> 1 package active dry yeast
> 2¼ cups warm water
> 2 egg yolks
>   Cooking oil
> 2½ teaspoons salt
> 1 cup nonfat dry milk
> 7 to 8 cups all-purpose flour
> 1½ cups firmly packed light-brown sugar
> 1 tablespoon ground cinnamon
>   Confectioners'-Sugar Frosting (see below)

Sprinkle granulated sugar and dry yeast into water in large bowl of electric mixer. Let stand for a few minutes; then stir until dissolved. Add egg yolks, ⅓ cup oil, the salt, milk and 2 cups flour. Beat at low speed. (Or beat with rotary beater.) Add enough remaining flour to make a stiff dough. Mix well. Cover and let rise until doubled in bulk. Divide dough in half and roll each half on a floured board to form a rectangle 14" x 10". Using a pastry brush, brush with oil. Sprinkle half the brown sugar and cinnamon over each rectangle. Roll up as for jelly roll. Pinch dough firmly together. Cut into 1" slices and lightly roll in a shallow dish of oil so that the finished rolls will separate more readily. Put in two greased pans, one 13″ x 9″ x 2″, the other 11″ x 7″ x 2″. Cover and let rise until doubled. Bake in preheated hot oven (400°F.) for about 20 minutes.

Confectioners'-Sugar Frosting

Add 2 to 3 tablespoons hot milk or water one teaspoon at a time to 2 cups confectioners' sugar and blend until frosting is of spreading consistency. Add ½ teaspoon vanilla extract and mix well.

Cream Coffee Rolls
MAKES 2½ DOZEN.

> 1 package active dry yeast
> ¼ cup warm water
> ¾ cup heavy cream
> 1 teaspoon salt
> 2 tablespoons sugar
>   Melted butter
> 1 egg, beaten
> 2½ cups all-purpose flour
>   Confectioners'-Sugar Frosting (see below)
>   Candied fruit (optional)

Sprinkle yeast into water. Let stand a few minutes, then stir until dissolved. Heat cream to lukewarm, add salt and sugar and stir until dissolved. Add ⅓ cup melted butter, yeast and egg. Add 1½ cups flour and beat well. Then stir in 1 cup flour. Cover with a damp kitchen towel and let rise until doubled in bulk. Punch down, cut off small pieces of dough and roll between hands to about the size of a pencil. Roll up pinwheel-fashion and with fingertip, spread a little melted butter over roll. Put in 2″ muffin cups and let rise until light. Bake in preheated hot oven (400°F.) about 15 minutes. While hot, spread tops with frosting. Decorate with candied fruit, if desired.

Confectioners'-Sugar Frosting

Add 2 to 3 tablespoons hot milk or water one teaspoon at a time to 2 cups confectioners' sugar and blend until frosting is of spreading consistency. Add ½ teaspoon vanilla extract and mix well.

Croissants
MAKES 16.

> 2 packages active dry yeast
> ½ cup lukewarm water
> ½ cup sugar
> 6 tablespoons butter
> 2 teaspoons salt
> 2 cups milk, scalded
> 7 to 8 cups sifted all-purpose flour
> 2 eggs, well beaten
> Melted butter

Soften yeast in water; let stand 5 minutes. In large bowl mix sugar, butter, salt and milk; cool to lukewarm, and mix well. Add 1 cup of the flour, and beat until smooth. Add softened yeast; mix well. Add about half of remaining flour; beat until smooth. Beat in eggs. Add enough remaining flour to make soft dough. Turn out on floured board, let stand 5 minutes, and knead 5 minutes, or until smooth and elastic. Put in large greased bowl, turn to bring greased side up. Cover with waxed paper and towel and let stand in warm place 1½ hours, or until doubled in bulk. Punch down, cover and let rise ½ hour. Turn out on lightly floured board. With rolling pin, roll raised dough in 12" circle ¼" thick; brush with melted butter. Cut in 16 wedges. Roll each wedge separately, beginning at base. Put on baking sheet with wedge point underneath, and shape into crescents. Cover and let rise about 15 minutes. Bake in preheated hot oven (425°F.) 15 minutes, or until browned. Can be frozen.

Southern Pecan Pie

Mincemeat-Pear Pie

Chilled Light Cheesecake with Blueberry Topping

Basic White Bread, Breadsticks, Round Rye Bread, Oatmeal Pull-Apart Loaves, Whole-Wheat Cinnamon Bread. Crescent Rolls

1. *Mixing*—Dough leaves sides of bowl and is ready for kneading.

2. *Kneading*—Fold dough, push with heels of hands, turn and repeat.

3. *Adequate Kneading Test*—Dough is smooth, elastic, springs back when lightly pressed and looks blistered beneath surface.

4. *Double-in-Bulk Test*—Dent remains when fingertips are lightly pressed half inch into dough.

5. *Punching Down*—With fist punch center of dough. Pull edges to center and turn dough over.

6. *Shaping*—Roll dough in rectangle, then roll as for jelly roll. Seal ends and seam with fingers.

7. *Second Rising*—Shaped loaf has risen enough and doubled when edge is lightly pressed with finger and dent remains.

8. *Cool on Rack*—Perfect breads have even, rounded tops, golden-brown crusts, texture with small, even holes, soft and moist crumbs.

Peanut Butter Cake

Saffron Bread, Slovene Potica, Moravian Sugar Cake, Sally Lunn,
Philadelphia Sticky Buns

Walnut Crescents, Spritz Cookies, Cherry Bonbons, Chocolate Triangles,
Cinnamon-Nut Diamonds, Sugar Cookies, Lizzies, Chocolate-Date Petits Fours,
Brandy Wafers, Molasses Ginger Cookies, Leckerli, Raspberry-Almond Cookies,
Apricot Foldovers

Danish Pastries
MAKES ABOUT 30.

    3 to 3½ cups all-purpose flour, spooned into cup
    2 packages active dry yeast
    ¼ cup warm water
    1 cup cold milk
    2 eggs, 1 slightly beaten
    2 tablespoons granulated sugar
 1½ cups cold margarine, sliced
       Filling (see below)
       Confectioners' sugar

Measure flour onto piece of waxed paper. Sprinkle yeast into the warm water and let stand 3 to 5 minutes; stir. Blend in milk, unbeaten egg, sugar and about half the flour. Beat with wooden spoon until smooth. Gradually stir in enough remaining flour to make a soft dough. Turn out on well-floured board and let rest while making Filling. Gently roll dough to a 14″ x 10″ rectangle. Cover two thirds of rectangle with slices of margarine, leaving 1″ at edges uncovered. Sprinkle with 2 tablespoons flour. Fold uncovered third of dough over margarine and press edges together. Gently roll to form a 14″ x 10″ rectangle, having long side parallel with front edge of board. Fold again from left and right, making 3 layers of dough. Turn one quarter-turn to the right. Repeat rolling, folding and turning 3 or 4 times, keeping to same size. (Rolling and folding make pastry flaky. If dough becomes sticky, wrap in waxed paper and chill 10 to 15 minutes between rolling and folding.) Roll to an 18″ x 15″ rectangle, rubbing flour on board and rolling pin as needed to prevent sticking. Cut in 3″ squares. Put filling in centers of squares and fold corners to center, pinching points together. Put on baking sheets and let rise at room temperature 1½ hours, or until almost doubled in bulk. Brush tops carefully with beaten egg and bake in preheated hot oven (425°F.) 10 to 12 minutes. Remove to rack to cool. Sift confectioners' sugar over tops.

Filling Mix 1 cup finely chopped almonds or other nuts, ½ cup sugar, 1 egg, and, if desired, ½ teaspoon almond extract.

Filled Butterhorns
The filling is a sweet meringue with finely chopped nuts.
MAKES 32.

>   2 cups all-purpose flour
>   1½ teaspoons granulated sugar
>   ½ teaspoon salt
>   ½ cup butter or margarine
>   1 package active dry yeast
>   2 tablespoons warm water
>   ¼ cup dairy sour cream, heated and cooled
>   2 egg yolks
>   Confectioners' sugar
>   Filling (see below)

Mix flour, sugar and salt. Cut in butter. Sprinkle yeast into warm water (110°F. to 115°F.). Let stand a few minutes; then stir until dissolved. Blend sour cream and egg yolks. Add yeast and mix well. Stir into flour mixture and blend well. Cover and refrigerate at least 3 hours, but not more than 24. Remove from refrigerator and let stand at room temperature until soft enough to handle. Divide dough in 4 parts. Shape one section at a time in a ball and roll on board sprinkled with confectioners' sugar; roll from center to edge to form an 8″ circle. Cover each circle not quite to edges with one fourth of the Filling. Cut each in 8 wedges. Roll up from base of wedge to point. Put on baking sheet point side down. Bake in preheated moderate oven (375°F.) 15 to 20 minutes. Cool and store airtight.

Filling Beat 2 egg whites until stiff peaks are formed. Gradually add ½ cup sugar and ½ teaspoon vanilla extract, beating until glossy. Fold in ½ cup finely chopped nuts.

Frosted Fruit Buns
MAKES 24.

  2 packages active dry yeast
 1¼ cups warm water
 3½ cups all-purpose flour
  6 tablespoons sugar
  ½ teaspoon cinnamon
   Grated rind of 1 orange
  1 teaspoon salt
  ¼ cup butter or margarine, softened
  1 egg
  ½ cup dried currants or seedless raisins
   Frosting (see below)

Sprinkle dry yeast into the warm water. Let stand a few minutes; then stir until dissolved. Add half the flour, the sugar, cinnamon, orange rind, salt, butter and egg. Beat until smooth. Add remaining flour and currants; mix well. Scrape batter from sides of bowl. Cover and let rise until doubled in bulk (about 30 minutes). Stir batter down, and spoon into 24 greased 2¼" muffin cups, filling half full. Let rise until light (20 to 30 minutes). Bake in preheated hot oven (425°F.) 10 to 15 minutes. Cool, and spread tops with frosting.

 Frosting Mix well 2 cups confectioners' sugar, ¼ teaspoon salt and 1 to 2 tablespoons hot milk or water.

Glazed Almond Knots
MAKES 16.

    1½ cups milk
     6 cups (about) unsifted all-purpose flour
     1 package active dry yeast
     3 tablespoons warm water
     4 egg yolks
     ⅔ cup sugar
     1 cup butter or margarine, melted
     ⅔ cup chopped almonds
        Grated rind of 2 large lemons
    ½ teaspoon salt
        Glaze (see below)
        Toasted slivered almonds

Scald milk, pour into large bowl and cool to lukewarm. Stir in 4
cups flour. Soften yeast in the warm water. Stir and beat into flour
mixture. Cover and let rise in a warm place until nearly doubled in
bulk (about 1 hour). Beat egg yolks with sugar until thick and
light. Stir into dough. Stir in melted butter until well blended. Add
almonds, lemon rind and salt. Gradually stir in enough remaining
flour to make a dough that is barely firm enough to handle. Turn
out on lightly floured board and knead, working in more flour
until dough is just firm enough to cut without sticking. (Keep
dough soft, adding no more flour than necessary.) Divide in 16
parts. Roll each part between palms of hands into a log about 6″
long. Tie loosely in a knot. Arrange knots on greased baking sheet.
Repeat, making 16 buns. Let rise in warm place until almost
doubled in bulk (about 1 to 1¼ hours). Bake in preheated hot
oven (400°F.) about 18 minutes. Drizzle Glaze over top while
buns are still warm. Top with toasted slivered almonds.

Glaze Stir together until smooth 1½ cups sifted confectioners'
sugar, 2 tablespoons white wine or orange juice and 2 tablespoons
melted butter or margarine.

Hot Cross Buns
MAKES 18.

 ⅓ cup granulated sugar
 ¾ teaspoon salt
 ½ teaspoon cinnamon
 1 package active dry yeast
 ⅓ cup margarine
 ⅔ cup milk
3⅓ cups unsifted all-purpose flour
 3 eggs
 ⅔ cup currants or raisins
 1 cup confectioners' sugar
 ½ teaspoon vanilla extract

In large bowl of electric mixer or other large bowl if mixer is not available, blend sugar, salt, cinnamon and dry yeast. Melt margarine in small saucepan, remove from heat and add milk. (Resulting mixture should be lukewarm.) Add to first mixture with 1 cup flour and blend. Beat at medium speed of mixer 1 minute or 150 strokes by hand with wooden spoon. Add 2 eggs and 1 yolk (reserving white) and beat well. Stir in remaining flour and the currants. Cover; let rise in warm place 1 hour. Stir down and store, covered, in refrigerator 2 hours or longer. Then stir down and shape with floured hands in eighteen 2″ balls. Put on greased baking sheets and brush with slightly beaten reserved egg white (set aside remainder for frosting). Let rise 30 minutes, or until light. Bake in preheated moderate oven (350°F.) 12 to 15 minutes, or until golden brown. Mix confectioners' sugar with egg white, adding a little water if necessary to make a smooth frosting of spreading consistency. Add vanilla and make a cross on top of each hot bun. Cool.

Philadelphia Sticky Buns

MAKES 18 BUNS.

Butter or margarine
1¼ cups packed light-brown sugar, divided
1½ cups coarsely chopped pecans
3½ to 4 cups all-purpose flour
½ cup granulated sugar
2 packages active dry yeast
1 teaspoon salt
¾ cup very warm (120° to 130°) water
2 eggs
½ cup currants or raisins
1 teaspoon cinnamon

Melt 1 cup butter in saucepan. Add 1 cup brown sugar and simmer, stirring, until mixture boils and sugar melts. Pour into two 9″ square pans, tilting to coat bottom, and sprinkle each equally with the pecans. Set aside. Measure flour onto waxed paper or into bowl. Combine 1 cup flour, the granulated sugar, yeast and salt in large bowl of electric mixer. Stir well and add ¼ cup softened butter and the water. Beat at low speed, scraping sides of bowl occasionally, 2 minutes. Add eggs and ½ cup flour. Beat at medium speed, scraping sides of bowl occasionally, 2 minutes. With spoon, gradually stir in enough additional flour to make a soft dough that leaves sides of bowl. Turn out on lightly floured surface, shape in ball and knead 5 to 10 minutes, or until smooth and elastic. Put in greased bowl, turning to grease top. Cover with plastic wrap or plastic bag and let rise in warm place free from drafts 1½ to 2 hours, or until doubled. Punch down, turn out on lightly floured surface and let rest 10 minutes. Divide dough in half. Roll each half in 12″ x 9″ rectangle. Brush each with 2 tablespoons melted butter. Combine remaining brown sugar, the currants and cinnamon and sprinkle half on each rectangle. Roll tightly, starting at short end, and pinch edges to seal. Cut each roll in nine 1″ slices. Arrange, flat side down, in prepared pans. Cover and let rise in warm place 1 hour, or until doubled. Bake in preheated 350° oven about 25 minutes. Cool on racks 10 minutes, then invert on platters to finish cooling.

Nut Pastries

The nuts which go in the filling are chopped walnuts.
MAKES ABOUT 4 DOZEN.

>   1 cup butter or margarine, softened
>   3 cups sifted all-purpose flour
>   1 package active dry yeast
>   2 tablespoons warm water
>   3 egg yolks
>   1 cup dairy sour cream
>   1 teaspoon vanilla extract
>   Nut Filling (see below)
>   Confectioners' sugar

Cut butter into flour. Soften yeast in the warm water. Add to flour mixture with remaining ingredients, except Nut Filling and sugar. Mix thoroughly and chill a few hours. Roll dough to ⅛″ thickness on floured board. Cut in 3″ squares. Put 1 teaspoon filling in center of each square. Moisten edges of pastry with water and pinch corners up and together. Bake on ungreased baking sheets in preheated moderate oven (375°F.) about 15 minutes. Cool and sprinkle with confectioners' sugar.

Nut Filling Force 4 cups walnuts through food chopper, using medium blade. Add 1 cup granulated sugar, 3 teaspoons vanilla extract and ½ cup milk; mix well.

Shrove Tuesday Buns

In Sweden, these are served in a bowl with warm milk and cinnamon every Tuesday during Lent.
MAKES 12.

> 3½ cups (about) all-purpose flour, spooned into cup
> ¼ cup granulated sugar
> ½ teaspoon salt
> 1 package active dry yeast
> ½ teaspoon crushed cardamom seed, or cinnamon
> ½ cup butter or margarine
> 1 cup milk
> 1 egg, at room temperature
>   Filling (see below)
> 1 cup heavy cream, whipped
>   Confectioners' sugar

Measure flour onto a piece of waxed paper. Combine 1½ cups flour, sugar, salt, dry yeast and cardamom seed or cinnamon in large bowl of electric mixer. Stir well. Melt butter and add milk. (Mixture should be lukewarm.) Gradually add to dry ingredients and beat at low speed, scraping sides of bowl occasionally, 2 minutes. Add egg and 1 cup flour. Beat at medium speed, scraping sides of bowl occasionally, 2 minutes, or until thick and elastic. With wooden spoon, gradually stir in enough remaining flour to make a soft dough that leaves sides of bowl. Turn out on lightly floured board, shape in a ball and knead 5 to 10 minutes, or until smooth and elastic. Put in greased bowl, turning to grease top. Cover with plastic wrap or put in plastic bag and let rise in warm place free from drafts 1 hour, or until doubled in bulk. Punch down, turn out on lightly floured board and knead until smooth. Shape in 12″ roll and cut in 12 equal pieces. Shape in smooth round buns and put on greased baking sheet. Let rise 30 minutes, or until almost doubled. Bake in preheated hot oven (400°F.) 10 to 12 minutes, or until golden brown and buns feel light. Remove to rack, cover with towel and cool. Cut slice off top of each and scoop out inside with fork, leaving a ¼″-thick shell. Reserve crumbs for filling. Spoon filling evenly into buns, add a generous spoonful of whipped cream, replace top and sprinkle with confectioners' sugar. Serve plain or in a bowl with warm milk and cinnamon.

Filling Mix reserved crumbs, ½ cup finely chopped almonds or other nuts, ½ cup confectioners' sugar, ¾ cup light cream and 1 teaspoon vanilla extract.

Slovene Potica

3 to 3½ cups all-purpose flour
⅓ cup sugar
1 teaspoon salt
1 package active dry yeast
¼ cup butter or margarine, softened
¾ cup very warm (120° to 130°) water
1 egg
Walnut Filling (below)
Confectioners'-Sugar Frosting (below)

Measure flour onto waxed paper or into bowl. Combine 1 cup flour, the sugar, salt and yeast in large bowl of electric mixer. Stir well. Add butter and water. Beat at low speed, scraping sides of bowl occasionally, 2 minutes. Add egg and ½ cup flour. Beat at medium speed, scraping sides of bowl occasionally, 2 minutes. With spoon, gradually stir in enough additional flour to make a soft dough that leaves sides of bowl. Turn out on lightly floured surface, shape in ball and knead 5 to 10 minutes, or until smooth and elastic. Put in greased bowl, turning to grease top. Cover with plastic wrap or plastic bag and let rise in warm place free from drafts 1½ to 2 hours, or until doubled. Punch down, turn out on lightly floured board and let rest 10 minutes. Roll to 20" x 15" rectangle. Spread evenly with filling to within 2" of edges. Roll as for jelly roll, starting with longest side. Dampen edges with fingers moistened with water and pinch to seal. Gently pull ends to make a roll 25" long. Form in snail shape, tucking end under to maintain shape while baking. Carefully transfer to large greased baking sheet. Cover loosely and let rise 1½ hours, or until light. Bake in preheated 325° oven about 45 minutes. Cool on rack. Spread top with frosting.

Walnut Filling Combine ¼ cup softened butter or margarine, ½ cup packed brown sugar, 1 egg (beaten), 1 tablespoon grated orange rind and 2 cups chopped walnuts.

Confectioners'-Sugar Frosting Combine 2 tablespoons melted butter or margarine, 1 cup confectioners' sugar and 1 to 2 tablespoons milk. Stir until smooth.

Quick Breads

QUICK BREADS have always been great favorites with Americans. Easy to make and richly satisfying, they seem especially well suited to our fast-paced way of life. In the collection of recipes offered here, you will find many old favorites as well as imaginative new variations. There are delicate tea breads and hearty whole-grain loaves, crusty corn breads, fruit filled muffins, coffee cakes, and many other treats to suit every taste and every occasion. Any of these breads will make a simple meal special or add just the right finishing touch to festive and holiday meals. In addition, they provide such nutritious goodness that they are ideal for snacks as well as at mealtimes.

The next time you want to celebrate an important day, honor a family hero or heroine, welcome a new neighbor or just please someone you care about, bake up a sweet-smelling loaf of Whole-Wheat Banana-Nut Bread, a batch of golden Apple-Nut Muffins, a Quick Cinnamon Coffee Cake or some light-as-air Popovers. The recipes are all here, and since quick breads require no kneading or rising time out of the oven, you can make most of them in just a little over an hour.

TIPS FOR MAKING QUICK BREADS

Have all the ingredients at room temperature. This is especially important in the case of butter, margarine and eggs. Butter or margarine should be soft enough to cream easily, but it should not be oily. You should be able to blend it quickly and thoroughly with the sugar and other ingredients. Egg whites at room temperature can be whipped to greater volume than they can when cold.

After you have combined all the ingredients—wet and dry—stir just enough to moisten the dry ingredients well. Batter should be moist but slightly lumpy. When you mix lightly in this way, your quick breads will have the right crumbly texture. Too much mixing activates the gluten in the flour, which toughens the end product.

When making muffins you can line muffin pan with either paper or foil muffin cups or grease muffin-pan cups well and pour batter directly into pan.

Cool loaf breads before you slice them. Many of them are fragile when warm and will crumble unless you wait until they cool. Individual recipes specify when and how long to cool in the pan and on a rack. Some breads—generally the moist, fruity ones—are actually better if they have a day to mature. They slice better and they taste better.

Wrap breads tightly in aluminum foil to store. Loaf breads keep well for several days at room temperature, slightly longer in the refrigerator. Muffins usually keep better in the refrigerator. Reheat in foil in a preheated 350°F. oven for about 15 minutes.

Most of these breads freeze well, although some may be slightly drier after freezing. To freeze, cool breads thoroughly, wrap tightly in plastic wrap and then in foil. Don't forget to date them. Most will keep successfully for about three months. Defrost at room temperature.

Almond Applesauce Bread

2 cups all-purpose flour
½ cup sugar
2 teaspoons baking powder
½ teaspoon salt
½ teaspoon baking soda
½ teaspoon cinnamon
½ teaspoon ground cardamom
1 can (5 ounces) toasted diced almonds
3 tablespoons butter or margarine, softened
1 egg
1 cup canned applesauce

Mix all ingredients, except almonds, butter, egg and applesauce in bowl. Reserve 3 tablespoons almonds and add remainder to first mixture. Cut in butter. Add egg and applesauce and mix only until dry ingredients are moistened. Pour into greased 9″ x 5″ x 3″ loaf pan and sprinkle with reserved almonds. Bake in preheated 350°F. oven 45 minutes, or until done. Turn out on rack and cool thoroughly before slicing.

Note If preferred, ¾ cup blanched or unblanched almonds, toasted, then chopped, can be substituted for the canned toasted almonds. Melted butter, margarine or liquid margarine can be used. Stir into batter just before pouring into pan.

Banana Nut Bread

> ½ cup butter or margarine
> ¾ cup sugar
> 3 eggs
> 2½ cups sifted all-purpose flour
> ½ teaspoon salt
> ¾ teaspoon baking soda
> 1 teaspoon baking powder
> 3 ripe bananas, mashed
> ½ cup chopped walnuts

Cream butter until light and fluffy. Gradually beat in sugar. Add eggs one at a time, and beat thoroughly. Sift together flour, salt, soda and baking powder and add to egg mixture. Stir in bananas and walnuts. Pour into a greased and floured 9″ x 5″ x 3″ loaf pan. Bake in a preheated 350°F. oven for 1 hour, or until done. Cool for ten minutes in the pan, then turn out on a wire rack to cool completely before cutting.

Whole Wheat Banana Nut Bread

> 1½ cups whole-wheat pastry flour
> 2 teaspoons baking powder
> ¼ teaspoon baking soda
> ½ teaspoon salt
> ½ cup chopped walnuts or other nuts
> 2 tablespoons chopped candied ginger
> ⅓ cup butter or margarine
> 1 cup packed light-brown sugar
> 2 eggs
> 1 cup (about 2 medium) mashed ripe bananas

Mix together flour, baking powder, soda, salt, nuts and candied ginger; set aside. Cream butter and sugar together until blended. Add eggs one at a time, beating after each until smooth. Add dry ingredients and banana and mix well. Put in 9″ x 5″ x 3″ loaf pan lined on bottom with waxed paper. Bake in preheated 350°F. oven 1 hour, or until done. Turn out on rack and peel off paper. Turn right side up and cool before cutting. Keeps well, wrapped and stored in cool place. Can also be frozen.

Blueberry-Orange Bread

     2 tablespoons butter
    ¼ cup boiling water
    ½ cup, plus 2 tablespoons orange juice
     4 teaspoons grated orange rind
     1 egg
     1 cup sugar
     2 cups sifted all-purpose flour
     1 teaspoon baking powder
    ¼ teaspoon baking soda
    ½ teaspoon salt
     1 cup washed fresh, or drained thawed frozen blueberries
     2 tablespoons honey

Melt butter in boiling water in small bowl. Add ½ cup orange juice and 3 teaspoons rind. Beat egg with sugar until light and fluffy. Sift together flour, baking powder, soda and salt, and add to egg mixture alternately with orange liquid, beating until smooth. Fold in berries. Bake in greased fancy 1½-quart loaf pan, or 9″ x 5″ x 3″ pan, in preheated moderate oven (325°F.) about 1 hour and 10 minutes. Turn out on rack on tray. Mix 2 tablespoons orange juice, 1 teaspoon rind and the honey; spoon over hot loaf. Let stand until cold.

Bran-Molasses Bread

    1 cup whole-bran cereal
    1 cup whole-wheat flour
    ½ cup raisins
    1 teaspoon baking powder
    ½ teaspoon baking soda
    ½ teaspoon salt
    1 egg
    ½ cup, plus 2 tablespoons buttermilk
    ¼ cup molasses

In large bowl combine cereal, flour, raisins, baking powder, soda and salt; set aside. Blend egg, buttermilk and molasses and add all at once to flour mixture; stir just until moist. Turn into greased 7½″ x 3¾″ x 2¼″ loaf pan. Bake in preheated 375°F. oven 25 minutes, or until pick inserted in center comes out clean. Cool in pan 10 minutes, then invert on rack and cool.

Buttermilk Nut Bread

    ⅓ cup margarine, softened
    ½ cup sugar
    1 egg
    2 cups all-purpose flour
    1 teaspoon salt
    2 teaspoons double-acting baking powder
    ¼ teaspoon baking soda
    ¾ cup chopped walnuts, filberts or other nuts
    1¼ cups buttermilk

Cream margarine and sugar until light and fluffy. Beat in egg. Sift dry ingredients and add nuts. Add to first mixture alternately with buttermilk, beating after each addition. Put in 9″ x 5″ x 3″ loaf pan lined on the bottom with waxed paper and bake in preheated slow oven (325°F.) 1 to 1¼ hours. Turn out on rack and peel off paper. Turn right side up and cool thoroughly before cutting.

Carrot-Nut Bread

3 eggs
1½ cups sugar
1 cup vegetable oil
2¼ cups whole-wheat flour
1¼ teaspoons baking soda
1½ teaspoons cinnamon
1½ teaspoons nutmeg
¾ teaspoon salt
2¼ cups finely grated raw carrots
1½ cups chopped walnuts
1¼ cups raisins

Beat eggs well, then add sugar and oil and beat until light. Mix flour, soda, cinnamon, nutmeg and salt. Add to egg mixture and stir until just moistened. Stir in remaining ingredients. Turn into greased 9″ x 5″ x 3″ loaf pan and bake in preheated 350°F. oven about 1¼ hours. Cool on wire rack 10 minutes, then remove from pan and cool.

Old-Time Corn Bread

2 eggs
1½ cups buttermilk
3 tablespoons lard, melted
1½ cups yellow cornmeal
1 teaspoon salt
1 cup all-purpose flour
¾ teaspoon baking soda

Beat together eggs, buttermilk and melted lard. Add remaining ingredients and mix well. Pour into greased 11″ x 7″ x 2″ pan and bake in preheated hot oven (400°F.) about 30 minutes.

Sour Cream Corn Bread

Sour cream gives a distinctive moistness and tenderness to corn bread.

> ¾ cup yellow cornmeal
> 1 cup unsifted all-purpose flour
> ¼ cup sugar
> 2 teaspoons double-acting baking powder
> ½ teaspoon baking soda
> ¾ teaspoon salt
> 1 cup dairy sour cream
> ¼ cup milk
> 1 egg, beaten
> 2 tablespoons shortening, melted

Mix all ingredients just enough to blend. Pour into greased 8″ square pan and bake in preheated hot oven (425°F.) about 20 minutes.

Cornmeal-Onion Batter Bread

MAKES 6 SERVINGS.

> 1 cup yellow cornmeal
> 1¼ teaspoons salt
> 2 teaspoons baking powder
> 2 cups milk
> 2 eggs
> ¼ cup chopped green onion
> 1 cup boiling water
> 2 tablespoons oil

Combine cornmeal, salt and baking powder in greased 1½-quart casserole. Stir in milk, eggs and onion and beat well with whisk. Stir in water and oil and mix well. Bake in preheated 375°F. oven 35 minutes or until puffed and golden brown. Serve at once.

Cranberry-Nut Bread

Boiling water
Juice and grated rind of 1 orange
2 tablespoons butter or margarine
1 cup sugar
1 egg
1 cup cranberries, washed, drained and chopped
½ cup chopped nuts
2 cups all-purpose flour
½ teaspoon salt
½ teaspoon baking soda

Add enough boiling water to orange juice to make ¾ cup liquid. Add grated rind and butter. Stir to melt butter. In another bowl, beat sugar and egg together and stir into orange mixture. Add cranberries and nuts. Sift together remaining ingredients and stir into first mixture. Pour into greased 9" x 5" x 3" loaf pan and bake in preheated slow oven (325°F.) for about 1 hour. Cool on rack and store overnight before slicing.

Honey-Pineapple Bread

3 cups all purpose-flour
3 teaspoons baking powder
¾ teaspoon baking soda
1½ teaspoons salt
3 eggs
½ cup vegetable oil
½ cup clover honey
1 can (8½ ounces) crushed pineapple
½ cup water
¾ cup chopped pecans or walnuts

Sift together dry ingredients. Beat eggs until thick and lemon-colored. Combine oil, honey, undrained crushed pineapple and the water, and mix with eggs. Add to dry ingredients, mixing only until blended. Fold in nuts and spread in greased 9″ x 5″ x 3″ loaf pan. Bake in preheated moderate oven (350°F.) 1 hour. Then reduce heat to 325°F. and bake 15 minutes longer, or until center is done. Cool in pan about 5 minutes, then turn out on rack. Cool completely before slicing. Loaf can be sliced thinner if cut the day after baking. Good with whipped cream cheese.

Honey-Raisin Quick Bread

         2 tablespoons butter or margarine, softened
        ⅓ cup honey
         3 tablespoons sugar
         2 eggs
        ⅔ cup whole-wheat flour
         1 cup all-purpose flour
      1½ teaspoons baking powder
        ½ teaspoon salt
        ½ teaspoon baking soda
        ½ cup buttermilk
        ½ cup raisins, scalded (see Note)
        ½ cup chopped nuts
         1 teaspoon grated lemon rind

Cream butter, honey and sugar thoroughly. Add eggs one at a time, beating after each until blended. Add whole-wheat flour. Then add other dry ingredients alternately with buttermilk, beating until blended. Add remaining ingredients and pour into greased 8½″ x 4½″ x 2½″ glass loaf pan. Bake in preheated slow oven (325°F.) about 50 minutes. Turn out on rack and cool thoroughly before slicing.

   Note To scald raisins, cover with boiling water and drain.

Sweet Lemon Bread

½ cup butter or margarine, softened
1 cup sugar
2 eggs
1½ cups sifted all-purpose flour
1 teaspoon baking powder
½ teaspoon salt
½ cup milk
    Juice and grated rind of 1 lemon
    Lemon glaze (optional)

Cream butter and sugar. Beat in eggs. Sift dry ingredients together and add to batter alternately with milk. Mix well. Stir in lemon juice and rind. Bake in greased 9″ x 5″ x 3″ loaf pan in preheated slow oven (300°F.) about 1 hour and 10 minutes. Remove to rack. If desired, pierce loaf top with cake tester in a number of places and pour over glaze made by mixing juice of 1 lemon and ½ cup sugar. Slice thin and serve at room temperature or cooled.

Orange-Nut Bread

2½ cups all-purpose flour
3 teaspoons double-acting baking powder
1 cup sugar
1 teaspoon salt
¼ cup vegetable shortening
1 egg
¾ cup milk
¼ cup orange juice
3 tablespoons grated orange rind
1 cup chopped walnuts or pecans

Combine flour, baking powder, sugar and salt in bowl and stir with fork to mix. Cut in shortening with pastry blender or fork. Beat egg slightly with fork and stir in milk, orange juice and rind. Add to dry ingredients, stirring only enough to dampen. Gently stir in nuts. Pour into greased 9″ x 5″ x 3″ loaf pan, spreading to corners and leaving a slight depression in center. Let stand 20 minutes. Bake in preheated 350°F. oven 55 to 60 minutes. Let stand 5 minutes, then turn out on rack to cool. Wrap and store overnight before slicing. Good with softened cream cheese.

Pumpkin Tea Loaf

> 2½ cups all-purpose flour
> ½ cup wheat germ
> 3 teaspoons baking powder
> 1½ teaspoons salt
> 1 teaspoon baking soda
> 1 teaspooon cinnamon
> ½ teaspoon nutmeg
> ½ teaspoon ginger
> ¼ teaspoon ground cloves
> 1½ cups sugar
> ½ cup vegetable oil
> 2 eggs
> 1½ cups canned pumpkin

Put flour, wheat germ, baking powder, salt, soda, cinnamon, nutmeg, ginger and cloves on sheet of waxed paper and stir to blend. Put sugar, oil and eggs in bowl and beat until creamy. Add pumpkin and mix until well blended. Add dry ingredients and mix only until ingredients are moistened. Spread in greased 9″ x 5″ x 3″ loaf pan and bake in preheated moderate oven (350°F.) 1 hour, or until done. Cool in pan on wire rack 10 minutes. Remove from pan and cool. Wrap and store overnight for easier slicing.

Soy-Prune Bread

> 1 cup pitted dried prunes
> ¾ cup all-purpose flour
> 1½ cups whole-wheat flour

¾ cup sifted soy flour
4½ teaspoons baking powder
1¼ teaspoons salt
¾ cup sugar
1 egg
4 teaspoons lemon juice
4 teaspoons grated lemon rind
1¼ cups milk
2 tablespoons vegetable oil

Soak prunes in water to cover ½ hour. Drain and cut in small pieces. Mix together the three flours, baking powder, salt and sugar. Beat egg in large bowl. Add prunes and remaining ingredients. Mix well, then add dry ingredients and stir only until blended. Spoon into greased 9″ x 5″ x 3″ loaf pan. Let rest free from drafts 20 minutes. Bake in preheated 325°F. oven 50 minutes, or until tester inserted in center comes out clean. Turn out and cool on wire rack.

White Soda Bread
MAKES 1 ROUND LOAF.

3 cups all-purpose flour
1½ teaspoons salt
1½ teaspoons baking soda
1½ teaspoons sugar
1 tablespoons butter or margarine
1⅓ cups (about) buttermilk

Put flour in mixing bowl. Mix salt and soda and add to flour with sugar. Mix well with fork. Blend butter into flour mixture with 2 knives, a pastry blender or fingers. Make a well in center, add buttermilk and stir until blended (dough should be dry enough to knead but not too dry). Knead on floured board about 30 seconds, then pat into greased 8″ round cake pan. Cut gashes across top in form of cross. Bake in preheated 400° oven 30 minutes, or until well browned. Cool on rack before cutting.

Apple-Nut Muffins
MAKES 12.

1½ cups all-purpose flour
2 teaspoons baking powder
¼ teaspoon salt
¾ cup sugar
⅓ cup oil
1 teaspoon vanilla extract
2 eggs
1 cup chopped unpeeled apple
¼ cup chopped nuts
½ cup evaporated milk

Combine flour, baking powder and salt; set aside. In large bowl mix sugar, oil and vanilla. Add eggs and mix until well blended. Add half the flour mixture and mix well. Stir in apple, nuts and milk. Add remaining flour mixture and mix just until blended. Grease bottoms of twelve 2½" muffin cups and divide batter among cups. Bake in preheated 350°F. oven about 25 minutes, or until pick inserted in center comes out clean and muffins are golden brown. Remove from cups and serve warm.

Blueberry Muffins
MAKES 16 TO 24.

2½ cups sifted all-purpose flour
2½ teaspoons baking powder
¼ teaspoon salt
½ cup sugar
1 cup buttermilk
2 eggs, beaten
1½ cups washed fresh blueberries
½ cup butter or margarine, melted
Granulated sugar

Sift flour, baking powder, salt and ½ cup sugar. Add buttermilk, eggs and melted butter and mix only until dry ingredients are dampened. Fold in berries. Spoon into greased muffin-pan cups filling two-thirds full. Sprinkle with granulated sugar. Bake in preheated hot oven (400°F.) 20 to 25 minutes.

Whole-Bran Muffins
MAKES 12.

```
    2  cups whole bran
 1¼  cups milk
    1  cup all-purpose flour
    1  tablespoon baking powder
  ¾  teaspoon salt
    2  tablespoons sugar
    1  egg, beaten
    1  tablespoon liquid or melted margarine or butter
```

Soak bran in the milk in mixing bowl 5 minutes. Stir together flour, baking powder, salt and sugar. Add egg and margarine to bran mixture, then add dry ingredients, stirring only enough to moisten. Fill greased muffin cups two-thirds full. Bake in preheated 400°F. oven about 25 minutes.

Cinnamon-Raisin Muffins
MAKES 12.

```
 1½  cups whole-wheat flour
  ⅓  cup packed brown sugar
    3  teaspoons baking powder
  ½  teaspoon salt
    1  teaspoon cinnamon
  ½  cup wheat germ
  ¾  cup unsulfured raisins
  ⅔  cup milk
  ⅓  cup soy or other cold-pressed oil
    2  eggs, slightly beaten
```

Mix flour, brown sugar, baking powder, salt, cinnamon, wheat germ and raisins in bowl. Add remaining ingredients and mix only until dry ingredients are moistened. Fill greased 2½″ muffin-pan cups two-thirds full and bake in preheated 400°F. oven about 20 minutes.

Sweet Cranberry Muffins
MAKES 12.

    2 cups all-purpose flour
    ½ cup sugar
    3 teaspoons baking powder
    ½ teaspoon salt
    ¼ cup shortening, melted
    1 egg
    1 cup milk
    1 cup cranberries, rinsed and drained
    Melted butter or margarine
    Sugar-cinnamon mixture (2 tablespoons sugar to 2 teaspoons cinnamon)

Mix flour, sugar, baking powder and salt in bowl. Add melted shortening, egg and milk, and stir to mix. Fold in cranberries and spoon into well-greased medium muffin-pan cups. Bake in preheated hot oven (400°F.) 20 to 25 minutes. Remove from pans and brush tops with melted butter. Sprinkle with sugar-cinnamon mixture and serve warm.

Hawaiian Pineapple Muffins
MAKES 24.

    4 cups all-purpose flour
    2 tablespoons baking powder
    ½ cup sugar
    1 teaspoon salt

4 eggs, beaten
1½ cups milk
½ cup butter or margarine, melted
1½ cups drained crushed pineapple

Sift dry ingredients. Add eggs, milk and butter. Stir until smooth. Add pineapple. Mix well. Spoon into greased 3″ muffin-pan cups filling three-quarters full. Bake in preheated hot oven (425°F.) 20 to 25 minutes.

Old-Fashioned Oatmeal Muffins
MAKES 12.

¾ cup old-fashioned rolled oats
¾ cup, plus 2 tablespoons all-purpose flour
2 tablespoons light-brown sugar
1½ teaspoons baking powder
½ teaspoon baking soda
½ teaspoon salt
1 teaspoon cinnamon
¼ cup butter or margarine
1 egg
¾ cup buttermilk
Sugar-cinnamon mixture (2 tablespoons sugar to 2 teaspoons cinnamon)

Combine oats, flour, brown sugar, baking powder, soda, salt and cinnamon in mixing bowl and mix well. Cut in butter. Beat egg and buttermilk together and pour over first mixture. Mix only until dry ingredients are moistened. Put twelve 2½″ paper-lined foil muffin cups on baking sheet and fill two-thirds full. Sprinkle tops with sugar-cinnamon mixture. Bake in preheated 425°F. oven 15 to 20 minutes. Serve warm with butter.

Note Muffins can be baked in greased muffin-pan cups, if preferred.

Peanut Butter Muffins
They're topped with a bit of apricot preserve.
MAKES 10.

$1\frac{3}{4}$ cups sifted all-purpose flour
$2\frac{1}{2}$ teaspoons double-acting baking powder
  2 tablespoons sugar
 $\frac{3}{4}$ teaspoon salt
  2 tablespoons wheat germ
 $\frac{1}{4}$ cup shortening, softened
 $\frac{1}{4}$ cup peanut butter
  1 egg, well beaten
 $\frac{3}{4}$ cup milk
   Apricot preserves

Sift flour, baking powder, sugar and salt into bowl. Add wheat germ. Cut in shortening and peanut butter. Mix egg and milk and add all at once to first mixture. Stir only until dry ingredients are dampened. Spoon into greased large muffin-pan cups filling only two-thirds full. Put about $\frac{1}{2}$ teaspoon preserves in center of each. Bake in preheated hot oven (400°F.) 25 minutes, or until done.

Soy-Raisin Muffins
MAKES 12.

 $\frac{1}{2}$ cup soy flour
$1\frac{1}{2}$ cups whole-wheat flour
  3 teaspoons baking powder
 $\frac{1}{2}$ teaspoon salt
  2 tablespoons sugar
  3 tablespoons margarine
  1 egg
  1 cup milk
 $\frac{1}{2}$ cup raisins

Mix dry ingredients and cut in margarine. Add egg and milk and mix lightly. Fold in raisins. Fill greased medium muffin-pan cups two-thirds full with the mixture and bake in preheated 425°F. oven 12 to 15 minutes.

Vermont Maple-Corn Muffins
MAKES 12.

   1 egg
  ⅓ cup milk
   2 tablespoons maple syrup
  ½ cup yellow cornmeal
  ¾ cup all-purpose flour
1½ teaspoons baking powder
  ¼ teaspoon salt
   3 tablespoons butter (or part butter, part margarine), melted

Beat egg. Add milk and syrup and beat again. Mix cornmeal, flour, baking powder and salt. Gradually stir in first mixture. Add melted butter. Spoon into tiny well-greased preheated muffin-pan cups, filling only three-quarters full. Bake in preheated hot oven (425°F.) 15 minutes, or until muffins are crisp and brown outside, tender and light inside. Serve hot with butter and maple syrup.

Blueberry Breakfast Roll

   1 cup washed fresh, or thawed drained frozen blueberries
    Sugar
   2 cups sifted all-purpose flour
2½ teaspoons baking powder
  ½ teaspoon salt
  ¼ cup butter
   1 egg
    Milk

Sprinkle fresh berries with 2 tablespoons sugar. (Omit for frozen if they contain sugar.) Sift together ¼ cup sugar, the flour, baking powder and salt. Cut in butter. Break egg into measuring cup; add milk to make ¾ cup. With fork, stir into first mixture. Roll out on floured board to a 12″ x 8″ rectangle. Sprinkle with berries, and roll up tightly. Slip onto a greased baking sheet, and bake in preheated moderate oven (375°F.) about 25 minutes. Slice, and serve hot with butter.

Apple Coffee Cake

        2 cups all-purpose flour
      ¼ cup sugar
        2 teaspoons baking powder
      ½ teaspoon salt
      ¼ cup butter or margarine, softened
        1 egg
      ⅔ cup milk
        2 small tart apples, peeled, cored and sliced thin (about 2 cups)
          Cinnamon-Nut Topping (see below)
      ¼ cup butter or margarine, melted

Mix flour, sugar, baking powder and salt. Cut in butter until mixture resembles coarse cornmeal. Beat egg and milk and pour over flour mixture; stir just until moistened. Spoon into greased 8″ x 8″ x 2″ pan. Arrange apples evenly on top. Sprinkle with topping and drizzle with melted butter. Bake in preheated 400°F. oven 30 minutes, or until pick inserted in center comes out clean and apples are tender. Cool in pan on rack.

Cinnamon-Nut Topping Mix ½ cup each packed brown sugar and chopped nuts, ½ teaspoon cinnamon and ¼ teaspoon nutmeg.

Cranberry Crumb Coffee Cake

> Cranberry Topping (see below)
> Crumb Topping (see below)
> ⅔ cup butter or margarine
> 1 cup sugar
> 2 eggs
> 2⅔ cups all-purpose flour
> 3 teaspoons baking powder
> 1 teaspoon salt
> 1 cup milk
> 2 teaspoons vanilla extract

Prepare Cranberry Topping and cool while preparing cake. Mix Crumb Topping and set aside. Cream butter and sugar until blended. Add eggs one at a time, beating thoroughly after each. Mix dry ingredients and add alternately with milk, beating after each addition until smooth. Add vanilla and spread in greased 13″ x 9″ x 2″ pan. Spread with Cranberry Topping, then sprinkle with Crumb Topping. Bake in preheated moderate oven (350°F.) about 35 minutes. Serve warm or cool.

Cranberry Topping Blend 2 teaspoons cornstarch with ½ cup water in large saucepan. Add 1 pound washed cranberries, 1 cup sugar and ¾ teaspoon cinnamon. Bring to boil and cook, stirring, until cranberries pop open and mixture is thickened.

Crumb Topping Mix ¼ cup flour and ⅔ cup packed brown sugar. Cut in ¼ cup softened butter, until crumbly.

Ginger Coffee Cake

2 cups all-purpose flour
½ cup packed brown sugar
1 teaspoon baking powder
½ teaspoon baking soda
½ teaspoon salt
1 teaspoon ginger
½ cup butter or margarine, softened
1 egg, slightly beaten
2 tablespoons molasses
1 cup buttermilk
Ginger-Nut Topping (see below)

Mix flour, sugar, baking powder, soda, salt and ginger. Cut in butter until mixture resembles coarse cornmeal. Beat egg, molasses and buttermilk and pour over flour mixture; stir just until moistened. Pour into greased 8″ x 8″ x 2″ pan. Sprinkle with topping. Bake in preheated 350°F. oven 30 minutes, or until pick inserted in center comes out clean. Cool in pan on rack.

Ginger-Nut Topping Mix ¼ cup each packed brown sugar and chopped nuts, and 1 teaspoon ginger.

Glazed Orange Coffee Cake

2 cups all-purpose flour
2 teaspoons double-acting baking powder
½ teaspoon salt
¼ cup butter or margarine, softened
⅓ cup sugar
1 egg, beaten
⅓ cup raisins
1 teaspoon grated orange rind
½ cup evaporated milk

⅓ cup orange juice
2 tablespoons water
   Orange Glaze (see below)
⅓ cup chopped pecans or walnuts

Stir together flour, baking powder and salt; set aside. In large bowl of electric mixer cream butter and sugar until fluffy; beat in egg. Stir in flour mixture, raisins and orange rind. In cup blend milk, orange juice and water, then add all at once to flour mixture, stirring just until moistened. Pour into greased 9″ x 9″ x 2″ pan and bake in preheated 425°F. oven 20 minutes, or until pick inserted in center comes out clean. Spoon glaze over cake, sprinkle with nuts and return to oven for 5 minutes. Cut in squares and serve warm.

Orange Glaze In small saucepan blend ⅓ cup sugar, ¼ cup butter or margarine, ¼ cup dairy sour cream, 1 tablespoon orange juice and ½ teaspoon grated orange rind and bring just to boil, stirring constantly (do not boil).

Pineapple-Nut Coffee Cake

2 cups all-purpose flour
1 teaspoon baking powder
1 teaspoon baking soda
½ cup butter or margarine, softened
1 cup sugar
1 teaspoon vanilla extract
¼ teaspoon salt
2 eggs
1 cup dairy sour cream
½ cup pineapple preserves
   Coconut-Nut Topping (see below)

Mix flour, baking powder and soda; set aside. In large bowl of electric mixer cream butter, sugar, vanilla and salt until fluffy. Add eggs one at a time and beat after each until blended. Stir flour mixture into creamed mixture alternately with sour cream; mix until smooth. Spread half the batter in greased 9″ x 9″ x 2″ pan; dot with preserves, then spread with remaining batter. Sprinkle with topping. Bake in preheated 350°F. oven 35 to 40 minutes, or until pick inserted in center comes out clean. Cool in pan on rack.

Coconut-Nut Topping Mix ¼ cup packed brown sugar, 2 tablespoons each flaked coconut and chopped nuts, 1 tablespoon softened butter or margarine and ¼ teaspoon cinnamon.

Sugar-Plum Coffee Cake

        2⅓ cups all-purpose flour
          4 teaspoons baking powder
          ½ teaspoon salt
          1 cup sugar
          ¼ cup shortening
          1 egg, well beaten
          ½ cup milk
          ½ cup orange juice
        1½ teaspoons grated orange rind
        10 (or more) fresh prune-plums
          ½ teaspoon cinnamon
          ¼ cup butter or margarine, softened

Sift together 2 cups flour, the baking powder, salt and ½ cup sugar. Cut in shortening until mixture is crumbly. Carefully stir in egg, milk, orange juice and rind, but do not beat. Put in greased round baking dish about 10″ x 2″. Cut plums in half and remove seeds. Then cut halves lengthwise. Arrange quarters on sides in pattern on top of batter. With fork, mix remaining flour and sugar, the cinnamon and butter. Sprinkle on plums and bake in preheated moderate oven (375°F.) about 35 minutes. Cut in wedges and serve hot.

Quick Cinnamon Coffee Cake

1½ cups sugar
½ cup chopped nuts
1 tablespoon cinnamon
½ cup butter or margarine
2 eggs
1 teaspoon vanilla extract
1 tablespoon lemon juice
2 cups all-purpose flour
½ teaspoon baking powder
1 teaspoon baking soda
1 teaspoon salt
1 cup dairy sour cream

Mix ½ cup sugar, the nuts and cinnamon; set aside. Cream butter and beat in remaining sugar and the eggs. Add vanilla and lemon juice. Mix dry ingredients and add alternately with sour cream. Spread half batter in greased 9″ square pan. Sprinkle with some of cinnamon mixture. Spread with remaining batter and sprinkle with remaining mixture. Bake in preheated moderate oven (350°F.) 35 minutes.

Cinnamon Bowknots
MAKES 12.

2 cups all-purpose flour
1 tablespoon baking powder
1 teaspoon salt
6 tablespoons shortening
⅔ cup milk
¼ cup butter or margarine, melted
2 tablespoons sugar mixed with 1 teaspoon cinnamon

Combine flour, baking powder and salt in bowl. Cut in shortening until mixture resembles coarse crumbs. Add milk all at once and stir with fork until mixture forms ball and no flour remains. Turn out on lightly floured surface and knead lightly 25 times. Roll out ½″ thick. Cut with floured 2½″ doughnut cutter. Twist each ring to form figure eight, place on ungreased cookie sheet and bake in preheated 450°F. oven 12 minutes, or until lightly browned. Dip tops in melted butter, then in sugar-cinnamon mixture.

Sour Cream Walnut Coffee Cake

So rich it's almost like pound cake.

> 3 cups all-purpose flour
> 1½ teaspoons baking powder
> 1½ teaspoons baking soda
> ½ teaspoon salt
> ¾ cup butter or margarine
> 1½ cups granulated sugar
> 3 eggs
> 2 teaspoons vanilla extract
> 1 pint dairy sour cream
> ¾ cup packed light-brown sugar
> 2 teaspoons cinnamon
> 1 cup coarsely chopped walnuts
> Confectioners'-Sugar Frosting (see below)

Mix flour, baking powder, soda and salt, and set aside. Cream butter in large bowl of electric mixer until soft. Gradually add granulated sugar and beat well. Add eggs one at a time, beating thoroughly after each; add vanilla. Then add flour mixture alternately with sour cream, blending after each addition until smooth. Mix brown sugar, cinnamon and walnuts together. Put about one third of batter in well-greased 10″ tube pan or bundt pan. Sprinkle with one third of nut mixture. Repeat until all batter and mixture are used. Bake in preheated moderate oven (350°F.) 1 hour, or until done. Let stand on wire rack about 5 minutes, then turn out of pan, leaving cake bottom up. While cake is still warm, put on board or serving plate and spread with frosting, allowing mixture to run down sides. Serve slightly warm or cold. Cake can also be frozen.

Confectioners'-Sugar Frosting Mix 1½ cups confectioners' sugar with enough water to make a frosting of spreading consistency. Add ½ teaspoon vanilla extract.

Note To bake in loaf pans, prepare batter as in above recipe and alternate layers of batter and nut mixture in thirds, as directed, in two greased 9″ x 5″ x 3″ loaf pans lined on bottoms with waxed paper. Bake in preheated moderate oven (350°F.) 50 minutes, or until done. Loosen from sides of pan and turn out on wire rack. Turn cakes right side up. Cool slightly, then drizzle frosting over tops, allowing some to run down sides. Serve warm or cool.

Quick Buttermilk Buns
MAKES 24.

  ½ cup butter or margarine, softened
  ¾ cup sugar
  1 egg
  1 cup buttermilk
  2½ cups all-purpose flour, lightly spooned into cup
  ¼ teaspoon salt
  ½ teaspoon baking soda
  ½ teaspoon baking powder
    Chopped nuts
    Granulated sugar

Cream butter, add ¾ cup sugar and cream until light and fluffy. Beat in egg. Stir in buttermilk alternately with sifted dry ingredients, mixing only until blended. Drop by heaping tablespoonfuls on lightly greased baking sheets. Sprinkle with nuts and sugar. Bake in preheated moderate oven (375°F.) about 15 minutes. Best when served warm. Good with milk or hot cocoa.

Bite-Size Caramel Buns
MAKES 24.

   2 cups all-purpose flour
   3 teaspoons double-acting baking powder
   ½ teaspoon salt
   ½ cup packed light-brown sugar
   ½ cup butter or margarine
   ¾ cup milk

Mix flour, baking powder, salt and brown sugar in bowl. Cut in butter until the size of peas. Add milk and mix only until blended. Divide into 24 greased 2½" muffin cups. Bake in preheated 375°F. oven about 15 minutes. Serve warm.

Orange Pinwheel Rolls
MAKES 24.

   2 cups all-purpose flour, spooned into cup
   3 teaspoons double-acting baking powder
   ½ cup, plus 2 tablespoons sugar
   ½ teaspoon salt
   ¼ cup shortening
   1 egg, beaten
   ½ cup milk
      Grated rind of 1 large orange
   2 tablespoons butter or margarine, melted

Sift flour, baking powder, 2 tablespoons sugar and the salt. Cut in shortening. Combine egg and milk and add to dry ingredients, stirring with fork only enough to moisten. Turn out on floured board and knead gently 30 seconds. Roll to a rectangle ¼" thick. Mix ½ cup sugar and the orange rind. Brush dough with the melted butter and sprinkle with half the orange mixture. Roll up and cut in ¾" slices. Put in 24 paper muffin cups and sprinkle with remaining orange mixture. Bake in preheated hot oven (425°F.) 15 to 20 minutes.

Whole-Wheat Sticky Buns
MAKES 12.

      Brown sugar
      Butter or margarine
      Pecan halves
1 cup whole-wheat flour
¾ cup all-purpose flour
3 tablespoons granulated sugar
4 teaspoons baking powder
½ teaspoon salt
1 egg, slightly beaten
1 cup milk
¼ cup oil

Measure 2 teaspoons brown sugar and 2 teaspoons butter into each of twelve 2½″ muffin cups. Place in 400°F. oven to melt. Remove and place 2 pecan halves in each cup. In bowl mix flours, granulated sugar, baking powder and salt; set aside. Blend well egg, milk and oil and add all at once to flour mixture; mix just until flour is moist; divide among muffin cups. Bake in preheated 400°F. oven 20 to 25 minutes, or until pick inserted in center comes out clean. Invert on platter and serve warm.

Hot Biscuits
MAKES 12 TO 18.

2 cups all-purpose flour
1 tablespoon baking powder
1 teaspoon salt
¼ cup solid white vegetable shortening
¾ cup (about) milk

Put flour, baking powder and salt in mixing bowl and mix well with fork. Cut in shortening with pastry blender or fingertips until mixture resembles coarse crumbs. With fork, blend in enough milk to make a soft dough. Turn out on lightly floured board and

knead gently 10 turns. Roll or pat out to ½″ thickness and cut
with floured 2″ cutter (or pat dough to an 8″ x 6″ rectangle, cut
in thirds lengthwise, then cut each third in 6 pieces crosswise to
make 18). Put on ungreased baking sheet and bake in preheated
450°F. oven 10 minutes, or until lightly browned.

DROP BISCUITS

Prepare biscuit dough, increasing milk to 1 cup to make a thick
batter. Drop from spoon onto ungreased baking sheet and bake as
directed.

HERB BISCUITS

Prepare biscuit dough, adding ¼ teaspoon thyme leaves and ½
teaspoon ground sage to dry ingredients. Proceed as directed.

ORANGE BISCUITS

Prepare biscuit dough, adding grated rind of 1 orange to dry
ingredients.

CHEESE BISCUITS

Prepare biscuit dough, adding ½ cup shredded sharp Cheddar
cheese and 2 tablespoons dried chives to dry ingredients. Pat
dough to a 7″ square. Cut in 16 squares and put in greased 8″
square pan. Brush lightly with melted butter or margarine and bake
in preheated 450°F. oven about 12 minutes.

CORNMEAL BISCUITS

Prepare biscuit dough, substituting ½ cup cornmeal for ½ cup
flour. Proceed as directed.

WHEAT-GERM BISCUITS

Prepare biscuit dough, substituting ½ cup wheat germ for ½ cup flour. Proceed as directed.

Whole-Wheat Banana Biscuits
MAKES ABOUT 20.

> 2 cups whole-wheat flour
> ¼ cup soy flour
> 3 teaspoons baking powder
> ½ teaspoon baking soda
> 1 teaspoon sugar
> 1 teaspoon salt
> ½ cup butter, softened
> ½ cup dairy sour cream
> ½ cup (about 1 medium) mashed ripe banana
> ¼ cup (about) milk

Put dry ingredients in bowl. Cut in butter until mixture resembles cornmeal. Add sour cream and mashed banana and enough milk to hold mixture together. Stir with fork only until dry ingredients are moistened. Turn out on lightly floured board and knead 10 turns. Roll gently to ½" thickness and cut in rounds with 2" cutter. Put on ungreased baking sheet, prick with fork and bake in preheated 450°F. oven 10 minutes, or until well browned. Serve at once with butter, and jam, if desired.

Cinnamon-Nut Biscuits
MAKES 12.

> ¼ cup sugar
> ¼ cup chopped walnuts or pecans
> ½ teaspoon cinnamon
> 2 cups buttermilk biscuit mix
> ½ cup cold water
> 3 tablespoons butter or margarine, melted

Mix sugar, nuts and cinnamon and set aside. Prepare mix according to package directions, using the cold water. Shape in ball and put on lightly floured waxed paper. Press down slightly, then cut in 12 pieces. Shape each in ball, roll in melted butter, then in nut mixture. Arrange in 8″ round layer-cake pan, pressing down slightly. Bake in preheated 400°F. oven 15 minutes, or until lightly browned and done. Serve warm.

Honey Scones
MAKES 8.

    2 cups all-purpose flour
    ¼ cup sugar
    1 tablespoon double-acting baking powder
    ½ teaspoon salt
    6 tablespoons butter or margarine
    ¼ cup milk
      Honey
    1 egg

Stir together flour, sugar, baking powder and salt. With pastry blender or two knives cut in butter until fine crumbs form. With fork blend milk, 2 tablespoons honey and the egg; stir all at once into flour. Turn out on floured board and knead a few strokes until dough holds together. Pat dough to make 9″ circle and cut in 8 wedges. Bake on greased baking sheet in preheated 400°F. oven 10 minutes, or until tops are browned. Brush tops with, or serve with, warm honey.

Raisin-Orange Scones
MAKES 8 TO 10.

    2 cups all-purpose flour
    ¼ cup, plus 2 tablespoons sugar
    1 tablespoon baking powder

1 teaspoon salt
⅓ cup shortening
½ cup raisins
1 teaspoon grated orange rind
1 egg
1 egg yolk
½ cup milk
1 egg white, beaten

Combine flour, ¼ cup sugar, the baking powder and salt. Cut in shortening until mixture resembles coarse crumbs. Stir in raisins and orange rind. Blend whole egg, yolk and milk and add all at once to flour mixture, stirring just until moist. Turn out on lightly floured surface and knead lightly 30 seconds. Roll or pat in 9″ circle ½″ thick; place on baking sheet and cut in 8 to 10 wedges. Brush with beaten egg white, sprinkle with 2 tablespoons sugar and bake in preheated 425°F. oven 12 minutes, or until golden. Serve warm.

Whole-Wheat Scones
MAKES 16.

2½ cups whole-wheat flour
2 cups all-purpose flour
1 teaspoon salt
2 teaspoons sugar
5 teaspoons baking powder
½ cup margarine
2 cups buttermilk
    Finely chopped nuts, grated Parmesan cheese, sesame seed or dillweed

Combine flours, salt, sugar and baking powder in mixing bowl. With fingertips, cut in margarine until well distributed. Add buttermilk and stir just until moistened. Spoon dough onto 2 greased baking sheets in 4″ to 6″ round cakes. Dip a dull knife in flour and mark each cake crosswise in 4 sections. Sprinkle with nuts, cheese, seeds or dill and press down with fingertips into dough. Bake in preheated 450°F. oven 12 minutes, or until well browned and done. Cool slightly on rack and break each in 4 pieces. Serve split, with butter or margarine.

Note Especially good toasted.

Popovers
MAKES ABOUT 12

>   2 large eggs
>   1 cup milk
>   1 cup all-purpose flour, lightly spooned into cup
>   ½ teaspoon salt

Break eggs into small bowl of electric mixer and beat with mixer or with rotary beater about 30 seconds. Add remaining ingredients and beat at medium speed 1 minute (do not overbeat). Mixture should be smooth. Half-fill 6 well-greased 8-ounce pottery or seven 5-ounce glass or pottery custard cups with the mixture. Bake in preheated 450°F. oven 25 minutes. Reduce heat to 350°F. and bake 15 to 20 minutes longer, or until popovers are a deep golden brown. About 3 minutes before popovers are done, quickly cut a slit in side of each to allow steam to escape. When done, remove at once from cups so that bottoms do not steam and soften. Serve at once with butter, and with jam, if desired. Or fill with creamed seafood, chicken, etc. Popovers can be made ahead and reheated later, or frozen. To reheat, put in shallow pan and set in preheated 350°F. oven 10 to 12 minutes.

Note To make popovers in blender, follow above recipe and blend eggs 15 seconds, or until foamy. Add remaining ingredients. Turn blender on and off 3 times, scraping down sides with rubber spatula after first blending (mixture should be smooth). Bake as directed.

CHEESE POPOVERS

Follow basic recipe, sprinkling popovers with ¼ cup grated Cheddar cheese just before baking.

HERB POPOVERS

Follow basic recipe, adding 1 teaspoon poultry seasoning to batter. Serve with creamed chicken. Or add ¼ teaspoon ground thyme to batter and serve with creamed seafood.

WHOLE-WHEAT POPOVERS

Follow basic recipe, substituting ¼ cup whole-wheat flour for ¼ cup all-purpose flour.

WHEAT-GERM POPOVERS

Follow basic recipe, adding 2 tablespoons wheat germ to batter.

Pies

AMERICANS LOVE PIE, and American cooks have created some of the best-tasting of all pies from native ingredients such as pumpkins, pecans, blueberries, and cranberries. But the all-time favorite American pie is fragrant, juicy apple pie. Some people love apple pie so much they eat it for breakfast. And we have heard of children who ask for it instead of birthday cake. Even so, there are many faithful supporters of lemon meringue, mince and deep-dish cherry. Whatever your own preferences, we think you will welcome this bountiful collection of superlative kitchen-tested recipes for pies of all sorts.

We have included best-ever recipes for Lemon Meringue Pie, Black-Bottom Pie and Banana Cream Pie that even a beginner can make with assurance. For holiday eating, we offer a luscious

147

Mince Pie With Cheddar-Cheese Crust, a Pumpkin Pie With Sesame-Seed Crust, and a classic Southern Pecan Pie. If you would like a light dessert, try Orange Chiffon, Cantaloupe Chiffon or Lemon-Honey Chiffon Pie. And naturally we have included some very special apple-pie recipes—three different kinds!

Pie-making used to be considered a talent you had to be born with or learn at your mother's knee. Good pie crust was considered a major achievement. Happily, that isn't true anymore. In recent years, a variety of easy-to-make pie crust recipes have been developed. Anyone can make these successfully and turn out outstanding pies every time.

Because pies are generally a rich and filling dessert, they go best with light meals—except at holidays. One great way to entertain is to have friends over for a Sunday supper of homemade soup followed by one of these superb-tasting pies. Or invite friends just for pie and coffee. In summer a main-course salad and a dessert of chiffon or cream pie is a great company meal. On Thanksgiving and Christmas, mince, pumpkin or apple pie is the time-honored and festive way to round out the holiday meal.

TIPS ON MAKING PIES

PIE PANS

Select a regulation pie pan with a slanting rim. A pan measuring 8″ across the top will hold enough pie for 4; a 9″ pie will serve 6 or more. Pastry browns best on the bottom when baked in a glass pie plate or dull-finish aluminum pie pan. If you bake in a foil pie pan, put it on a baking sheet so that the bottom crust will brown evenly.

HOW TO MAKE PERFECT PIECRUST

For a 9″ two-crust pie, choose piecrust recipe you prefer and proceed according to directions. Divide dough in half and shape into balls. Wrap dough in plastic wrap and chill in refrigerator for at least a half hour, longer if possible.

To roll pastry, place ball of dough on a lightly floured board and flatten dough with your hand. Rolling pin should also be lightly floured or, even better, it should be covered with a stockinet cotton knit cover, which should also be lightly floured. Rolling from the center outward, roll the dough into a circle about 2″ larger than the pie pan. Lift rolling pin a little as you get to the edge, so that edges will not get too thin.

To transfer pastry to pie pan, gently fold it over the rolling pin, lift carefully onto pie pan and unroll. Press pastry lightly into bottom and sides of pan with fingertips. Be careful not to stretch pastry or it will shrink when baked. Also, make sure there are no holes in the crust or the juices will run out. Put in filling according to recipe. Roll out top crust. Transfer as before. Tuck overhang under edge of bottom crust and seal rim by fluting the edge as follows: place your left index finger on the outside of the pastry rim, pinch dough slightly with right index finger and thumb. Repeat all around rim of pie. Make slits in top crust to allow steam to escape.

For a 9″ lattice-crust pie, line pie pan with bottom crust as above. Trim edge and add filling. Roll out second ball of dough into a circle, but in this case cut pastry into ½″ strips with a knife. Moisten rim of bottom crust with water and then transfer strips to form a lattice-like top crust. Press ends of strips into bottom crust with the tines of a fork. Or let about ¾″ of bottom crust hang over side of pie pan and fold this overhang over on top of the ends of the lattice strips. Flute with fingers.

For a baked pie shell, roll out one half of dough. Line pan as above, tucking edge of crust overhang under and fluting. Prick pastry with fork all over to prevent puffing. Bake in a preheated 450°F. oven for 12 to 15 minutes until well browned. Pie dough will keep for about a week in the refrigerator. It also freezes well.

STORING PIES

For best flavor and texture eat pies when fresh. If you must keep leftovers for a day or two, cover with plastic wrap or foil and store on a pantry shelf. You can reheat two-crust or lattice-crust pies for a few minutes in a preheated 325°F. oven. If you refrigerate pies, let them stand at room temperature about 15 minutes before reheating. You should always store cream, custard and chiffon pies in the refrigerator, and these may be served directly from the refrigerator.

FREEZING PIES

Pie shells can be frozen baked or unbaked. Frozen baked shells will keep 4 months; unbaked shells, 2 months. To thaw baked shells, unwrap and let stand at room temperature. Or put in a preheated 350°F. oven about 6 minutes. Unbaked shells can be baked in the frozen state.

Fruit pies are best if baked before freezing.

Do not freeze custard, cream or meringue pies. Custard and cream fillings separate; meringues toughen and shrink.

Freeze pies first, then wrap and store. Use heavyweight plastic wrap and seal with freezer tape, heavy-duty foil, sealed with a tight double fold, plastic bags or other airtight containers. Label and date. Fruit pies will keep 4 to 6 months. Store chiffon pies only 1 month.

To heat baked pies, unwrap and let stand 30 minutes; heat in a preheated 350°F. oven just until warm.

To thaw chiffon pies, unwrap and let stand at room temperature 2 to 4 hours. Chiffon pies may be eaten while still partially frozen.

Perfect Piecrust
Always tender, even with excess handling.
MAKES FIVE 9″ CRUSTS.

> 4 cups all-purpose flour
> 1 tablespoon sugar
> 2 teaspoons salt
> 1¾ cups solid vegetable shortening (*not* lard, butter, margarine or oil) at room temperature
> ½ cup water
> 1 tablespoon white or cider vinegar
> 1 large egg

In large bowl mix well with fork flour, sugar and salt. Add shortening and mix with fork until crumbly. In small bowl beat water, vinegar and egg; add to flour mixture and stir until moistened. Divide dough in 5 portions and shape each in flat circle. Wrap each in plastic wrap or waxed paper and chill at least 30 minutes. Lightly flour both sides of dough circle; roll out on lightly floured surface. For baked pie shell place in pie pan; prick bottom and sides with fork; bake in preheated 450°F. oven 12 to 15 minutes, or until golden brown. For 1- and 2-crust pies follow pie recipe.

Note Dough can be kept refrigerated up to 3 days.

Whole-Wheat Pie Shell
MAKES ONE 9″ PIE SHELL.

> 1¼ cups whole-wheat flour
> ½ teaspoon salt
> ½ cup solid white vegetable shortening
> Cold water

Put flour and salt in bowl, then cut in shortening with pastry blender or 2 knives. Mixing with fork, add enough cold water to hold mixture together. Pull into ball and roll on floured board to ⅛″ thickness. Fit in 9″ pie pan, trim edges and flute. Prick with fork and bake in preheated 450°F. oven about 12 minutes.

Cream-Cheese Pastry

Especially good for open fruit pies—blueberry, pear, peach—or for citrus-flavored chiffon pies.
MAKES 1 TWO-CRUST PIE OR 2 PIE SHELLS.

2 cups all-purpose flour
¾ teaspoon salt
⅔ cup solid vegetable shortening
12 ounces cream cheese

Mix flour with salt. Work in vegetable shortening and cream cheese until blended. Roll dough into a ball and chill. When ready to use, roll out on lightly floured board.

Tart Pastry

Use for tart shells or open fruit pies.
MAKES TWELVE 3½″ TART SHELLS.

2 cups all-purpose flour
3 tablespoons sugar
¾ cup butter or margarine
1¼ teaspoons grated lemon rind
3 hard-cooked egg yolks, mashed
2 raw egg yolks
½ teaspoon salt

Make a well in center of flour, working on a table or in a bowl. Put all remaining ingredients in well. (Butter should not be ice cold, nor so soft it is oily.) Using fingertips, make a paste of center ingredients, gradually incorporating flour to make a firm, smooth ball of paste. Work as quickly as possible so butter won't become greasy. When bowl or tabletop has been left clean, chill dough until firm enough to roll between sheets of waxed paper. Makes twelve 4½″ rounds to fit over backs of, or inside, 3½″ tart pans. Bake in preheated hot oven (425°F.) 10 minutes. Cool before removing from pans.

Crumb Shell

MAKES ONE 9″ PIE SHELL.

1¼ cups fine graham-cracker, vanilla-wafer, cornflake or
    gingersnap crumbs
¼ cup butter, softened
2 to 4 tablespoons sugar
1 egg (optional)

Mix the crumbs and the butter. Add sugar to taste, depending on
the sweetness of the crumbs you're using. If you wish a firm
graham-cracker crust that cuts without crumbling, add the egg
and flute the edges. Press the crumbs into a 9″ pie pan. Bake 8
minutes in a preheated 375°F. oven (10 minutes in a 350°F. oven
if you've added the egg).

Old-Time Apple Pie

    Pastry for 9″ two-crust pie
6 cups sliced peeled tart cooking apples (about 2 pounds)
½ cup granulated sugar
¼ cup packed light-brown sugar
2 tablespoons all-purpose flour
¼ teaspoon salt
⅛ teaspoon nutmeg or cinnamon
⅛ teaspoon grated lemon rind
2 teaspoons lemon juice
1 tablespoon butter or margarine

Line 9″ pie pan with pastry. Lightly mix apples, sugar, brown
sugar, flour, salt, nutmeg, lemon rind and lemon juice and fill
pie shell, laying apple slices flat. Dot with the butter. Roll out top
crust and cut slits in several places for steam to escape. Moisten
edges of both crusts well with cold water and adjust top crust.
With fingers or fork, pinch two crusts together to make a tight
seal around pie. Bake in preheated very hot oven (450°F.) 15 min-

utes. Reduce heat to 350°F. and bake 45 to 50 minutes longer. Serve warm or at room temperature.

Cheese-Custard Apple Pie

   3 cups thinly sliced peeled apples
  ¾ cup sugar
  ¼ teaspoon cinnamon
  ⅛ teaspoon nutmeg
     Unbaked 9″ pie shell
  2 eggs
  ¼ teaspoon salt
  ¾ cup milk
  ¾ cup small-curd creamed cottage cheese
  1 teaspoon vanilla extract
  ¼ cup raisins

Mix apples, ¼ cup sugar and the spices and put in pie shell. Bake in preheated hot oven (425°F.) 15 minutes. Combine ½ cup sugar and remaining ingredients, except raisins, and beat until thoroughly blended. Pour over apple mixture in pie shell and sprinkle with raisins. Reduce oven heat to 325°F. and bake 40 minutes longer, or until set. Let pie stand until it reaches room temperature before serving.

Applesauce-Ginger Pie

   3 eggs
  1 jar (15 ounces) applesauce
  ½ cup sugar
  ½ cup light molasses
  1 teaspoon ginger
  ½ teaspoon nutmeg
  ¼ teaspoon salt
  1 teaspoon grated lemon rind

1 tablespoon lemon juice
Unbaked 9″ pie shell
1 cup heavy cream, whipped

In large mixing bowl, beat eggs slightly with fork; add apple-sauce, sugar, molasses, ginger, nutmeg, salt, lemon rind and juice and mix thoroughly; pour into pie shell. Bake on lowest rack in preheated 400°F. oven about 55 minutes, or until knife inserted near center comes out clean. Cool, then chill. Top with whipped cream before serving.

Banana Cream Pie

½ cup sugar
6 tablespoons all-purpose flour
¼ teaspoon salt
2½ cups milk
2 egg yolks or 1 whole egg
1 tablespoon butter
½ teaspoon lemon or vanilla extract
3 ripe bananas
Baked 9″ pie shell
½ cup shredded coconut
½ cup heavy cream, whipped

Mix sugar, flour and salt in top part of double boiler. Gradually stir in milk and cook over boiling water until thickened, stirring constantly. Cover and cook for 10 minutes longer, stirring occasionally. Beat egg and add to it a small amount of milk mixture before stirring into remaining mixture in double boiler. Cook for 2 minutes over hot, not boiling, water, stirring constantly. Remove from heat and add butter and extract; cool. Slice 2 bananas into baked shell. Pour cooked mixture over bananas at once. Chill for at least 1 hour. Put coconut in shallow pan and toast by baking in preheated moderate oven (350°F.) for 10 minutes, or until lightly browned, stirring occasionally; cool. Just before serving, spread pie with whipped cream. Peel remaining banana and score lengthwise with fork; slice thin and arrange around edge of pie; put toasted coconut in center.

Black-Bottom Pie
Rich blend of flavors for a company dessert.

    1 envelope unflavored gelatin
1¾ cups milk
    4 eggs, separated
    1 cup granulated sugar
    4 teaspoons cornstarch
   ½ teaspoon salt
    2 squares (1 ounce each) unsweetened chocolate
    1 teaspoon vanilla extract or rum
      9" Gingersnap Crumb Crust, baked and chilled (see below)
    3 tablespoons rum
    1 cup heavy cream whipped with 2 tablespoons confectioners' sugar

Sprinkle gelatin over ¼ cup milk and set aside to soften. Scald remaining 1½ cups milk. In heavy medium-size saucepan beat together egg yolks, ½ cup granulated sugar, the cornstarch and salt until well blended. Gradually beat in scalded milk. Beat over low heat until custard is smooth and thickened (do not boil). Remove ½ cup custard to small saucepan and set aside. Add softened gelatin to remaining hot custard and stir until dissolved. Melt 1½ squares chocolate and beat into the ½ cup custard until smooth. If lumps form, return to low heat and beat until smooth. Beat in vanilla. Spread on crumb crust. Chill until firm. Meanwhile to custard-gelatin mixture add the 3 tablespoons rum and chill until mixture mounds when dropped from spoon. In large bowl of mixer beat egg whites until stiff but not dry; gradually beat in remaining ½ cup granulated sugar until stiff; fold in custard mixture thoroughly. Pour over chocolate layer. Chill until set. Put whipped cream on top with pastry tube or spoon.

Shave or chop fine remaining ½ square chocolate and sprinkle over cream. Chill before serving.

Gingersnap Crumb Crust Mix 1¼ cups fine gingersnap crumbs with ⅓ cup butter or margarine until well blended. Press firmly onto sides and bottom of greased 9″ pie pan. Bake in preheated 350° oven 10 minutes. Chill.

Fresh Blueberry Pie

```
3½  cups blueberries
 1  tablespoon lemon juice
 1  cup packed light-brown sugar
 3  tablespoons flour
    Pastry for 9″ two-crust pie
 2  tablespoons margarine
```

Mix blueberries, lemon juice, brown sugar and flour and put in pastry-lined 9″ pie pan. Dot with margarine. Moisten edges of both crusts and adjust top crust. With fingers or fork, pinch two crusts together to make a tight seal around the pie. Cut a few slits to allow steam to escape. Bake in preheated hot oven (400°F.) about 35 minutes. Serve slightly warm, or cool.

Blueberry-Lemon Chiffon Pie

```
 1  envelope unflavored gelatin
 ½  cup cold water
 ¼  cup lemon juice
 ½  teaspoon salt
 ¾  cup sugar
 3  eggs, separated
 1  pint blueberries
    Baked 9″ pie shell
    Whipped cream (optional)
```

Soften gelatin in the cold water and lemon juice in top of double boiler. Add salt and ½ cup sugar. Put over boiling water and stir until dissolved. Beat egg yolks until well mixed. Then add hot mixture slowly, stirring. Put back in double boiler and cook, stirring over low heat until mixture thickens slightly. Remove from heat and chill until mixture begins to set. Beat egg whites until stiff. Gradually add remaining sugar and beat well. Fold in gelatin mixture and blueberries and pour into baked shell. Chill 1½ hours, or until set. Spoon whipped cream around edge, if desired.

Cantaloupe Chiffon Pie

        1 medium cantaloupe, peeled
        1 envelope unflavored gelatin
        3 eggs, separated
        ¾ cup sugar
        ½ teaspoon salt
        ¼ cup fresh lemon juice
        1 cup heavy cream, whipped
            Crumb Shell made with graham crackers, baked and chilled (see p. 153)

Shred fine or purée in blender half of cantaloupe, or enough to make 1 cup pulp. Put in top part of small double boiler. Soften gelatin in the pulp. Add slightly beaten egg yolks, ¼ cup sugar, and the salt. Cook over boiling water, stirring, until thickened. Add lemon juice and cool. Cut remaining cantaloupe into small cubes and add to cooled mixture. Beat egg whites until foamy; gradually beat in ½ cup sugar and beat until stiff, but not dry. Fold meringue and half of cream into cantaloupe mixture. Pour into cold crust; decorate top with remaining whipped cream and chill until firm.

Cranberry-Glazed Cheese Pie

½ cup graham-cracker crumbs
1 tablespoon brown sugar
2 tablespoons margarine, melted
1 envelope unflavored gelatin
¼ cup cold water
1 teaspoon grated lemon rind
¾ cup milk
1 cup dairy sour cream
1 package (3¾ ounces) lemon-flavor instant pudding
1 cup small-curd creamed cottage cheese
Cranberry Glaze (see below)

Mix crumbs, brown sugar and melted margarine and spread evenly in 9″ pie pan. (Mixture will be loose.) Chill while making filling. Soften gelatin in the cold water, then dissolve over hot water or low heat. Put in bowl with lemon rind, milk, sour cream and lemon pudding and beat quickly until blended and thick. Fold in cheese and turn into shell. Chill while preparing glaze. Spread with glaze and chill firm.

Cranberry Glaze In saucepan, bring to boil 1½ cups washed and drained cranberries and ½ cup water. Simmer 10 minutes, then add ½ cup granulated sugar, ¼ cup packed brown sugar and dash of salt. Cook, stirring, 1 to 2 minutes, or until syrupy. Remove from heat and stir in ¼ cup chopped walnuts or other nuts. Cool.

Greek-Style Cheese Pie With Prunes

A rather soft unbaked cheese filling in a crumb crust.

        Walnut Crumb Crust (see below)
 1 package (8 ounces) cream cheese, softened
 3 tablespoons honey
        Grated rind and juice of 1 lemon
 ¼ teaspoon cinnamon
 1 cup plain yogurt
 1 cup finely snipped ready-to-eat prunes

Prepare crust, bake and cool thoroughly. Cream cheese until very light and fluffy. Add honey, lemon rind and juice and the cinnamon; cream until well blended. Carefully fold in yogurt a little at a time until smooth. Fold in prunes. Pour into crust and chill at least 24 hours before serving.

Note Handle yogurt gently; overfolding may break down curds.

Walnut Crumb Crust Combine 1¼ cups fine vanilla-wafer crumbs, ¼ cup finely chopped walnuts and 2 tablespoons sugar. Work in 5 tablespoons softened butter or margarine and press firmly on bottom and sides of 9″ pie pan. Bake in preheated 375°F. oven 8 minutes.

Deep-Dish Cherry Pie

 1 quart pitted fresh dark sweet cherries
 ½ cup sugar
        Grated rind of ½ lemon
        Grated rind of ½ orange
        Juice of ½ lemon
 ⅓ cup light corn syrup
        Pastry for 9″ one-crust pie
 1 cup heavy cream (optional)

Mix all ingredients, except pastry and cream. Put in shallow baking dish about 10″ x 6″ x 2″. Cover with rolled pastry, cut slits in top for steam to escape, fold edges under and flute. Bake in preheated 425°F. oven 25 minutes, or until pastry is lightly browned. Serve warm, with cream, if desired.

Georgia Chess Pie

This is a very rich pie, so serve it in small wedges.

    ½ cup butter or margarine, softened
    1½ cups sugar
    3 eggs
    1 teaspoon cornmeal
    1 teaspoon vinegar
    1 tablespoon vanilla extract
    1 teaspoon cornstarch
    1 cup flaked coconut
      Unbaked shallow 9″ pie shell without fluted rim

Cream butter and sugar until light. Add eggs one at a time, beating thoroughly after each. Add cornmeal, vinegar, vanilla and cornstarch, and beat well. Stir in coconut and pour into shell. Bake in preheated slow oven (325°F.) 1 hour, or until firm. Serve slightly warm, or cool.

Chocolate Meringue Pie

    1¼ cups sugar
    ½ teaspoon salt
    ¼ cup cornstarch
    3 cups milk
    3 squares (1 ounce each) unsweetened chocolate
    3 eggs, separated
    1 tablespoon butter
    1½ teaspoons vanilla extract
      Baked 9″ pie shell

In heavy saucepan, mix sugar, salt and cornstarch. In another saucepan, scald milk and add chocolate; stir until chocolate is melted; beat until smooth with rotary beater. Gradually stir into first mixture and cook over medium heat, stirring, until thickened. Boil 1 minute; remove from heat. Beat egg yolks slightly; stir in small amount of chocolate mixture. Stir yolks into mixture in saucepan and cook, stirring, 1 minute. Add butter and vanilla; cool slightly and pour into pie shell. Top with Meringue, below; bake. Cool well.

Meringue Beat number of egg whites specified in recipe with ⅛ teaspoon salt per white until frothy. Gradually add sugar, using 2 tablespoons for each egg white, and beat until stiff, but not dry. Pile lightly on pie, being sure filling is completely covered. Bake in preheated hot oven (400°F.) 5 minutes, or until lightly browned.

Chocolate Cheese Pie

     Butter Crust (see below)
1½ cups small-curd creamed cottage cheese
 1 package (3 ounces) cream cheese
 3 eggs
¾   cup sugar
 2 squares semisweet chocolate, grated
¾   cup dairy sour cream
     Chocolate curls (optional)

Prepare crust and, while baking, prepare filling. Beat cheeses together in large bowl of electric mixer until fairly smooth. Add eggs one at a time, beating well after each. Add sugar and beat until blended. Sprinkle half the chocolate in crust and pour in half the cheese mixture. Repeat. Bake in preheated 325°F. oven 1 hour, or until knife inserted near center comes out clean. Put pie on wire rack and spread with sour cream. Cool completely, then sprinkle with chocolate curls, if desired. Store any leftover pie in refrigerator.

Butter Crust Beat in medium bowl of electric mixer until smooth ½ cup softened butter or margarine, 1 cup flour and 2 tablespoons confectioners' sugar. Press evenly on bottom and sides of 9″ pie pan. With fork, press edge of crust to edge of pan. Prick crust bottom. Bake in preheated 400°F. oven about 10 minutes.

Fresh-Coconut Cream Pie

>   1 medium coconut (see Note below)
>   2 cups milk
>   Sugar
>   ¼ teaspoon salt
>   3 tablespoons cornstarch
>   4 eggs, separated
>   1 tablespoon butter or margarine
>   1 teaspoon vanilla extract
>   Yellow food coloring (optional)
>   Baked 9″ pie shell
>   ¼ teaspoon cream of tartar

Follow directions for preparing coconut below. Grate coconut and reserve liquid for other use. Reserve 2 cups coconut and add remainder (about 1 cup) to the milk and scald. Cool to room temperature and squeeze through several thicknesses of cheesecloth; discard coconut. If necessary, add enough more milk to liquid to make 2 cups. In heavy saucepan, mix ⅓ cup sugar, the salt and cornstarch and add beaten egg yolks. Stir in milk, add butter and cook, stirring, over low heat until thickened; let bubble a little. Cool and stir in vanilla and 1 cup reserved coconut. Add a few drops food coloring, if desired. Pour into pie shell. Beat egg whites until frothy, add cream of tartar and beat until stiff. Gradually beat in ½ cup sugar. Spread on filling and sprinkle with remaining coconut. Bake in preheated slow oven (325°F.) about 15 minutes. Turn off heat, open oven door and let pie stand in oven 10 minutes. Remove from oven and let reach room temperature before serving.

Note See directions for preparing fresh coconuts on pp. 18–19. If fresh coconut is not available, substitute 2 cans (3½ ounces each) flaked coconut and proceed as directed. Reduce sugar in filling to ¼ cup.

Deep-Dish Cranberry-Applesauce Pie

 4 cups cranberries
 1 cup sugar
 1 teaspoon cinnamon
 2 tablespoons flour
 2 cups canned applesauce
 1 package (10 ounces) piecrust mix
  Cream or vanilla ice cream (optional)

Pick over and wash cranberries, then force through food chopper, using coarse blade. Add sugar, cinnamon, flour and applesauce, and mix well. Put in shallow 1½ quart baking dish. Prepare pie-crust mix as directed on label. Roll out about 1″ larger than top of baking dish. Fit on dish, cut slits in top for steam to escape, fold edges under and flute. Bake in preheated 425°F. oven 30 to 40 minutes, or until browned (set pan on rack under pie to catch any spillovers). Serve with cream or vanilla ice cream, if desired.

Never-Fail Custard Pie

 2½ cups milk
 ½ cup sugar
 ½ teaspoon salt
  Dash of nutmeg
 ½ teaspoon vanilla extract
 3 large eggs, slightly beaten
  Vegetable oil
  Unbaked 9″ pie shell

Scald milk, add sugar, salt, nutmeg and vanilla and mix well. Gradually pour over eggs, stirring. Grease a deep 9″ pie pan with oil and pour in custard mixture. Set pan in larger shallow pan and pour in hot water to depth of about 1″. Bake in preheated 300°F. oven 55 minutes, or until set. Remove pan of custard from water, let stand until cold, then chill. Bake pie shell in pie pan exactly like one containing custard, and cool. Just before serving, carefully loosen custard from sides of pan, using small spatula. Shake gently to loosen custard from bottom and carefully but quickly slide from pan into baked shell. Allow filling to settle down into crust a few minutes before serving.

COCONUT CUSTARD PIE

Use above recipe, sprinkling custard just before baking with ½ cup flaked coconut. Bake as directed.

CARAMEL CUSTARD PIE

Follow above recipe, but caramelize the sugar. (To do this, heat sugar in heavy skillet over low heat, stirring until brown and syrupy.) Gradually stir into hot milk and continue stirring until blended. Proceed as directed.

Date Chiffon Pie

> 1 envelope unflavored gelatin
> 6 tablespoons sugar
> ¼ teaspoon salt
> 1 cup milk
> 2 eggs, separated
> 1 teaspoon vanilla extract
> ¾ cup heavy cream, whipped
> 1 cup pitted dates, cut in small pieces
> Sesame-Seed Pie Shell (see below)

In top part of small double boiler, mix gelatin, 4 tablespoons sugar and the salt. Add milk and egg yolks and beat slightly to blend. Put over simmering water and cook, stirring, until mixture thickens slightly and coats a metal spoon. Remove from heat, add vanilla and chill until thickened but not firm. Beat egg whites until soft peaks form. Gradually add remaining sugar and beat until stiff. Fold into gelatin mixture with cream and dates. Pour into cold baked shell and chill until firm.

Toasted Sesame Seed

Put sesame seed in shallow baking pan or pie pan and toast in moderate oven (350°F.), stirring several times, about 20 minutes. Cool before using.

Sesame-Seed Pie Shell

Put 1 cup all-purpose flour, ½ teaspoon salt and ¼ cup Toasted Sesame Seed in bowl and cut in ⅓ cup solid vegetable shortening. Mixing with fork, add cold water a little at a time until dry ingredients just hold together. Shape in ball and roll out on lightly floured board to ⅛″ thickness. Line 9″ pie pan and flute edges. Prick well with fork and bake in preheated very hot oven (450°F.) 12 minutes, or until golden brown; cool.

Lemon Chess Pie

        2 cups sugar
        1 tablespoon flour
        1 tablespoon cornmeal
        4 eggs
       ¼ cup butter, softened
       ¼ cup light cream
        2 tablespoons grated lemon rind
       ¼ cup lemon juice
           Unbaked 9″ pie shell
           Whipped cream

Combine sugar, flour and cornmeal in large bowl and toss lightly with fork to mix. Add eggs, butter, cream, lemon rind and juice; beat with rotary or electric beater until smooth and thoroughly blended and pour into pie shell. Bake on lowest rack in preheated 375°F. oven 45 minutes, or until golden brown. Cool. Top with whipped cream.

Lemon Meringue Pie

This pie has been a favorite of Woman's Day readers for more than twenty years.

          3 large eggs
      1½ cups sugar
          7 tablespoons cornstarch
        ¼ teaspoon salt
      1½ cups hot water
          2 tablespoons butter or margarine
          1 teaspoon grated lemon rind
        ½ cup lemon juice
            Baked 9″ pie shell
            Meringue

Separate eggs while cold, putting whites into large bowl of mixer (reserve at room temperature for meringue). Put yolks in small bowl and beat slightly; set aside. In heavy medium saucepan stir together sugar, cornstarch and salt. Stir in the hot water until smooth. Bring to boil, stirring constantly. Reduce heat and let bubble 8 minutes, stirring constantly. Remove from heat. Stir several spoonfuls of hot mixture into yolks, mixing thoroughly. Then stir yolks into cornstarch mixture in saucepan. Stir over medium heat 5 minutes; remove from heat. Stir in butter and lemon rind. Stir in lemon juice in fourths; mix until smooth. Cool thoroughly at room temperature. Spread filling in pie shell. Spread Meringue on filling, making certain it touches crust at all points. Bake in preheated 350°F. oven 12 minutes, or until lightly browned. Cool in draft-free place 2 to 3 hours before cutting.

Meringue

In small saucepan blend 1 tablespoon cornstarch with 2 table-spoons cold water. Stir in ½ cup boiling water. Bring to boil over medium heat, stirring constantly. Cook and stir 2 minutes or until thickened. Set aside and cool to room temperature. Add 1 teaspoon lemon juice to 3 egg whites (reserved from filling) and beat until soft peaks form. Gradually add 6 tablespoons sugar, beating well after each addition. Continue beating until stiff peaks form. Beat in cornstarch mixture until blended.

Note Pie is best *not refrigerated* before serving, but refrigerate if keeping more than 3 hours, or if any is left over.

Lemon-Honey Chiffon Pie

       1 envelope unflavored gelatin
      ¼ cup cold water
       4 eggs, separated
      ¾ cup honey
      ¼ teaspoon salt
       1 teaspoon grated lemon rind
      ½ cup lemon juice
         Baked 9″ pie shell
      ½ cup heavy cream, whipped (optional)

Soften gelatin in the cold water. Beat egg yolks and combine with honey, salt, lemon rind and lemon juice. Cook over hot water, stir-ring, until thickened. Add gelatin and stir to dissolve. Cool, stirring. When cold, fold in stiffly beaten egg whites and turn into shell. Chill 2 to 3 hours, or until firm. Top with whipped cream, if desired.

Lime Pie

       1 cup, plus 2 tablespoons sugar
      ⅓ cup cornstarch

  ½ teaspoon salt
  ¼ cup cold water
1½ cups hot water
  6 tablespoons fresh lime juice
  3 eggs, separated
  3 tablespoons butter or margarine
  1 tablespoon grated lime rind
    Baked 9″ pie shell
  6 tablespoons sugar
  ⅛ teaspoon salt
    Fresh lime slices for garnish

Combine 1 cup plus 2 tablespoons sugar, cornstarch, salt and cold water in a saucepan. Mix well. Add hot water and cook over low heat, stirring constantly, until very thick. Stir in fresh lime juice. Return to heat and cook until thickened. Beat egg yolks lightly; beat in a small amount of hot mixture; then add yolks to hot mixture. Cook for about 2 minutes, stirring constantly. Add butter and lime rind. Cool. Pour into cold pie shell. Beat egg whites until stiff but not dry. Beat in 6 tablespoons sugar and the salt gradually, beating until blended. Spread over top of pie. Bake for 20 minutes in preheated slow oven (300°F.). Serve cold, garnished with fresh lime slices.

Mince Pie With Cheddar-Cheese Crust

1½ cups all-purpose flour
  ½ cup finely shredded sharp Cheddar cheese
  ½ teaspoon salt
  ½ cup shortening
  2 to 3 tablespoons ice water
  4 cups prepared mincemeat
    Grated rind and juice of 1 lemon (optional)
    Pecan halves (optional)

Stir together flour, cheese and salt. Cut in shortening until crumbly. Sprinkle with ice water, a tablespoon at a time. With hands form in ball; wrap and chill at least 30 minutes. On lightly floured surface roll out two thirds of pastry to circle ⅛″ thick. Lightly fit into 9″ pie pan. Combine mincemeat, lemon rind and juice and spoon into pastry-lined pie pan. Roll out remaining dough and cut in seven ½″ strips. Arrange on pie lattice fashion. Trim edges and flute rim. Place pecan half on mincemeat in each diamond. Bake on lowest rack in preheated 400°F. oven about 40 minutes, or until golden brown. Serve slightly warm.

Note If crust browns too quickly, cover rim with foil strip.

Mincemeat-Pear Pie

   1 jar (28 ounces) prepared mincemeat
   2 firm unpeeled pears, cored and chopped (about 2 cups)
   2 tablespoons brandy or grated peel of 1 lemon
     Pastry for 2-crust 9-inch pie
     Beaten egg or milk
     Ice cream or Cheddar cheese

Stir together mincemeat, pears and brandy; set aside. Roll out two-thirds of pastry and line 9″ pie pan, fluting edge; spoon in mincemeat mixture. Roll out remaining pastry ⅛″ thick. Using cookie cutter or other pattern, cut out 8 holiday shapes; arrange on mincemeat. Brush pastry with egg. Bake in preheated 400° oven 40 minutes, covering pie loosely with foil after about 20 minutes. Serve slightly warm topped with ice cream or cheese. Makes 8 servings.

Note Baked pie can be frozen. Thaw in wrapping at room temperature. Heat in preheated 325° oven about 20 minutes.

Orange Chiffon Pie

   2 envelopes unflavored gelatin
   2 cups orange juice
   ½ teaspoon salt

3 eggs, separated
1 tablespoon lemon juice
1½ teaspoons vanilla extract
2 egg whites
6 tablespoons sugar
Baked 9″ pie shell
Whipped cream
Mandarin orange sections

Sprinkle gelatin over orange juice in top of double boiler. Add salt and egg yolks; mix well. Place over boiling water and cook, stirring constantly about 5 minutes, or until mixture thickens slightly and gelatin dissolves. Remove from heat; stir in lemon juice and vanilla. Chill in refrigerator just until mixture mounds slightly when dropped from spoon. Beat the 3 reserved and 2 additional egg whites until stiff but not dry; gradually add sugar, beat until very stiff, gently fold in gelatin mixture and turn into pie shell. Chill in refrigerator until set. Garnish with whipped cream and orange sections.

Deep-Dish Peach Pie

¼ cup granulated sugar
½ cup packed light-brown sugar
⅛ teaspoon mace
1½ tablespoons quick-cooking tapioca
4 cups sliced peeled firm-ripe peaches
2 tablespoons lemon juice
Pastry for 1-crust pie
Heavy cream (optional)

Combine sugar, brown sugar, mace and tapioca. Add peaches and lemon juice and toss gently to mix. Turn into 9″ square baking dish. Roll pastry to about an 11″ square. Put over peaches, pressing to side of dish. Cut a few slits in top with knife to permit steam to escape. Bake in preheated hot oven (425°F.) 40 minutes, or until crust is browned and filling is bubbly. Serve warm with cream.

Pear Tart

            1 cup dry white wine
        ¼ cup sugar
        ⅛ teaspoon ginger
            4 ripe but firm Comice or Anjou pears
            1 cup heavy cream
            1 tablespoon cornstarch
            3 egg yolks, beaten
            3 tablespoons sugar
            2 teaspoons almond extract
                Baked 9″ or 10″ pie shell
        ½ cup apricot jam
            1 tablespoon hot water

Combine wine, sugar and ginger. Bring to boil and simmer for 3 minutes. Peel pears, cut into halves and core them. Poach pears in wine syrup for 10 minutes, or until just tender. Drain pears and reserve syrup. Boil syrup down to measure 1 cup, or add water to bring up to 1 cup. Blend cream and cornstarch to smooth paste. Stir into syrup. Cook over low heat, stirring constantly, until mixture thickens. Beat egg yolks with sugar and almond extract. Stir syrup gradually into egg-yolk mixture. Replace over low heat and cook, stirring constantly, until thickened. Cool, and spread over pie-shell bottom. Arrange pears on top, rounded side up and pointed end to the center. Heat apricot jam and thin with water. Drizzle over pears.

Southern Pecan Pie
Extra delicious served with whipped cream.

        ½ cup sugar
            1 cup dark corn syrup
        ¼ teaspoon salt
            2 tablespoons all-purpose flour
            2 eggs

    1 teaspoon vanilla extract
    1 tablespoon butter or margarine, melted
1¼ cups pecan halves
    Unbaked 8″ pie shell
    Whipped cream (optional)

In small bowl of electric mixer beat well sugar, syrup, salt, flour and eggs. Stir in vanilla, butter and pecans. Pour into shell. Bake in preheated 300°F. oven 1 hour and 20 minutes, or until set. Cool thoroughly before serving.

Texas Pecan Pie

    1 cup dairy sour cream
    2 eggs, separated
    1 cup sugar
    ¼ cup all-purpose flour
    ⅛ teaspoon salt
    ¼ teaspoon lemon extract
    1 cup packed light-brown sugar
    1 cup pecan halves
    Unbaked 9″ pie shell

In top part of small double boiler, mix sour cream, egg yolks, sugar, flour and salt. Put over simmering water and cook, stirring, until fairly thick. Remove from heat, add flavoring and cool. Beat egg whites until almost stiff. Then add brown sugar and beat until stiff. Fold in pecans. Pour filling into pie shell and spread with pecan topping. Bake in preheated slow oven (300°F.) about 15 minutes. Cool before cutting.

Pumpkin Pie With Sesame-Seed Crust

>   ½ package piecrust mix
>   2 tablespoons sesame seed
> 1½ cups canned pumpkin
>   ¾ cup packed light-brown sugar
>   ½ teaspoon ginger
>   1 teaspoon cinnamon
>   Dash of ground cloves
>   ½ teaspoon salt
>   1 tall can evaporated milk (13 ounces)
>   2 tablespoons butter or margarine
>   2 eggs
>   ½ teaspoon lemon extract
>   Nutmeg
>   Whipped cream, sweetened, and slivered Brazil nuts
>   (optional)

Prepare piecrust mix as directed on label, adding sesame seed. Roll to fit 9″ pie pan, put in pan and flute edges. In saucepan, mix pumpkin, brown sugar, ginger, cinnamon, cloves, salt, milk and butter. Heat, stirring, until butter is melted. Remove from heat and add 1 egg and 1 egg yolk, slightly beaten, and the lemon extract. Fold in remaining egg white, stiffly beaten. Pour into lined pan and sprinkle with nutmeg. Bake in preheated hot oven (425°F.) 8 minutes. Turn temperature control to 325°F. and bake 30 minutes longer, or until set; cool. If desired, top with whipped cream and sprinkle with nuts.

Buttermilk Raisin Pie

>   3 cups raisins (15-ounce box)
>   3 egg yolks, beaten
>   1 cup buttermilk
>   1 tablespoon vinegar
>   ¾ cup sugar

2 tablespoons all-purpose flour
1 tablespoon grated orange rind
½ teaspoon salt
    Pastry for 9″ two-crust pie
1 egg beaten with 1 tablespoon water

Plump raisins by placing in bowl and covering with boiling water; let stand. With fork, beat together yolks, buttermilk and vinegar; add sugar, flour, orange rind and salt and mix well. Drain raisins and stir into egg mixture. Spoon into pastry-lined 9″ pie pan, adjust top crust and seal and flute edge. Cut vents in crust and brush with egg-white mixture. Bake in preheated 375°F. oven 50 minutes. Cool on wire rack.

Rhubarb-Orange Pie

    Pastry for 9″ lattice-top pie
4 cups rhubarb in 1″ pieces
1 orange, peeled and diced
¾ cup packed light-brown sugar
¾ cup granulated sugar
¼ teaspoon nutmeg
⅓ cup all-purpose flour
⅓ cup butter or margarine, melted

Roll out about two thirds of pastry and arrange in 9″ pie pan, letting about ¾″ hang over side of pan. Mix remaining ingredients, except butter, and put in lined pan. Pour butter over top. Roll remaining pastry to 10″ circle and cut in ½″ strips. Weave strips on top of pie. Press ends to bottom crust and fold overhang over on top of the ends; flute. Bake in preheated hot oven (425°F.) 40 to 45 minutes.

Bayou Sesame Pie

> 3 eggs
> 1 cup dark corn syrup
> ½ cup light corn syrup
> 1 teaspoon vanilla extract
> ¼ teaspoon salt
> 1 tablespoon all-purpose flour
> ½ teaspoon cinnamon
> ¼ teaspoon nutmeg
> 2 tablespoons butter or margarine, melted
>   Unbaked 9" pie shell
> ⅓ cup sesame seed

Put eggs in medium mixing bowl and beat slightly. Then add corn syrups, vanilla, salt, flour, cinnamon, nutmeg and butter and beat until smooth and blended. Pour into pie shell and sprinkle with sesame seed. Bake in preheated moderate oven (375°F.) 40 minutes, or until firm. Cool before cutting. Serve in small wedges (pie is rich).

Strawberry Devonshire Tart

> Pastry Shell (see below)
> 1 package (3 ounces) cream cheese, softened
> 3 tablespoons dairy sour cream
> 1 to 1½ quarts strawberries
>   Water
> 1 cup sugar
> 3 tablespoons cornstarch
>   Red food coloring (optional)

Make Pastry Shell and cool. Beat cream cheese until fluffy; add sour cream and beat until smooth. Spread on bottom of shell and refrigerate. Wash and hull strawberries. Mash enough uneven ones to make 1 cup. Force through sieve and, if necessary, add water to make 1 cup. Mix sugar and cornstarch. Add ½ cup water and sieved berries. Cook over medium heat, stirring, until mixture is clear and thickened, then boil about 1 minute. Stir to cool slightly and add a little red food coloring if desired. Fill Pastry Shell with remaining berries, tips up, and pour mixture over top. Chill 1 hour.

Pastry Shell

Combine 1 cup all-purpose flour and 1 tablespoon sugar, then work in with fingertips, 6 tablespoons butter, at room temperature but not soft. Add 1 egg yolk and 1 tablespoon ice water and work with fingers until dough holds together (work well but don't over-work). Pat into flat round, wrap and chill until firm enough to roll. Then roll between sheets of waxed paper to fit a 9" loose-bottom tart pan. Remove top paper and turn pastry over pan, centering. Let pastry slip down into pan and gently pull off paper. Use fingertips to press pastry into pan; even off rim and chill shell. Bake in preheated 375°F. oven 15 minutes, or until lightly browned. Prick dough with fork whenever it begins to bubble (this helps to keep shell flat).

Sweet Potato Pie

    2½ pounds sweet potatoes
    ½ cup packed light-brown sugar
    ¼ cup butter, melted
    ½ teaspoon nutmeg
    ¼ teaspoon cinnamon
    3 eggs beaten with
    ¼ cup milk
        Unbaked 9" pie shell
        Whipped cream
        Crystallized ginger
        Candied citron

Boil sweet potatoes in jackets until tender, drain, peel and mash. Measure out 4 cups in large mixing bowl and blend in sugar, butter, nutmeg and cinnamon. Stir in egg mixture until thoroughly blended, pour into pie shell and bake on lowest rack in preheated 325°F. oven 40 minutes, or until lightly browned. Cool on wire rack. Garnish with mounds of whipped cream around rim of pie and sliced ginger and citron.

Vanilla Pie

        1 cup light-brown sugar
        1 tablespoon, plus 1 cup all-purpose flour
        1 egg, well beaten
        ¼ cup dark corn syrup
        1 teaspoon vanilla extract
        1 cup water
        ½ teaspoon cream of tartar
        ½ teaspoon baking soda
        2 tablespoons butter
        2 tablespoons lard or shortening
          Unbaked 9″ pie shell

Mix ½ cup brown sugar, 1 tablespoon flour, the egg, syrup and vanilla. Gradually add the water, mixing until smooth. Bring to full rolling boil, then set aside to cool. Mix remaining sugar, 1 cup flour, cream of tartar and soda; cut in butter and lard until mixture is crumbly. Pour liquid into pie shell and sprinkle with flour mixture. Bake in preheated 350°F. oven about 40 minutes.

Walnut Rum Pie

        3 eggs
        1 cup light corn syrup
        1 cup coarsely chopped walnuts
        ½ cup sugar
        ¼ cup light rum
        ¼ teaspoon salt

Unbaked 9″ pie shell
Whipped cream

In medium bowl, beat eggs slightly with fork; add syrup, walnuts, sugar, rum and salt, mix well and pour into pie shell. Bake on lowest rack in preheated 325°F. oven about 55 minutes. Cool. Top with whipped cream.

Cakes

CAKES AND FESTIVE OCCASIONS seem to go together. It is hard to imagine birthdays, weddings and holiday celebrations without these very special creations of the baker's art. But cakes also add a bright and cheerful note to everyday meals and simple gatherings. And there are so many wonderful kinds to choose from— gold cakes, white cakes, chocolate cakes, pound cakes, spice cakes, fruitcakes, cheesecakes! In this appealing collection we have included a full selection of every kind, from lavish to simple quick-to-make versions. We think you will find many delightful cakes that suit your taste, your schedule and your budget.

Baking a cake at home from scratch has a kind of magic to it. Combining simple good things into a batter, pouring it into pans and then baking it until it is transformed into a light and fragrant cake give a feeling of real accomplishment. At every step there are many small satisfactions. Even licking the bowl is a treat. And the delectable smell that baking gives to a house is a big part of the enjoyment. However, all these preliminaries are nothing compared to the pleasure of sharing a freshly baked cake with family and friends. Home-baked cakes taste so good.

Choosing the right cake for the right occasion takes some thought. If you plan to serve a cake for dessert, make sure that the meal itself is rather light and choose a cake that gives the meal balance. It is generally best to bake rich, frosted layer cakes for birthdays and other occasions where the cake is the main thing you are serving, so that people can give it their full attention and can appreciate it more. For dessert, you might want to try Apple Cake With Cream-Cheese Frosting, Honey-Nut Spice Cake or Blueberry Upside-Down Cake. A sliver of Almond Torte might be just right. Or a Chiffon Cheesecake. There are all sorts of interesting possibilities.

TIPS FOR MAKING AND BAKING CAKES

EQUIPMENT

For easy, accurate measurement, use a set of standard measuring spoons, a nest of measuring cups for dry ingredients and a measuring cup for liquids with a pouring lip and a rim above the 1-cup line. A rubber spatula and a sifter are essential items for preparing batter. Use shiny aluminum or glass baking pans.

For layer cakes, use pans about 1½" deep. Waxed paper, plain white or brown paper can be used to line pan bottoms. Cut paper slightly smaller than pan so that it will not touch edge but will completely cover bottom. Greasing the bottom of pan will keep the paper from slipping when batter is poured in.

PROCEDURE

For best results, use only ingredients specified and follow directions exactly. Make all measurements level unless otherwise specified. Spoon granulated sugar and sifted confectioners' sugar into cup. Level off with flat knife. Do not shake down. Use kind of flour specified. Large eggs were used in making these cakes; substituting eggs of another size is not recommended. You can use either fresh whole milk or evaporated milk diluted with an equal amount of water. Ingredients such as shortening, milk and eggs should be at room temperature (72°F. to 80°F.). It is advisable not to double recipes.

OVEN TEMPERATURE

Correct oven temperature is of great importance when baking cakes. If your oven has no thermostatic control, try using an oven thermometer and adjusting the heat accordingly. You may want to use a thermometer in any case to check the accuracy of your control. When baking in glass loaf pans, use an oven temperature 25° less than that specified in recipe.

STORING BAKED CAKES

Frosted cakes keep best. It's helpful to store cakes in a cake saver, deep bowl or an airtight container.

Cover the cut surface of cake with waxed paper or transparent plastic wrap; if necessary, hold wrapping in place with toothpicks inserted at an angle into cake. Cakes with perishable fillings or frostings should be stored, covered, in the refrigerator. It is best to freeze cakes unfrosted.

Company Gold Cake

This is an especially delicious gold cake. Save the egg whites for an angel food cake (p. 204) or make the delightful Silver Cake With Lady Baltimore frosting and filling (see pp. 191–92).

> 11 egg yolks
> 2 cups sugar
> ½ cup butter or margarine
> 1 cup milk, scalded
> 2⅓ cups sifted cake flour
> 3 teaspoons double-acting baking powder
> ½ teaspoon salt
> 1 teaspoon vanilla extract
> Caramel Frosting (see below)

Beat egg yolks until thick and lemon-colored. Gradually beat in sugar. Add butter to hot milk and let stand until butter melts. Add sifted flour, baking powder and salt to first mixture alternately with milk and butter. Add vanilla. Pour into 3 ungreased 8″ x 8″ x 2″ pans. Bake in preheated moderate oven (325°F.) 30 minutes. Cool and frost.

Caramel Frosting

> 2 cups light brown sugar
> 1 cup granulated sugar
> 2 tablespoons light corn syrup
> 3 tablespoons butter
> ¼ teaspoon salt
> ⅔ cup light cream
> 1 teaspoon vanilla extract

In a large saucepan combine all ingredients. Bring to a boil, cover and cook 3 minutes. Uncover and cook until candy thermometer indicates a temperature of 236°F. or until a small amount of mixture forms a soft ball when dropped into cold water. Cool 5 minutes; then beat until thick. If too stiff, add a little hot water.

Orange Gold Cake
When you're expecting an honored guest, try this one.

> ¾ cup butter, softened
> 1¼ cups sugar
> 8 egg yolks
> Grated rind of 1 orange
> ⅓ cup orange juice
> 2¾ cups sifted cake flour
> 2¾ teaspoons double-acting baking powder
> ½ teaspoon salt
> ⅔ cup milk
> Orange Butter Frosting (see below)

Cream butter and sugar until light. Add egg yolks, one at a time, beating well after each addition. Add orange rind and juice. Add sifted flour, baking powder and salt alternately with milk, beating until smooth. Pour into two 9″ layer-cake pans lined on the bottom with paper. Bake in preheated moderate oven (375°F.) about 20 minutes. Cool and frost.

Orange Butter Frosting

Combine grated rind of 1 orange and 1 lemon and ¼ cup orange juice. Let stand 10 minutes; strain, if desired. Cream ¼ cup butter until light. Add 1 egg yolk, dash salt and 2 teaspoons lemon juice. Gradually beat in 1 pound confectioners' sugar (about 2⅓ cups). Add reserved orange juice and beat in.

Missouri Buttermilk Coconut Cake

    ¾ cup butter, softened
    1½ cups sugar
     3 eggs
    2½ cups sifted cake flour
     1 teaspoon baking powder
     ½ teaspoon baking soda
     ½ teaspoon salt
     1 cup buttermilk
     1 teaspoon vanilla
     1 teaspoon lemon extract
       Frosting (see below)
       Flaked coconut

Cream butter and sugar until light and fluffy. Add eggs one at a time, beating thoroughly after each addition. Sift dry ingredients 3 times. Combine buttermilk and flavorings and add alternately with dry ingredients to first mixture, beating after each addition until smooth. Pour into two 9″ layer-cake pans lined on the bottom with waxed paper. Bake in preheated moderate oven (350°F.) 30 to 35 minutes. Remove from oven and let stand 5 minutes. Then turn out on racks and peel off paper. Turn right side up, cool and put layers together with frosting. Spread remaining frosting on top and sides of cake and sprinkle with coconut.

Frosting

Beat 2 egg whites with ⅛ teaspoon salt until almost stiff. Gradually add ¾ cup sugar and beat 5 minutes, or until mixture is very stiff and sugar is almost completely dissolved. Add 1 teaspoon vanilla extract.

Chicken and Stuffing Bake

1 box (6 oz.) chicken
flavored stuffing mix
6 skinless, boneless chicken
breast halves (about 1½ lb.)
1 can cream of mushroom soup
⅓ cup milk
1 tsp. chopped parsley

1. Preheat oven to 400°F. Prepare stuffing mix according to package directions but do not let stand.

2. Spoon stuffing across center of 2-qt. shallow baking dish. Arrange 3 chicken pieces on each side of stuffing, overlapping if necessary.

3. Combine soup, milk and parsley. Pour over chicken. Cover with foil; bake 15 min. Uncover; bake 10 min. or until chicken is no longer pink. Stir sauce before serving.

6 servings.

VARIATION: Add ½ cup each chopped carrot, celery and onion with seasoning packet while preparing stuffing mix.

Burnt-Sugar Cake

Burnt sugar lends it a distinctive old-fashioned flavor.

1¾ cups sugar
¾ cup boiling water
⅔ cup butter or margarine, softened
1 teaspoon vanilla extract
2 eggs, separated
3 cups sifted cake flour
3 teaspoons double-acting baking powder
½ teaspoon salt
¾ cup milk
    Burnt-Sugar Frosting (see below)
    Pecan halves

In small heavy skillet or saucepan, heat ¾ cup sugar, stirring, until a brown syrup forms and mixture begins to smoke. Very gradually stir in boiling water and remove from heat. Cool thoroughly. Cream butter and 1 cup sugar until light. Gradually beat in ½ cup burnt-sugar syrup. (Reserve remainder for Frosting.) Add vanilla, then egg yolks, one at a time, beating well after each addition. Add sifted flour, baking powder and salt alternately with milk, beating until smooth. Fold in stiffly beaten egg whites. Pour into two 8″ layer-cake pans lined on the bottom with paper. Bake in preheated moderate oven (375°F.) about 25 minutes. Cool and frost. Top with nut halves.

Burnt-Sugar Frosting Cream ⅓ cup butter or margarine. Beat in 1 pound (about 2⅓ cups) confectioners' sugar, ½ teaspoon salt, 1 teaspoon vanilla extract, burnt-sugar syrup reserved from cake and enough cream or evaporated milk (about 2 tablespoons) to make of spreading consistency.

Peanut Butter Layer Cake
You mix the batter in one bowl.

⅓ cup butter or margarine, softened
2¼ cups sifted cake flour
1½ cups sugar
3 teaspoons double-acting baking powder
1 teaspoon salt
⅓ cup peanut butter
1 cup milk
2 eggs
1 teaspoon vanilla extract
Chocolate Peanut-Butter Frosting (see below)

Cream butter. Sift in flour, sugar, baking powder and salt. Add peanut butter and ⅔ cup milk. Mix until all flour is dampened. Beat 2 minutes at low speed of electric mixer, or 300 vigorous strokes by hand. Add ⅓ cup milk, eggs and vanilla and beat 2 minutes. Pour into two 9″ layer-cake pans, lined on the bottom with paper. Bake in preheated moderate oven (375°F.) about 25 minutes. Cool and frost.

Chocolate Peanut-Butter Frosting

Cream together ½ cup peanut butter and ⅓ cup unsweetened cocoa. Add 2⅔ cups sifted confectioners' sugar, ¼ teaspoon salt, 1 teaspoon vanilla extract and about ½ cup cream or evaporated milk. Beat until smooth.

Banana Cream Layer Cake
All ingredients should be at room temperature.

1½ cups sifted cake flour
1½ teaspoons double-acting baking powder
½ teaspoon salt
¾ cup cold water
Grated rind of ½ lemon

   3 eggs, separated
     Sugar
     Lemon juice
   1 cup heavy cream, whipped and sweetened
   3 fully ripe medium bananas, sliced

Sift together flour, baking powder and salt 3 times. Add the water and lemon rind to egg yolks and beat with rotary beater or electric mixer until tripled in volume. Add 1 cup plus 2 tablespoons sugar a few tablespoons at a time, beating well after each addition. Then add sifted dry ingredients a small amount at a time, beating slowly and gently with beater. Beat egg whites until foamy, add 1½ teaspoons lemon juice and 3 tablespoons sugar and continue beating until mixture stands in soft peaks. Fold into flour mixture. Pour batter in 2 ungreased round 9″ layer-cake pans 1½″ deep. Bake in preheated moderate oven (350°F.) 25 to 30 minutes. Turn upside down on wire racks and let stand until cold. Remove from pans. Just before serving, spread half the whipped cream on one layer of cake. Cover with banana slices dipped in lemon juice. Top with remaining cake layer and decorate with whipped cream and bananas.

Note For a small family, reserve 1 cake layer for another meal. Cut remaining layer in half and fill with cream and bananas.

Silver Cake
Egg whites give it the silvery hue.

   ⅔ cup butter, softened
  1½ cups sugar
   1 teaspoon vanilla extract
   ½ teaspoon almond extract
  2½ cups sifted cake flour
  2½ teaspoons double-acting baking powder
   ⅔ cup milk
   ½ teaspoon salt
   ½ teaspoon cream of tartar
   4 egg whites

Cream butter and sugar until light. Add flavorings. Add sifted flour and baking powder alternately with milk, beating until smooth. Add salt and cream of tartar to egg whites. Beat until stiff, but not dry. Fold into first mixture. Pour into two 9″ layer-cake pans lined on the bottom with paper. Bake in preheated moderate oven (375°F.) 20 to 25 minutes. Cool and frost as desired.

LADY BALTIMORE CAKE

Make Silver Cake, above. Make Fluffy White Frosting, below. To one third of frosting add 6 chopped dried figs and ½ cup each chopped raisins and nuts. Spread between layers. Use remaining frosting for top and sides of cake.

Fluffy White Frosting

In top part of double boiler combine 2 egg whites, 1½ cups sugar, ⅛ teaspoon salt, ⅓ cup water and 2 teaspoons light corn syrup. Put over boiling water and beat with rotary beater or electric mixer 7 minutes, or until mixture will stand in stiff peaks. Add 1 teaspoon vanilla extract.

Two-Minute White Cake

You need not beat the egg whites separately.

⅓ cup vegetable shortening
1 cup sugar
2 egg whites
½ teaspoon vanilla extract
1¾ cups sifted cake flour
2 teaspoons double-acting baking powder
½ teaspoon salt
½ cup milk

In mixing bowl put shortening, sugar, egg whites, vanilla, flour, baking powder, salt and milk. Beat vigorously 2 minutes by hand or at medium speed of electric mixer. Pour into two 8″ layer-cake pans lined on the bottom with waxed paper. Bake in preheated 375°F. oven 20 minutes. Turn out on racks and peel off paper. Cool and frost.

Quick Walnut Cake

And quick it is! You toss the unbeaten egg whites right into the batter.

> 2 cups sifted cake flour
> 1 cup chopped walnuts
> 1⅓ cups sugar
> ½ teaspoon salt
> ½ cup butter, softened
> 1 cup milk
> 3 teaspoons baking powder
> 4 egg whites
> 1 teaspoon vanilla extract

Sprinkle small amount of flour on nuts and mix to coat. Put remaining flour in bowl with sugar and salt. Cut in butter. Add ⅔ cup milk and mix until dry ingredients are moistened. Then beat 1 minute. Mix in baking powder. Add remaining milk, egg whites and vanilla. Beat 2 minutes, then fold in nuts. Pour into two 8″ layer-cake pans lined on the bottom with waxed paper. Bake in preheated moderate oven (350°F.) about 35 minutes. Turn out on racks and peel off paper. Cool and frost as desired.

Chocolate Shadow Cake

Dark, velvety cake with rich chocolate flavor, topped with butter-cream frosting and semisweet-chocolate shadow.

4 squares (1 ounce each) unsweetened chocolate
½ cup hot water
1½ cups sugar
½ cup butter, softened
1 teaspoon vanilla extract
3 eggs
2 cups sifted cake flour
1 teaspoon baking soda
½ teaspoon salt
⅔ cup milk
Buttercream Frosting (see below)
Chocolate Shadow (see below)

Melt chocolate in ½ cup hot water in top part of double boiler over hot water. Cook, stirring, until thickened. Add ½ cup sugar and cook, stirring, 2 to 3 minutes. Remove from water and cool. Cream butter, then gradually add remaining sugar and cream until light and fluffy. Add vanilla; add eggs one at a time, beating thoroughly after each. Add chocolate mixture and blend well. Fold in sifted dry ingredients alternately with milk, beginning and ending with flour mixture. Pour into two 9″ layer-cake pans lined on bottom with waxed paper. Bake in preheated moderate oven (350°F.) 30 to 35 minutes, or until cake tester comes out clean. Cool in pans 5 minutes, then turn out on wire racks to cool thoroughly. Peel off paper. Spread frosting between layers and on top and sides of cake. Pour Chocolate Shadow over top, allowing some to run down sides of cake. Let chocolate set before cutting.

Buttercream Frosting Beat together thoroughly ¾ cup softened butter, 2 egg yolks and 1 teaspoon vanilla extract. Gradually add 2¼ cups confectioners' sugar, beating until smooth.

Chocolate Shadow Melt ½ cup semisweet chocolate pieces in top of double boiler over hot water. Blend in 3 to 4 tablespoons warm water, or enough to make mixture smooth and thin enough to pour.

Chocolate-Nut Layer Cake

> ½ cup butter, softened
> 2 cups sugar
> 2 eggs
> 4 squares (1 ounce each) unsweetened chocolate, melted and cooled
> 2 cups sifted cake flour
> 2 teaspoons baking powder
> ½ teaspoon salt
> 1½ cups milk
> 1 cup chopped nuts
> 1 teaspoon vanilla extract
> Chocolate Fudge Frosting (see below)
> Chopped nuts (optional)

Cream butter and sugar until light and fluffy. Add eggs one at a time, beating thoroughly after each. Beat in chocolate. Sift flour, baking powder and salt together; add alternately with milk to first mixture, beating until smooth. Add nuts and vanilla. Pour into two 9″ layer-cake pans lined on the bottom with waxed paper. Bake in preheated moderate oven (350°F.) about 35 minutes. Turn out on racks and peel off paper. Turn right side up. Cool and spread frosting quickly between layers and on top and sides of cake. Sprinkle with chopped nuts while frosting is still soft, if desired.

Chocolate Fudge Frosting

Put 3 cups sugar, 3 tablespoons light corn syrup, 1 cup milk, and 4 squares unsweetened chocolate in large saucepan. Cook over medium heat, stirring until sugar is dissolved. Cool at 232°F. on a candy thermometer until a small amount of mixture forms a very soft ball in very cold water, stirring occasionally to prevent scorching. Remove from heat, add ⅓ cup butter or margarine without stirring and cool until lukewarm, about 1 hour. Add 1 teaspoon vanilla extract and beat until frosting is creamy.

Note If frosting stiffens before spreading is completed, add ½ to 1 teaspoon water and beat until smooth.

Sweet Chocolate Cake

Some people use the Coconut-Pecan Filling as the frosting on this cake, omitting the chocolate frosting and spreading the filling on the tops of all three layers. It's delicious either way.

> 1 package (4 ounces) sweet cooking chocolate
> ½ cup boiling water
> 1 cup butter or other shortening
> 2 cups sugar
> 4 eggs, separated
> 1 teaspoon vanilla extract
> 2½ cups sifted cake flour
> 1 teaspoon baking soda
> ½ teaspoon salt
> 1 cup buttermilk
>   Coconut-Pecan Filling (see below)
>   Chocolate Cream-Cheese Frosting (see below)

Melt chocolate in water; cool. Cream butter and sugar; add egg yolks, one at a time, beating thoroughly after each addition. Add vanilla and chocolate; mix well. Add sifted dry ingredients alternately with buttermilk; beat until smooth. Fold in stiffly beaten egg whites. Pour into three 8″ or 9″ layer-cake pans lined on bottom with paper. Bake in preheated 350°F. oven, about 35 minutes. Cool. Fill, and frost.

Coconut-Pecan Filling

In a saucepan combine 1 cup evaporated milk (undiluted), 1 cup sugar, 3 egg yolks, ½ cup butter or margarine, and 1 teaspoon vanilla extract. Cook over medium heat 12 minutes, stirring, until mixture thickens. Add 1 can flaked coconut and 1 cup chopped pecans. Beat until thick.

Chocolate Cream-Cheese Frosting

Cream 2 tablespoons butter and 4 ounces cream cheese together until well blended. Add 1½ ounces unsweetened chocolate (melted), 1½ cups confectioners' sugar, ¼ cup heavy cream, ½ teaspoon vanilla extract and a dash salt. Mix until well blended.

One-Bowl Chocolate Cake
A moist, red cake.

> ½ cup shortening, softened
> 1¾ cups sifted cake flour
> 1½ cups sugar
> 1¼ teaspoons baking powder
> ½ teaspoon baking soda
> 1 teaspoon salt
> 1 cup milk
> 1 teaspoon vanilla extract
> 2 eggs
> 2 squares (1 ounce each) unsweetened chocolate, melted
> ½ teaspoon red food coloring

Cream shortening. Sift dry ingredients into shortening. Add milk and vanilla; beat 2 minutes. Add remaining ingredients, and beat 1 minute. Pour into 9″ square pan lined on bottom with paper. Bake in preheated 350°F. oven, 1 hour. Cool, and frost as desired.

Chocolate Cake, Hungarian Style

This light, sponge-type cake contains no flour and has a mild chocolate flavor.

> 5 large eggs
> ¼ teaspoon salt
> 1 cup sifted confectioners' sugar
> ¼ cup sifted unsweetened cocoa
> 1 teaspoon vanilla extract
> 1 cup heavy cream, whipped and sweetened
> Chocolate Glaze (see below)
> Toasted sliced almonds (optional)

Separate eggs and beat whites with the salt until stiff, but not dry. Beat in confectioners' sugar 1 tablespoon at a time, then fold in cocoa. Beat yolks until thick and lemon-colored and fold into cocoa mixture. Add vanilla. Spread in 15″ x 10″ x 1″ pan lined with waxed paper and greased. Bake in preheated moderate oven (350°F.) about 20 minutes. Turn out on towel sprinkled with confectioners' sugar. Very gently peel off waxed paper, using a small spatula to separate cake from paper if it sticks. Cool and cut crosswise in quarters. Put layers together with whipped cream. Spread with glaze; decorate with almonds, if desired. Chill and slice.

Chocolate Glaze Over boiling water, melt 1 tablespoon butter and 1 square unsweetened chocolate. Remove from boiling water. Add ½ cup sifted confectioners' sugar, 2 tablespoons boiling water, dash of salt and ½ teaspoon vanilla extract; beat until smooth and glossy.

Rich Mocha Layer Cake With Creamy Mocha Frosting

>   2 packages (6 ounces each), or 1 package (12 ounces)
>   semisweet chocolate pieces
>   1¾ cups cake flour
>   1 cup sugar
>   2 teaspoons instant-coffee powder
>   1 teaspoon baking powder
>   ½ teaspoon salt
>   ½ teaspoon baking soda
>   1 cup milk
>   ¼ cup butter or margarine, softened
>   3 eggs
>   2 teaspoons vanilla extract
>   Few drops red food coloring (optional)
>   Creamy Mocha Frosting (see below)

Melt chocolate over hot (not boiling) water; set aside. Sift flour, sugar, instant coffee, baking powder, salt and soda into large bowl of electric mixer. Add chocolate, milk and butter. Blend, then beat at medium speed of electric mixer for 2 minutes. Add remaining ingredients, except frosting, and beat 2 minutes longer. Pour into two 9″ layer-cake pans lined on bottom with waxed paper. Bake in preheated 350°F. oven about 30 minutes. Let stand in pans on wire racks 10 minutes, then turn out and peel off paper. Turn right side up and cool completely. Spread frosting between layers and on top and sides of cake.

Creamy Mocha Frosting

Melt 1 package (6 ounces) semisweet chocolate pieces over hot (not boiling) water and cool to room temperature. Beat 1 cup butter or margarine until creamy. Blend in chocolate and 2 egg yolks. Beat in 1¼ cups confectioners' sugar and 1 teaspoon instant-coffee powder.

Honey-Nut Spice Cake

    ½ cup margarine or butter
    ½ cup sugar
    ¾ cup clover honey
    1 egg
    ½ cup coarsely chopped nuts
    2 cups sifted cake flour
    1 teaspoon baking powder
    ¼ teaspoon soda
    ¼ teaspoon salt
    1 teaspoon cinnamon
    ¼ teaspoon ground cloves
    ¼ teaspoon ginger
    ½ cup water
    1½ cups dairy sour cream
    2 tablespoons chopped candied ginger

Cream margarine and sugar until light. Add ½ cup honey, the egg and nuts and beat 1 minute. Sift together dry ingredients; add alternately with the water to the creamed mixture and beat thoroughly. Pour into two greased and waxed-paper-lined 8″ layer-cake pans. Bake in preheated moderate oven (350°F.) about 30 minutes. Turn out on racks and peel off paper; cool. Mix remaining honey and sour cream. Spread between layers and on top of cake. Sprinkle with ginger.

Molasses Spice Cake

If you like fruitcake, you will surely enjoy this one.

    ½ cup shortening
    1 cup molasses
    1 egg
    2½ cups sifted cake flour
    1¼ teaspoons baking powder
    ¾ teaspoon baking soda

½ teaspoon salt
½ teaspoon ginger
½ teaspoon allspice
¾ cup buttermilk
    Fruit Filling (see below)
    Fluffy White Frosting (see below)

Cream shortening. Beat in molasses and egg. Add sifted flour, baking powder, soda, salt, ginger and allspice alternately with buttermilk, beating until smooth. Pour into two 8″ layer-cake pans lined on the bottom with paper. Bake in preheated moderate oven (375°F.) about 30 minutes. Cool. Spread filling between layers and frosting on top and sides.

Fruit Filling Chop 1 cup pitted stewed prunes and ½ cup stewed raisins. Add ½ cup chopped nuts, 2 tablespoons citrus marmalade, ⅛ teaspoon salt and 2 tablespoons prune juice.

Fluffy White Frosting In top part of a double boiler combine 2 egg whites, 1½ cups granulated sugar, ⅛ teaspoon salt, ⅓ cup water and 2 teaspoons light corn syrup. Put over boiling water and beat with rotary beater or electric mixer 7 minutes, or until mixture will stand in stiff peaks. Add 1 teaspoon vanilla extract.

Fresh-Coconut Cake
MAKES TWO 9″ x 5″ x 3″ CAKES.

    1 cup shortening
    2 cups sugar
3½ cups sifted cake flour
    2 teaspoons baking powder
    1 teaspoon salt
    1 cup milk
    1 teaspoon vanilla extract
    ⅔ cup grated fresh or canned flaked coconut
    6 egg whites

Cream shortening. Gradually add sugar and beat until light. Add sifted dry ingredients alternately with milk to first mixture, blending well. Add vanilla and fold in coconut and stiffly beaten egg whites. Put in 2 well-greased 9″ x 5″ x 3″ loaf pans and bake in preheated moderate oven (350°F.) about 1 hour.

Note If desired, greased pans can be lightly sprinkled with coconut before adding batter.

Mississippi Pecan Cake
Tender cake, chock-full of nuts. Can be frozen.

> ½ cup butter or margarine
> 2 cups sugar
> 1 teaspoon vanilla extract
> 1 egg
> 3 egg yolks
> 2½ cups all-purpose flour
> 3 teaspoons baking powder
> ¾ teaspoon salt
> 1 cup water
> Pecan Mixture (see below)

Cream butter, sugar, vanilla and whole egg until fluffy. Add egg yolks one at a time and beat well after each. Stir flour, baking powder and salt together. Add to creamed mixture alternately with water. Stir until smooth. Grease 10″ tube pan and line *bottom only* with waxed paper. Pour half the batter into pan. Drop Pecan Mixture by spoonfuls on batter, then top with remaining batter. Bake in preheated 325°F. oven 1 hour and 25 minutes or until pick inserted in center comes out clean. Cool cake in pan on rack; turn out.

Pecan Mixture In large bowl of electric mixer combine 3 egg whites, ¼ teaspoon salt and ¼ cup water. Beat at high speed until stiff but not dry. Stir together ½ cup sugar, 2 tablespoons all-purpose flour and 1 teaspoon baking powder. Gradually beat into whites until stiff. Fold in 1 pound (4 cups) pecans, ground.

Chocolate-Frosted Marble Cake

A tender, buttery white cake complemented by dark chocolate cake and rich chocolaty frosting.

4 squares (4 ounces) semisweet chocolate or ¾ cup (4 ounces) chocolate pieces
1 cup butter, softened
2 cups sugar
8 egg whites (separate one at a time, using 6 yolks for frosting)
3¼ cups sifted cake flour
2 teaspoons double-acting baking powder
⅛ teaspoon salt
1 cup milk
2 teaspoons vanilla extract
Rich Chocolate Frosting (see below)

Melt chocolate over hot water in top part of double boiler. Remove from water and cool. With waxed paper, line bottom of 4″-deep 10″ tube pan. Cream butter in large mixing bowl. Gradually add sugar and cream until light and fluffy. Add egg whites one or two at a time, beating well after each. Fold in sifted dry ingredients alternately with mixture of milk and vanilla, beginning and ending with flour mixture. Add one third of batter (about 2 cups) to melted chocolate and blend well. Pour half the remaining white batter into lined pan. Spoon in chocolate batter and pour remaining white batter on top. Run small spatula through batter several times to marbleize. With rack in center of oven, bake in preheated moderate oven (350°F.) 50 to 60 minutes. Cool on cake rack 10 minutes. Run spatula around edges of cake and around tube. Turn out on rack, remove paper, cool and turn top up. Spread with frosting, including center part. Make swirls with small spatula.

Rich Chocolate Frosting Cream 6 tablespoons softened butter in large mixing bowl. Add 6 squares unsweetened chocolate (melted), 3⅓ cups sifted confectioners' sugar and ⅓ cup water. Mix well. Add 6 egg yolks one at a time, beating well after each.

Add 1½ teaspoons vanilla extract and beat until smooth. Chill 10 minutes before frosting cake.

Angel Food Cake

One of the most glorious of American cakes, angel food makes a wonderful party dessert. Use the egg yolks for Company Gold Cake (see p. 186), or one of our other special gold cakes.

> 1 cup sifted cake flour
> 1½ cups sugar
> 1½ cups egg whites (10 to 12 medium-size eggs)
> ¼ teaspoon salt
> 1½ teaspoons cream of tartar
> 1½ teaspoons vanilla extract
> ½ teaspoon almond extract

Sift flour and ¾ cup of the sugar together 3 times. Beat egg whites with salt and cream of tartar in large bowl at high speed of electric mixer until light and fluffy. Sprinkle remaining sugar over egg whites, 2 tablespoons at a time, beating thoroughly after each addition. Continue beating until stiff peaks form. Fold in extracts. Sift dry ingredients, 2 tablespoons at a time, over beaten egg whites. Fold in gently but thoroughly with a wire whip or rubber spatula. Pour batter into ungreased tube pan (10″ x 4″). Make sure that there is not a trace of any fat or grease in pan, or cake won't rise. Cut gently through batter to remove large air bubbles. Bake in preheated moderate oven (350°F.) for 40 to 50 minutes, or until crust is golden brown and cracks are very dry. Invert pan immediately and place on funnel or bottle. Cool cake in upside-down pan for at least 1 hour. Cut cake out of pan with a sharp knife. Using two forks, separate cake into pieces or slice with a sawing motion using a knife with serrated edge.

Note Cake can be decorated and frosted with fruits, icings, or whipped cream, or it can be scooped out and filled with ice cream, custard, whipped cream or fruit for a delicious dessert.

Spongecake

  6 eggs, separated
1½ cups granulated sugar
1½ cups sifted cake flour
  1 teaspoon baking powder
½ teaspoon salt
⅓ cup cold water
  2 teaspoons vanilla extract
  1 teaspoon lemon extract
  1 teaspoon grated lemon rind
½ teaspoon cream of tartar
   Confectioners' sugar

Beat egg yolks until very thick and lemon-colored. Gradually add sugar, beating constantly. Add sifted flour, baking powder and salt alternately with water, flavorings and rind, blending lightly. Beat egg whites with cream of tartar until stiff, but not dry. Gradually and gently fold egg-yolk mixture into beaten whites. Pour into ungreased 10″ tube pan. Bake in preheated slow oven (325°F.) about 1 hour. Turn pan upside down with tube over neck of funnel or bottle. Cool and remove from pan. Put on serving plate and dust top with confectioners' sugar.

Lemon-Filled Cake Roll

  4 eggs
¾ teaspoon baking powder
¼ teaspoon salt
¾ cup granulated sugar
¾ cup sifted cake flour
  1 teaspoon lemon juice
   Confectioners' sugar
   Lemon Filling (see below)

Grease a 15″ x 10″ x 1″ jelly-roll pan with vegetable shortening, line with waxed paper and grease paper. Beat eggs, baking powder and salt until thick and pale. Gradually add sugar, beating about 10 minutes. Fold in flour and lemon juice. Spread in pan and bake in preheated hot oven (400°F.) about 13 minutes. Invert pan on sheet of waxed paper generously sprinkled with confectioners' sugar. Remove pan and peel paper off cake. While still warm, roll cake lengthwise in the waxed paper and let stand until cool. Unroll and spread with Lemon Filling. Reroll and carefully wrap in waxed paper; chill. Sprinkle with confectioners' sugar before serving.

Lemon Filling In top part of double boiler, mix 3 eggs, 1 egg yolk and 1 cup sugar. Stir in grated rind and juice of 1 lemon and ½ cup butter or margarine. Put over simmering water and cook, stirring frequently, 30 minutes. Remove from heat and cool.

Strawberry Cake Roll

    1 cup sifted cake flour
    1 teaspoon double-acting baking powder
  ¼ teaspoon salt
    3 eggs
    1 teaspoon vanilla extract
    1 cup granulated sugar
  ¼ cup water
  ¼ cup confectioners' sugar
    1 cup sliced fresh strawberries
    1 pint strawberry ice cream, softened
    1 package (1 pound) frozen sliced strawberries, thawed
    2 tablespoons brandy (optional)

Sift flour, baking powder and salt. Beat eggs with vanilla until fluffy and light-colored. Gradually beat in granulated sugar. Stir in the water. Fold in sifted dry ingredients carefully but thoroughly. Turn into waxed-paper-lined 15″ x 10″ x 1″ baking pan. Bake in preheated 350°F. oven 15 minutes, or until done. Sift confectioners' sugar evenly onto smooth dish towel. Turn hot cake out on towel and carefully peel off paper. Roll up cake from end, jelly-roll fashion; cool. Add fresh strawberries to ice cream. Unroll cake and spread with ice cream mixture; reroll, wrap in foil and freeze. Thaw 10 minutes before serving. When ready to serve, mix thawed berries with brandy and serve as sauce on sliced roll.

Blueberry Upside-Down Cake

¾ cup margarine
½ cup packed brown sugar
2 cups washed fresh blueberries
2 teaspoons grated lemon rind
½ cup granulated sugar
1 egg
1½ cups all-purpose flour
2 teaspoons baking powder
½ teaspoon salt
½ cup milk

Melt ¼ cup margarine in 9″ square pan. Sprinkle with the brown sugar. Mix berries and lemon rind and put in pan, distributing evenly. Cream remaining margarine. Add granulated sugar and beat until light. Add egg and beat well. Mix dry ingredients and add alternately with milk to first mixture, beating after each addition until smooth. Spread on berries. Bake in preheated 375°F. oven about 30 minutes. Let stand 10 minutes, then turn out on serving dish.

Pineapple Upside-Down Cake

An old favorite that keeps winning new friends. This cake is just right after a light supper.

¼ cup butter or margarine
½ cup firmly packed dark-brown sugar
6–8 slices of pineapple, cut into halves
¼ cup shortening
⅔ cup granulated sugar
1 egg
2¼ cups sifted all-purpose flour
1 tablespoon baking powder
½ teaspoon salt
1 cup milk

Cream butter and stir in brown sugar. Spread mixture in the bottom of an 8″ square pan. Top with pineapple. Cream shortening until light and fluffy. Gradually beat in granulated sugar. Stir in egg. Sift flour with baking powder and salt. Add dry ingredients alternately with milk, beginning and ending with flour. Pour batter over fruit in pan. Bake in preheated moderate oven (375°F.) for about 35 minutes. Turn upside down onto serving plate.

Old-Fashioned Spice Cake

½ cup vegetable shortening
1 cup granulated sugar
3 eggs
1⅓ cups all-purpose flour
1 teaspoon baking soda
½ teaspoon salt
2 teaspoons cinnamon
1 teaspoon ground cloves
1 teaspoon ginger
1 teaspoon crushed cardamom seed

1 cup dairy sour cream
Fine dry bread crumbs
Confectioners' sugar

Cream shortening. Gradually add granulated sugar and beat well. Add eggs one at a time, beating thoroughly after each. Mix dry ingredients and add alternately with sour cream to first mixture, blending well. Grease well a 2-quart fluted tube pan, sprinkle with crumbs and shake out excess. Put batter in pan and bake in preheated slow oven (325°F.) about 50 minutes. Let cool in pan on wire rack 10 minutes before turning out. Cool and sprinkle with confectioners' sugar.

Pumpkin Spice Cake

2¼ cups sifted cake flour
  3 teaspoons double-acting baking powder
¼ teaspoon baking soda
½ teaspoon salt
  1 teaspoon cinnamon
¼ teaspoon ginger
½ cup granulated sugar
½ cup margarine, at room temperature
  1 cup packed light-brown sugar
¾ cup canned pumpkin
½ cup buttermilk
  1 egg
  2 egg yolks
    Creamy Molasses Frosting (see below)

Sift flour, baking powder, soda, salt, cinnamon, ginger and sugar. Put margarine in large bowl of electric mixer (or other mixing bowl if mixer is not available) and stir just to soften. Add flour mixture, brown sugar, pumpkin and ¼ cup buttermilk. Beat 2 minutes at low speed of mixer, or 300 vigorous strokes by hand. Add remaining buttermilk, 1 egg and 2 egg yolks and beat 1 minute longer, or 150 strokes by hand. Pour into greased and floured 13" x 9" x 2" pan. Bake in preheated moderate oven (350°F.) 45 minutes, or until done. Cool in pan; spread with frosting.

Creamy Molasses Frosting Cream ⅓ cup margarine until fluffy. Add 1 cup confectioners' sugar, 1 egg white and 1 teaspoon vanilla extract and mix well. Gradually beat in 2 cups of confectioners' sugar alternately with 1 tablespoon molasses and about 1½ tablespoons milk. Blend well.

Dark Gingerbread

> ½ cup butter or margarine
> ½ cup sugar
> 1 egg
> 2¼ cups all-purpose flour
> 1½ teaspoons baking soda
> 1 teaspoon cinnamon
> 1 teaspoon ginger
> ½ teaspoon ground cloves
> ½ teaspoon salt
> 1 cup dark molasses
> 1 cup hot water

Cream butter and sugar until blended. Add egg and beat until light. Mix dry ingredients together. Stir molasses and hot water together and add alternately with dry ingredients to first mixture, beating well. Pour into greased 9" square pan and bake in preheated 350°F. oven 40 minutes.

Spicy Southern Gingerbread

> 2 eggs
> ¾ cup packed brown sugar
> ¾ cup light molasses
> ¾ cup butter, melted

   2½ cups all-purpose flour
   2 teaspoons baking powder
   2 teaspoons ginger
   1½ teaspoons cinnamon
   ½ teaspoon ground cloves
   ½ teaspoon nutmeg
   ½ teaspoon baking soda
   ½ teaspoon salt
   1 cup boiling water
     Whipped cream

Beat eggs, brown sugar, molasses and melted butter together. Mix together dry ingredients and add with the boiling water to first mixture. Beat well, then pour into well-greased 13″ x 9″ x 2″ baking pan. Bake in preheated 350°F. oven about 35 minutes. Serve with whipped cream.

Applesauce-Nut Cake

   ½ cup vegetable shortening
   1 cup packed light-brown sugar
   1 cup canned applesauce
   2¼ cups all-purpose flour
   ½ teaspoon salt
   ½ teaspoon baking soda
   1 teaspoon double-acting baking powder
   ½ teaspoon ground cloves
   ½ teaspoon cinnamon
   ¼ teaspoon nutmeg
   1 cup chopped walnuts
     Confectioners' sugar, or Lemon Frosting (see below)

Cream shortening and brown sugar until light. Add applesauce. Mix dry ingredients and gradually beat into first mixture. Add nuts and pour into 9″ x 5″ x 3″ loaf pan lined on bottom with waxed paper. Bake in preheated slow oven (325°F.) 1 hour, or until done. Let stand on wire rack about 5 minutes, then turn out and peel off paper. Turn right side up. Cool and sprinkle with confectioners' sugar, or frost.

Lemon Frosting

Combine 2 cups confectioners' sugar with 1 teaspoon grated lemon rind and enough lemon juice (2 to 3 tablespoons) to make a frosting of spreading consistency.

Apple Cake With Cream-Cheese Frosting

> 2 eggs
> 2 cups sugar
> ½ cup vegetable oil
> 1 teaspoon vanilla extract
> 2 cups all-purpose flour
> ½ teaspoon salt
> 1 teaspoon baking soda
> 2 teaspoons cinnamon
> ¼ teaspoon nutmeg
> 4 cups diced peeled apples
> 1 cup chopped walnuts
> Cream-Cheese Frosting (see below)

Beat eggs until light and fluffy. Gradually add sugar, oil and vanilla. Sift together flour, salt, soda, cinnamon and nutmeg and add to first mixture. Stir in apples and walnuts. Put in greased 13″ x 9″ x 2″ pan and bake in preheated 350°F. oven about 45 minutes. Let cool in pan on rack 10 to 15 minutes, then spread with frosting.

Cream-Cheese Frosting Mix 1 package (3 ounces) cream cheese, at room temperature, 3 tablespoons butter or margarine, softened, pinch of salt, ½ teaspoon vanilla extract and 1½ cups confectioners' sugar together until smooth.

Banana Loaf Cake

  ½ cup butter or margarine, softened
  ¾ cup light-brown sugar, lightly packed
  ¾ cup granulated sugar
  1 teaspoon vanilla extract
  1 egg
  1 egg yolk
  1 cup mashed very-ripe banana (see Note)
  2 cups all-purpose flour
  1 teaspoon baking powder
  ½ teaspoon baking soda
  ½ teaspoon salt
  ¾ cup buttermilk

Cream butter. Gradually add sugars and beat until fluffy. Add vanilla, whole egg and yolk and beat well. Blend in banana, then add mixed dry ingredients alternately with buttermilk, beating after each addition until smooth. Pour into well-greased 9″ x 5″ x 3″ loaf pan and bake in preheated slow oven (325°F.) 55 minutes, or until done. Cool in pan on wire rack 10 minutes. Turn out.

Note For 1 cup mashed banana, mash 2 medium bananas with fork or potato masher (do not whirl in blender).

Carrot Cake With Cream-Cheese Frosting

  2¼ cups all-purpose flour
  2½ teaspoons cinnamon
  1½ teaspoons baking soda
  1 teaspoon salt
  4 eggs
  2 cups sugar
  1½ cups grated carrot (about 3 large)
  1½ cups oil
      Cream-Cheese Frosting (see below)

Mix flour, cinnamon, soda and salt; set aside. In large bowl of electric mixer beat eggs with sugar until fluffy and lemon-colored. Add carrots and oil and mix well. Add flour mixture and stir to mix well. Pour into greased 13″ x 9″ x 2″ pan and bake in preheated 350°F. oven 45 minutes or until pick inserted in center comes out clean. Cool in pan on rack, then spread with frosting.

Cream-Cheese Frosting Beat together 1 package (3 ounces) softened cream cheese and ¼ cup softened butter or margarine. Add 2¼ cups confectioners' sugar and 1 teaspoon grated lemon rind; beat until of spreading consistency.

Pineapple-Carrot Cake

    2½ cups all-purpose flour
    ½ teaspoon salt
    1 teaspoon baking soda
    1 teaspoon cinnamon
    1 can (8 ounces) crushed pineapple
    1½ cups oil
    3 eggs
    2 cups granulated sugar
    2 cups finely shredded peeled carrots (4 medium)
    Confectioners' sugar

Stir together flour, salt, soda and cinnamon; set aside. Purée pineapple with the syrup in blender. Pour into large bowl of electric mixer, add oil, eggs and granulated sugar and beat well. Beat in carrots. Beat in flour mixture thoroughly. Pour into greased floured 13″ x 9″ x 2″ pan and bake in preheated 350°F. oven about 45 minutes. Cool in pan; sprinkle with confectioners' sugar and cut in squares.

Apricot-Brandy Pound Cake

    1 cup butter or margarine, softened
2½ cups sugar
    6 eggs
    1 teaspoon vanilla extract
    1 teaspoon orange extract
    1 teaspoon rum extract
    ½ teaspoon lemon extract
    3 cups sifted cake flour
    ¼ teaspoon baking soda
    ½ teaspoon salt
    1 cup dairy sour cream
    ½ cup apricot brandy

Cream butter. Gradually add sugar and beat until light. Add eggs one at a time, beating thoroughly after each. Add flavorings, then sifted dry ingredients alternately with sour cream and brandy. Blend well. Put in greased 3-quart bundt pan and bake in preheated slow oven (325°F.) about 1 hour and 15 minutes. Cool in pan on rack.

Best-Ever Pound Cake

1½ cups lightly salted butter (not sweet or whipped)
2⅔ cups sifted all-purpose flour (see below)
    ¼ teaspoon baking soda
    ½ teaspoon mace
2¼ cups granulated sugar
    2 tablespoons lemon juice
    2 teaspoons vanilla extract
    8 large eggs, separated
    ¼ teaspoon salt
    ¾ teaspoon cream of tartar
      Confectioners' sugar (optional)

With pastry brush and softened butter from the 1½ cups, grease bottom and sides of 3½-quart cast-iron bundt pan with nonstick coating or 10″ x 4″ aluminum tube pan. Dust pan with flour (*not* from the 2⅔ cups), turn pan upside down and shake to remove excess. Turn on oven; set at 300°F. If oven has no control, use a portable oven thermometer and keep correct temperature by controlling heat. Sift flour into bowl, then spoon lightly into measuring cup for dry ingredients and fill heaping full. Do not shake down or pack with spoon. Level off with metal spatula. Put flour in sifter with soda, mace and 1¼ cups granulated sugar. Sift into bowl containing butter and blend well with fingers. Stir lemon juice and vanilla into unbeaten egg yolks. Add a small amount at a time to butter mixture, blending well with fingers after each addition. With electric mixer or rotary beater, beat egg whites with the salt until whites stand in soft glossy points, but not until dry. Gradually add remaining granulated sugar, beating after each addition until blended. With spoon or rubber spatula, gently fold in cream of tartar. With hands, gently fold whites into batter until whites are distributed evenly throughout. Spoon into pan, smoothing top with back of spoon. Set pan down hard on counter to remove any air bubbles. Bake about 2 hours. Cake is done when it shrinks from sides of pan and surface springs back when pressed lightly with finger. Turn off heat and leave cake in oven 30 minutes. Remove from oven and let stand in pan on wire rack 30 minutes. Loosen sides with spatula, turn cake out on rack and let stand until completely cold. Put cake on serving plate; sprinkle with confectioners' sugar, if desired.

Note To store cake, cover with cake cover or loosely with foil or plastic wrap, tucking it in tightly under plate. Store in cool place. Stored this way, cake will keep several weeks. If frozen, then wrapped well and stored in freezer, cake will keep almost indefinitely.

Chocolate Pound Cake
Tender and buttery.

 1 cup butter or margarine, softened
1¼ cups granulated sugar
 5 eggs, separated
 1 teaspoon vanilla extract
 2 squares (1 ounce each) unsweetened chocolate, melted and cooled
 2 cups sifted all-purpose flour
 ½ teaspoon baking powder
 ½ teaspoon salt
  Confectioners' sugar (optional)

Cream butter and 1 cup granulated sugar. Add egg yolks, one at a time, beating well after each; add vanilla. Blend in chocolate. Add sifted flour, baking powder and salt; beat until smooth. Beat egg whites until stiff, but not dry. Gradually beat in remaining granulated sugar. Fold into first mixture. Pour into greased 9" x 5" x 3" loaf pan, lined on bottom with paper. Bake in preheated 300°F. oven, about 1 hour and 45 minutes. When cool, sift confectioners' sugar over top, if desired.

Ginger Pound Cake

 1 cup butter or margarine, softened
 2 cups packed light-brown sugar
 4 eggs, separated
 3 cups all-purpose flour
 1 teaspoon baking powder
 1 teaspoon nutmeg
 1 tablespoon ground ginger
 1 teaspoon salt
 2 tablespoons minced candied ginger (optional)
 ½ cup light cream

Cream butter. Gradually add sugar and beat until light. Add egg yolks one at a time, beating thoroughly after each. Sift dry ingredients and add candied ginger, if used. Add to first mixture alternately with cream, blending well. Fold in stiffly beaten egg whites. Put in greased 9″ tube pan lined on the bottom with waxed paper. Bake in preheated moderate oven (350°F.) about 1 hour. Turn out on rack and peel off paper.

Moroccan Pound Cake

⅔ cup margarine
½ cup vegetable shortening
2 cups granulated sugar
4 eggs
3 cups all-purpose flour
3 teaspoons baking powder
¼ teaspoon salt
1 cup milk
1 teaspoon vanilla extract
½ cup raisins
¾ cup chopped unsalted mixed nuts (any combination)
1 tablespoon cocoa
1 tablespoon cinnamon
Confectioners' sugar

Cream margarine, shortening and granulated sugar until light. Add eggs one at a time, beating thoroughly after each addition. Add sifted dry ingredients alternately with milk, beating until smooth. Add vanilla, raisins and nuts. Pour three quarters of batter into a greased 10″ tube pan lined on the bottom with waxed paper. Mix remaining batter with cocoa and cinnamon and spoon onto batter in pan. Run a knife through batter to marbleize. Bake in preheated moderate oven (350°F.) about 1 hour and 15 minutes. Let stand in pan 5 minutes, then turn out on rack, peel off paper, cool and sprinkle with confectioners' sugar.

Peanut Butter Cake

>   2 cups flour
>   3 tablespoons baking powder
>   ¾ teaspoon salt
>   1 cup chunky peanut butter
>   ¼ cup shortening
> 1½ cups packed dark-brown sugar
> 1½ teaspoons vanilla
>   3 eggs
>   1 cup milk
>   Fine dry bread crumbs (optional)
>   Chocolate Glaze (below)
>   About ¼ cup salted roasted blanched peanuts

Stir together flour, baking powder and salt; set aside. In large bowl of mixer cream peanut butter and shortening. Beat in sugar until well mixed, then add vanilla. Beat in eggs until fluffy. At low speed stir in flour mixture alternately with milk, beginning and ending with flour mixture. Pour into well-greased 12-cup fluted tube pan heavily coated with bread crumbs. Bake in preheated 350° oven 40 to 45 minutes or until pick inserted in cake comes out clean. Cool in pan 10 minutes, then turn out on rack to cool completely. Decorate with Chocolate Glaze and peanuts arranged as flower petals. Makes 16 to 18 servings.

Note Can also be baked in greased 13″ x 9″ x 2″ pan 40 minutes. Cool in pan. Cut in about 2″ squares. Makes about 24.

Chocolate Glaze Melt ½ cup semisweet chocolate pieces or 3 squares (3 ounces) semisweet chocolate in heavy saucepan over very low heat. Gradually stir in 2 to 3 tablespoons hot water until chocolate is thin enough for glazing.

Praline Cake
Like a pound cake in texture, with a delicious praline flavor.

   1 cup butter, softened
½ cup hydrogenated shortening
   1 pound light-brown sugar
   5 eggs
   3 cups unsifted all-purpose flour
¼ teaspoon baking soda
½ teaspoon baking powder
¾ cup milk
   2 teaspoons vanilla extract
   2 cups chopped pecans
     Confectioners' sugar

Cream butter, shortening and brown sugar until light and fluffy. Add eggs, one at a time, beating well after each addition. Add sifted dry ingredients alternately with milk, beating until smooth after each addition. Stir in vanilla and nuts. Pour into well-greased heavy bundt pan (a scalloped 3-quart tube pan). Put in cold oven and turn heat control to 300°F. Bake about 1 hour and 40 minutes. Let stand 5 minutes, then turn out on rack to cool. Before serving, sift confectioners' sugar lightly over top. Store airtight.

Sand Cake

   1 cup sifted all-purpose flour
   1 cup sifted cornstarch
   2 teaspoons baking powder
½ teaspoon salt
   1 cup butter or margarine, softened
   1 cup sugar
     Grated rind of 1 lemon
   2 tablespoons brandy
   6 eggs, separated

Sift together flour, cornstarch, baking powder and salt. In large bowl of electric mixer cream butter; gradually add sugar and continue to cream until light and fluffy. Beat in rind and brandy; add egg yolks one at a time, beating well after each. Continue beating, gradually adding dry ingredients. Beat egg whites until stiff, but not dry; gently fold into batter. Turn into greased 10″ tube pan and bake in preheated 350°F. oven 45 minutes. Cool pan on rack 5 minutes, then turn cake out on rack to cool.

Almond Torte

Rich with almonds and butter cream. Chill several hours or overnight for best flavor.

> 1 cup toasted blanched almonds
> ½ cup fine dry bread crumbs
> 6 eggs, separated
> ⅛ teaspoon salt
> 1 cup sugar
> ½ teaspoon almond extract
> Praline Butter Cream (see below)
> ¼ cup toasted sliced almonds (optional)

Grease bottoms of two 9″ square cake pans. Line with waxed paper cut to fit. Grease paper and set aside. Finely grate blanched almonds in blender or put through nut grinder. Combine with bread crumbs and set aside. In large bowl of electric mixer beat egg whites and salt at medium speed until soft peaks form. Increase speed to high and gradually beat in sugar, beating until stiff peaks form. Stir almond extract into egg yolks to break up and blend. Fold about a quarter of egg-white mixture into egg yolks, then pour this mixture over remaining egg-white mixture. Sprinkle with almond-crumb mixture a few tablespoons at a time, folding in gently but thoroughly after each addition. Divide batter evenly between pans and bake on rack in center of preheated 350°F. oven 30 to 40 minutes, or until tops are light brown and spring back when touched lightly with finger. Cool completely in pans on wire racks. Run small spatula around edges, invert on racks and peel off waxed paper. To assemble torte, sandwich layers with about a quarter of the Praline Butter Cream. Frost tops and sides with remaining cream. Chill several hours. Before serving, sprinkle with sliced almonds, if desired.

Praline Butter Cream Cook and stir ¼ cup unblanched almonds and ¼ cup sugar in small heavy skillet over medium heat until sugar is melted and golden brown and almonds are lightly toasted. Pour praline mixture on greased baking sheet to cool. When hard, break in small pieces, then grate in blender; set aside. Combine ¾ cup sugar and ⅓ cup water in small saucepan and bring to boil over medium heat (do not stir). Cook just until a thin syrup forms and a drop placed between thumb and index finger feels sticky (be careful not to burn fingers), or until candy thermometer reads 220°F. (about 6 minutes). Pour hot syrup in thin stream over 4 well-beaten egg yolks, beating constantly. Cool, beating occasionally. Cream 1 cup butter or margarine, then gradually beat in egg-sugar mixture until smooth and thick. Fold in praline.

Chocolate-Pecan Torte

A moist, rich, not very sweet cake, brownielike in texture (not a high, fluffy cake).

    1½ cups (9 ounces) semisweet chocolate pieces
    ½ cup butter, softened
    ½ cup sugar
    4 egg yolks
    4 egg whites, stiffly beaten
    1 cup pecans, chopped in blender or minced
    ¼ cup all-purpose flour
    ½ cup apricot preserves
       Whipped cream (optional)

Melt 1 cup chocolate in top of double boiler over hot water. Cool. Cream butter and sugar until light. Add egg yolks one at a time, beating thoroughly after each. Blend in chocolate. Fold egg whites into batter with nuts and flour. Blend well. Pour into 9″ layer-cake pan lined on bottom with waxed paper. Bake in preheated moderate oven (350°F.) about 25 minutes. Turn out on wire rack. Spread top and sides with apricot preserves while cake is still warm. Melt remaining chocolate and spread thin layer on top of preserves. Cool cake, cut in thin wedges and serve, with whipped cream, if desired.

Linzer Torte

> 1 cup unsalted butter
> 1 cup granulated sugar
> 2 egg yolks
> 2 hard-cooked egg yolks, sieved
>   Grated rind and juice of 1 lemon
> 1 tablespoon brandy
> ½ pound almonds, ground
> 2 cups sifted all-purpose flour
> 1 teaspoon baking powder
> 1 cup raspberry or apricot jam
>   Confectioners' sugar

Cream butter and gradually beat in granulated sugar. Add egg yolks, hard cooked egg yolks, lemon juice and rind, and brandy. Blend well. Stir in almonds, and sifted flour and baking powder. With fingers, work ingredients to a smooth dough. Press half of dough in loose-bottomed 9″ layer-cake pan. Make bottom of torte thicker than sides. Cover bottom with ¾ cup jam. Chill remaining half of dough until easier to handle. Roll dough in ⅜″-thick strips and arrange crisscross over jam-covered dough. Bake in preheated moderate oven (350°F.) 45 to 50 minutes, or until pale gold in color. Before serving, fill spaces between strips with ¼ cup jam. Dust with confectioners' sugar.

Sacher Torte

The world-famous chocolate torte from the Hotel Sacher in Vienna.
Make layer 24 hours before frosting.

    ¾ cup butter or margarine, softened
    ¾ cup sugar
    6½ squares (6½ ounces) semisweet chocolate, melted and
        cooled
    8 eggs, separated
    1 cup cake flour, stirred and lightly spooned into measur-
        ing cup
    2 egg whites
    2 tablespoons apricot jam or preserves, slightly heated
      Chocolate Fondant Frosting (see below)
      Whipped-cream rosettes (optional)

Grease 9″ springform pan well and set aside. In large bowl of electric mixer cream butter; gradually beat in sugar until light and fluffy. Beat in chocolate, then the 8 egg yolks, about 2 at a time, until well blended. Stir in flour. Beat the 10 egg whites until stiff, but not dry; add about a third to chocolate mixture and blend well. Fold in remaining egg whites gently but thoroughly. Pour into pan and bake on rack in center of preheated 275°F. oven about 1 hour 15 minutes, or until torte pulls away from sides of pan and pick inserted in center comes out clean. Cool in pan on wire rack 10 minutes. Run small spatula around edge, remove ring and cool torte thoroughly. Cover loosely with waxed paper and let stand 24 hours. To assemble, remove torte from cake-pan bottom and put on serving platter. (Top may be slightly soggy so cut off a thin layer, if desired.) Spread top of torte with jam. Pour Chocolate Fondant Frosting on center of torte and with small spatula quickly spread over top and sides of cake. Decorate top with large whipped-cream rosettes piped through pastry bag with fluted tip, or top each wedge with a dollop of whipped cream.

Chocolate Fondant Frosting Melt 7 squares (7 ounces) semisweet chocolate in top of double boiler over hot water. Combine 1 cup sugar and ⅓ cup water in small saucepan and bring to boil over medium heat (do not stir). Cook 3 to 5 minutes, just until thin syrup forms and a drop placed between thumb and index finger feels sticky (be careful not to burn fingers), or until candy thermometer reads 220°F. Gradually add syrup to chocolate and stir until well blended and frosting coats spoon but is still glossy.

Note Do not overcook syrup or frosting will be dull and sugary.

Brazil Nut Fruitcake
Lots of fruits and nuts held together by a little bit of batter.
MAKES 2.

    1 pound shelled Brazil nuts
    1 pound pitted dates
    ¾ pound candied cherries
    1 pound candied pineapple
    ¾ cup sifted all-purpose flour
    ¾ cup sugar
    ½ teaspoon baking powder
    ½ teaspoon salt
    3 eggs
    1 teaspoon vanilla extract

Combine nuts, dates, cherries and pineapple in large bowl. Sift flour, sugar, baking powder and salt; mix with fruit. Beat eggs until foamy; add vanilla. Add to nut-and-fruit mixture; mix well. Pack into 2 greased waxed-paper lined 1-quart molds. Bake in preheated slow oven (300°F.) about 1½ hours. Remove from pan and peel off paper. Cool.

Dark Fruitcake
MAKES 2.

    1½ cups packed brown sugar
      4 eggs, separated
      3 cups all-purpose flour
      1 teaspoon baking powder
      2 teaspoons salt
      1 tablespoon cinnamon
      1 teaspoon allspice
      1 teaspoon ground cloves
      1 cup fruit juice
     ¾ pound citron, shaved
     ½ pound candied pineapple, chopped
      1 pound candied cherries, halved
     ½ pound dried figs, chopped
      1 cup raisins
      1 pound nuts, chopped (about 4 cups)
      1 cup butter, melted, or vegetable oil

Mix sugar and egg yolks vigorously 2 minutes. Sift 2 cups flour with baking powder, salt and spices. Add to first mixture alternately with fruit juice, mixing until smooth. Fold in stiffly beaten egg whites. Mix remaining flour with fruits and nuts, coating well. Add to first mixture with butter and mix well. Press into two greased 9″ x 5″ x 3″ loaf pans lined on the bottom with waxed paper. Bake in preheated very slow oven (275°F.) about 4 hours.

Busy-Day Dark Fruitcake

      1 cup raisins
      1 cup diced mixed candied fruits
      1 cup broken walnut meats
    2⅓ cups all-purpose flour
      1 teaspoon baking powder
     ¼ teaspoon baking soda
     ½ teaspoon salt

½ teaspoon nutmeg
½ teaspoon allspice
½ teaspoon cinnamon
½ teaspoon ground cloves
½ cup butter, margarine or other shortening
1 cup sugar
1 egg
¼ cup molasses
⅔ cup canned applesauce
   Additional candied fruit and nut halves (optional)

Mix raisins, candied fruits and nuts and set aside. Mix flour, baking powder, soda, salt and spices. Cream butter and sugar together until fluffy. Add egg and molasses and beat well. Add dry ingredients alternately with applesauce, beating after each addition until smooth. Stir in fruit-nut mixture and pour into well-greased 1½-quart glass casserole. If desired, decorate top with candied fruit and nuts. Cover and bake in preheated slow oven (325°F.) about 1¾ hours. Turn out on rack, then turn right side up to cool. This cake keeps several weeks if well wrapped. Can also be frozen.

Vanilla Cupcakes
MAKES 12.

½ cup butter or margarine, softened
1 cup sugar
½ teaspoon vanilla extract
2 eggs
1½ cups sifted cake flour
1¼ teaspoons baking powder
¼ teaspoon salt
⅓ cup milk
   Favorite frosting
   Candied fruit (optional)
   Colored sugar (optional)

Cream butter. Gradually beat in sugar, a little at a time. Beat in vanilla extract and eggs, one at a time, beating well after each addition. Sift together cake flour, baking powder and salt. Add to first mixture alternately with milk, beating until smooth. Grease twelve 2¾″ muffin-pan cups. Line cups with waxed paper. Half fill them with batter. Bake in preheated moderate oven (375°F.) for about 20 minutes. Cool. Frost with any favorite frosting. Decorate with candied fruit and colored sugar, if desired.

Dundee Cake

Of all of Scotland's delicious fruitcakes, this is probably the best known and loved.

>   1 cup butter
>   1 cup sugar
>   5 eggs
>   ½ cup blanched almonds
>   2½ cups sifted all-purpose flour
>   1 teaspoon baking powder
>   ½ teaspoon salt
>   1 cup golden raisins
>   1 cup currants
>   ½ cup chopped mixed candied fruit
>   1 tablespoon grated orange rind
>   2 tablespoons orange juice
>   Almond halves
>   Strips of citron
>   Candied cherries

Cream butter and sugar together. Beat in eggs, one at a time. Grate the almonds or whirl in an electric blender; add to batter. Sift flour, baking powder and salt together into a bowl. Mix in the raisins, currants and candied fruit. Add to batter, mixing well. Stir in grated orange rind and juice. Grease a 9″ tube pan. Pour in batter, pressing down to eliminate any air bubbles. Decorate top with almond halves and strips of citron and candied cherries.

Bake in preheated slow oven (300°F.) about 1 hour and 15 minutes.

Note If golden raisins are unavailable, dark seedless raisins can be substituted.

Kentucky Fruitcake
MAKES 3.

 4 cups all-purpose flour
 1 pound butter, softened
2¼ cups sugar
 1 cup dark molasses
 12 eggs, well beaten
 2 teaspoons baking powder
 1 cup milk
 1 tablespoon cinnamon
 1 tablespoon ground allspice
 2 nutmegs, grated or 1½ teaspoons ground nutmeg
 ½ cup sherry or port
 ½ cup brandy
 2 packages (15 ounces each) seeded raisins, chopped
 1 package (11 ounces) currants
 ½ pound each dried figs, citron, candied pineapple and cherries, chopped
 2 pounds almonds, chopped
 Thin slices citron and red candied pineapple

Put flour in shallow pan and brown in preheated slow oven (300°F.) about 30 minutes, stirring occasionally. (Browned flour is used in many old-fashioned cakes.) Remove from oven and cool. Cream butter. Gradually add sugar and beat until light. Beat in molasses, then eggs. Add 3 cups of the flour, and the baking powder dissolved in the milk; blend thoroughly. Add the spices mixed with the liquors. Dredge fruits and nuts with remaining flour and stir into mixture. Grease three 9" tube pans or loose-bottomed pans and dust with flour. Press batter into pans and bake in preheated very slow oven (250°F.) 2½ to 3 hours. Turn out on racks and cool thoroughly. Decorate with cornucopias of citron and red candied pineapple.

Light Candied Fruitcake

Best made 4 to 6 weeks ahead to allow for aging and increased flavor.
MAKES 3.

> 1 cup coarsely chopped pitted prunes or dates
> 1 cup golden raisins
> 1 cup diced candied pineapple
> 1 cup minced candied orange peel
> 1 cup candied cherries, thinly sliced
> 1 cup chopped almonds or pecans
> 2½ cups all-purpose flour
> 2 teaspoons baking powder
> 1½ teaspoons salt
> 1 tablespoon cinnamon
> 1 teaspoon allspice
> ½ teaspoon ground cloves
> 1¼ cups shortening
> 1½ cups sugar
> 6 eggs
> ½ cup pineapple or other fruit juice
> Candied-cherry halves and/or whole almonds for decoration (optional)
> Brandy (optional)

Mix fruits and chopped almonds with 1 cup flour. Stir together remaining 1½ cups flour, baking powder, salt, cinnamon, allspice and cloves; set aside. Cream shortening and sugar, beating until light. Add eggs one at a time, beating well after each. Add flour mixture alternately with fruit juice. Pour over fruit-nut mixture and blend well. Pack batter lightly in three greased 8″ x 4″ x 2″ loaf pans lined on bottom with waxed paper. Decorate with cherry halves and/or almonds, if desired. Bake in preheated 250°F. oven about 3 hours or until cake is firm and pick inserted in center comes out clean. (Place shallow pan of water on bottom rack of oven while cake is baking.) Loosen edges of cake; let stand 20 minutes, then remove from pan. If desired, wrap in cheesecloth soaked in brandy before wrapping in foil. Store in refrigerator. If desired, cheesecloth may be resoaked in brandy as it becomes dry. Will keep 2 months.

Scottish Seed Cake

A delicate fruitcake, scented with caraway. Rosewater was formerly used as one of the flavoring ingredients.

½ cup butter or margarine
½ cup sugar
3 eggs
2 cups sifted all-purpose flour
2 teaspoons baking powder
¼ teaspoon mace or nutmeg
⅓ cup milk
¼ cup each finely chopped candied orange peel, lemon peel and citron
¼ cup chopped blanched almonds
2 teaspoons caraway seed

Cream butter and sugar together. Beat in eggs, one at a time. Sift flour with baking powder and mace. Add alternately with milk to first mixture, beating well after each addition. Mix in fruit and nuts. Grease a 9" x 5" x 3" loaf pan. Pour in batter. Sprinkle with caraway seed. Bake in preheated slow oven (325°F.) about 1 hour. Turn out on rack to cool. Cut in thin slices to serve.

Surprise Banana Cupcakes
MAKES 12.

¼ cup butter or margarine, softened
⅔ cup sugar
1 egg
1 cup all-purpose flour
1 teaspoon baking powder
½ teaspoon salt
½ teaspoon baking soda
½ cup mashed ripe banana
2 tablespoons milk
½ teaspoon vanilla extract
Jam or jelly

Cream butter and sugar; add egg and beat until well blended. Mix flour, baking powder, salt and soda. Combine banana, milk and vanilla. Add dry ingredients to creamed mixture alternately with banana mixture and mix well. Drop by heaping tablespoonfuls into 12 greased muffin-pan cups or paper baking cups. Drop ½ teaspoonful jam into each, then top with another tablespoonful batter. Bake in preheated 375°F. oven 20 to 25 minutes.

Coconut Cupcakes
MAKES 24.

3 cups shredded coconut
3 egg whites
⅔ cup sugar
⅓ cup cake flour
½ teaspoon baking powder
⅛ teaspoon salt
¼ cup finely chopped pecans
Candied cherries, halved

Chop coconut, 1 cup at a time, in blender until fine (or force through fine blade of food grinder); set aside. Beat egg whites until foamy; gradually add sugar and continue to beat until stiff peaks form. Fold in coconut, sifted dry ingredients and nuts. Using about 1 tablespoon batter for each, spoon into 2″ paper-lined foil baking cups and top each with a cherry half; bake in preheated 325°F. oven 25 minutes, or until lightly browned. Store in airtight container.

Spicy Fudge Cupcakes
Wonderful for lunch boxes.
MAKES 28.

    ⅓ cup shortening
    1 cup sugar
    1 teaspoon vanilla extract
    2 eggs
    2 squares (1 ounce each) unsweetened chocolate, melted and cooled
    ½ teaspoon baking soda
    2 cups sifted cake flour
    1 teaspoon baking powder
    1 teaspoon cinnamon
    ½ teaspoon salt
    ½ cup hot water
    ½ cup buttermilk
    ½ cup molasses

Cream shortening, sugar and vanilla. Add eggs, one at a time, beating thoroughly after each addition. Add chocolate, and blend. Add sifted dry ingredients alternately with liquids, beating until smooth. Half fill greased 2½″ muffin-pan cups with batter. Bake in preheated 350°F. oven 25 minutes. Serve plain, or frost. Can be frozen.

Fruit Cupcakes
MAKES 12.

½ cup butter or margarine, softened
½ cup sugar
3 eggs
1 cup all-purpose flour
¾ teaspoon baking powder
½ teaspoon salt
1 cup chopped mixed candied fruits
1 cup chopped pecans
¾ cup currants
¾ cup golden raisins
¼ cup bourbon
Confectioners' sugar

In large bowl of electric mixer, cream butter and sugar until fluffy; add eggs one at a time, beating well after each. Stir together flour, baking powder and salt; add to creamed mixture, beating until smooth. With wooden spoon, stir in candied fruits, pecans, currants, raisins and bourbon and blend well. Fill 12 greased 2½″ muffin-pan cups to top. (We used a bundt muffin pan.) If you prefer, line muffin-pan cups with paper baking cups. Bake in preheated 300°F. oven 40 minutes, or until pick inserted in center comes out clean. Cool 10 minutes on rack, then turn out on rack to cool further. Sprinkle with confectioners' sugar if desired. Store airtight in cool place.

Angel Cheesecake

1 pound small-curd creamed cottage cheese
1 pound cream cheese
1 cup sugar
5 eggs
Dash of salt
1 teaspoon vanilla extract

Grated rind of 1 orange (1 teaspoon)
½ cup dairy sour cream
  Topping (see below)
  Chopped nuts (optional)

Force cottage cheese through mill or sieve. Add cream cheese and beat until fluffy. Gradually add sugar, beating constantly. Add eggs one at a time, beating well after each addition. Add salt, vanilla, grated rind and sour cream. Beat at low speed to blend well. Pour into 11" x 7" pan (pan will be full). Bake in preheated moderate oven (350°F.) 55 minutes, or until set. Remove from oven and let stand 15 minutes.

Topping Beat 1½ cups sour cream with 3 tablespoons sugar and 1 teaspoon vanilla extract and spread over top. Sprinkle with chopped nuts, if desired. Cool on rack away from drafts. This cake is easier to cut if allowed to stand in refrigerator overnight.

Cheesecake Deluxe

5 packages (8 ounces each) cream cheese
1¾ cups sugar
3 tablespoons all-purpose flour
¼ teaspoon salt
  Grated rind of 1 lemon
  Grated rind of ½ orange
5 eggs
2 egg yolks
1 cup heavy cream
  Cookie-Dough Crust (see below)
  Toasted chopped blanched almonds

Have ingredients, except ¾ cup cream, at room temperature. Beat cheese until fluffy. Mix sugar, flour and salt. Gradually blend into cheese, keeping mixture smooth. Add grated rinds, then eggs and yolks one at a time, beating well after each. Stir in ¼ cup cream. Turn into Cookie-Dough Crust. Bake in preheated very hot oven

(475°F.) 15 minutes. Turn control to 200°F. and bake about 1
hour. Turn off heat and let cake stand in oven 15 minutes. Remove
and cool in pan. (This cake will shrink somewhat.) Remove sides
of pan. Just before serving, top with ¾ cup cream, whipped, and
sprinkle with almonds.

Cookie-Dough Crust Mix 1 cup flour and ¼ cup sugar. Add
grated rind of 1 lemon, 1 egg yolk and ½ cup of softened butter
or margarine, and mix well; chill. Roll one third of dough to
cover bottom of 9″ springform cake pan. Bake in preheated hot
oven (400°F.) 8 minutes, or until lightly browned. Butter sides of
pan and insert bottom with the crust. Cool. Roll remaining dough
in two strips 14″ long and 3½″ wide. Press onto sides of pan.

Chiffon Cheesecake

        16 zwieback
         1 cup, plus 3 tablespoons sugar
        ¼ cup butter, softened
        1½ pounds (3 cups) small-curd creamed cottage cheese
         3 eggs, separated
        ¼ cup all-purpose flour
           Dash of salt
           Grated rind and juice of 1 lemon
         1 cup heavy cream, whipped

Crush zwieback fine with rolling pin (or whirl in electric blender).
Mix crumbs with 3 tablespoons sugar and the butter. Press half of
mixture firmly on bottom of buttered 9″ springform cake pan.
Force cheese through ricer or food mill, or whirl in blender. Beat
egg yolks until thick. Add ¾ cup sugar, the flour, salt, cheese,
lemon rind and juice; mix well. Beat egg whites until foamy.
Gradually add ¼ cup sugar and beat until stiff. Fold with the
cream into cheese mixture. Pour into crumb-lined pan. Sprinkle
with remaining crumbs. Bake in preheated slow oven (300°F.) 1
hour and 15 minutes. Turn off heat and let stand in oven 45 min-

utes. Remove from oven and cool in pan. (Cake will shrink somewhat.)

Chilled Light Cheesecake with Blueberry Topping
MAKES 10 TO 12 SERVINGS.

        1 cup fine vanilla-wafer crumbs
        3 tablespoons butter or margarine, melted
        2 envelopes unflavored gelatin
      ½ cup sugar
        3 eggs, separated
        1 cup water
        1 pound cream cheese, softened
          Grated peel of 1 lemon
        1 teaspoon lemon juice
    1½ cups heavy cream, divided
          Blueberry Glaze (see below)
        1 pint blueberries, divided (reserve 1 cup for glaze)

Mix crumbs and butter. Using back of spoon, press mixture firmly and evenly in bottom of 9″ springform pan. Bake in preheated 350° oven 10 minutes; cool. In heavy saucepan mix gelatin and sugar. Stir in egg yolks and water; blend well; let stand 1 minute. Stir over low heat until gelatin is completely dissolved and mixture thickens slightly, 7 to 9 minutes. Remove from heat; cool. In large bowl of mixer cream cheese until fluffy. Gradually beat in gelatin mixture until smooth. Stir in lemon peel and juice. With clean beaters beat egg whites in small bowl of mixer until stiff but not dry. Fold into cheese mixture. Whip 1 cup cream until stiff; fold into cheese mixture. Pour into prepared pan; chill until firm. Spoon on Blueberry Glaze. Chill until set. Top with blueberries. Unlatch and remove side from pan. Whip remaining ½ cup cream until stiff. Put into pastry bag. Using rosette tip, pipe rosettes around rim of cake. Or simply spoon on small dollops of whipped cream.

Blueberry Glaze In small saucepan cook reserved 1 cup blueberries with 2 tablespoons water until berries burst, about 3 minutes. Press through fine sieve into ⅓-cup measure; set aside. In same saucepan mix 2 teaspoons unflavored gelatin and ¼ cup each sugar and water. Let stand 1 minute. Add strained blueberries. Stir over medium heat until gelatin is completely dissolved. Flavor with dash of cinnamon or lemon juice to taste. Chill until consistency of unbeaten egg whites, 5 to 10 minutes. Makes about ¾ cup.

Strawberry-Glazed Cheesecake

    1¼ cups fine zwieback crumbs
        Grated rind of 1½ lemons
    1¾ cups, plus 2 tablespoons sugar
     ¼ cup butter or margarine
     1 pound cream cheese
     2 teaspoons all-purpose flour
        Dash of salt
     2 eggs
     1 tablespoon heavy cream
     1 quart strawberries
     ¼ cup water
    1½ tablespoons cornstarch
        Red food coloring (optional)

Mix crumbs, two thirds of rind, 2 tablespoons sugar and the softened butter. Press onto bottom and sides of 8" x 8" x 2" pan. Combine cheese, 1 cup sugar, the flour, remaining rind and salt. Add eggs one at a time, mixing well after each; add cream. Turn into crumb-lined pan. Bake in preheated very hot oven (450°F.) 5 minutes. Reduce heat to 200°F. and bake 1 hour longer. Cool. Wash and hull berries. Crush enough to fill 1 cup; keep remainder whole. Put crushed berries, ¾ cup sugar, the water and cornstarch in saucepan. Bring to boil; boil 2 minutes, stirring constantly. Stir in 1 teaspoon butter and a few drops red food coloring, if desired.

Cool. Arrange whole berries on top of cooled cheesecake, and spoon glaze over berries and top of cake.

Low-Calorie Cheese Pie

    1 envelope unflavored gelatin
1⅓ cups unsweetened pineapple juice
    1 pound small-curd creamed cottage cheese
  ½ teaspoon noncaloric liquid sweetener
    2 egg whites, stiffly beaten
      Fruit (optional)

Soften gelatin in ⅓ cup cold juice. Heat remaining juice, add to gelatin and stir until dissolved. Chill until mixture begins to thicken. Beat cheese until fluffy, then gradually beat in gelatin mixture. Add liquid sweetener and fold in egg whites. Pour into 9″ pie pan and chill 1 hour, or until set. Top with slices of fresh or canned fruit, if desired.

Cookies

Baking fragrant, delectable homemade cookies is easy, quick and a lot of fun. It is one of the joys of childhood that stays with us as adults. What could be nicer than baking a batch of crisp chocolate-chip cookies, chewy nut-filled brownies, or spicy raisin-studded gingerbread men? And there is the special pleasure of making and decorating all sorts of festive cookies at Christmastime —cinnamon stars, sugar-cookie Santas, gingerbread angels, chocolate bells and lemony Christmas trees. There are so many wonderful cookies to choose from that deciding which recipes to include here was not easy. After much thought and munching, we have selected a number of all-time favorites as well as some outstanding new delights.

Some cookies are easier to make than others. Beginners might like to start with drop or bar cookies, which are especially easy because they need no shaping, rolling or chilling. After a few baking sessions, you will be ready to take on more challenging recipes. Very often people bake the same cookies over and over again. And while we think it is nice to have traditional favorites, we like to try a new recipe from time to time to widen our horizons. We have discovered some wonderful cookies that way.

Cookies make marvelous gifts—not only at Christmas but throughout the year. Almost everyone seems to welcome a gift of homemade cookies. And when you know the recipient well, you can choose cookies that will just suit his or her taste. Bake three kinds of peanut butter cookies for a peanut butter fan. Or surprise a chocolate lover with Dark-Chocolate Brownies, Crisp Chocolate-Chip Cookies and Chocolate-Filled Almond Hearts. It's a wonderful way to express affection.

TIPS FOR MAKING AND BAKING COOKIES

COOKIE SHEETS

You don't have to grease cookie sheets unless the recipe specifies it. Try the new baking sheets that never need greasing. They come in attractive colors. If you're using aluminum sheets, shiny ones give browner cookies. Choose sheets at least 2″ narrower and shorter than the oven rack so heat can circulate.

MIXING

Measure ingredients accurately. Don't make substitutions such as cocoa for chocolate, or omit ingredients. Don't use self-rising flour. Make cookies of the size specified in the recipe.

When rolling dough, be careful not to work in a lot of flour. For easier rolling, use a pastry cloth or cotton rolling-pin cover. Cut with floured cutter, using a fairly plain one if dough is soft and tender.

BAKING

Space cookies to allow for spreading. Because ovens vary, watch cookies closely. Check for doneness just before minimum baking time is up. If some cookies are thinner than others, you may have to remove them and bake the remainder a bit longer.

COOLING

Unless otherwise specified in the recipe, remove baked cookies from the sheet to a wire rack as soon as you take them from the oven. Don't stack them until they have cooled thoroughly.

STORING

Store unbaked cookie dough, tightly covered, in refrigerator up to 2 weeks.

Store bar cookies in baking pan, tightly covered in a cool place.

Store soft cookies in tightly covered container in a cool place. If cookies tend to dry out, put a piece of bread or a wedge of apple in container with them to maintain moisture.

Store crisp cookies in a container with loose-fitting cover in a cool place. If cookies soften, place on cookie sheet in preheated slow oven (300°F.) for about 5 minutes to recrisp.

Do not store soft and crisp cookies together.

FREEZING

Most cookie dough, and baked cookies, may be frozen. Storage life: 6 months to 1 year. Shape stiff dough into rolls or bars and wrap carefully. Put soft dough in freezer containers and cover tightly. Cool baked cookies and pack carefully in freezer boxes or transparent plastic bags.

Thaw soft dough until easy to handle. Thaw stiff dough until it can be sliced. Thaw baked cookies at room temperature for about 15 to 20 minutes.

MAILING

Select cookies that keep their fresh flavor for at least a week under average conditions and are thick and firm enough so they do not break easily.

Wrap separately, or back to back in pairs, in transparent plastic wrap or foil. Pack in crumpled tissue paper in a firm box so cookies cannot slide around. Gift wrap box, if desired, then cover with corrugated cardboard. Put in a slightly larger box and mark it "FRAGILE."

FIVE BASIC TYPES OF COOKIES

DROP COOKIES

These are generally thick and round with a thin crisp crust and a soft center. Drop dough from a spoon onto a cookie sheet, pushing dough from spoon with another spoon or a spatula. Drop cookies spread more than other types during baking and need to be placed about 2″ apart. Try to make cookies all the same size so that they will be done at the same time.

BARS AND SQUARES

These are about the easiest and quickest to make. The ingredients are mixed, spread in a pan and baked. The pan should always be the size recommended: if too large, the cookies will be thin and dry; if too small, they will be thick and may not bake through properly. When cool, use a sharp knife and a sawing motion to cut.

MOLDED OR SHAPED COOKIES

The dough for these cookies is high in fat and is usually chilled to make handling easier. Pieces of the dough may be shaped into balls then, often, flattened, either with a fork in a crisscross pattern, or with the bottom of a glass dipped into sugar; or they can be molded into an infinite variety of shapes: fingers, crescents, rings, acorns, etc.

ROLLED COOKIES

These cookies are crisp and tender. The dough is stiff and, often, you chill it. Roll the dough out on a lightly floured board or between 2 sheets of waxed paper, in which case less flour will be needed and the cookies will be more tender. Scraps of dough should be collected and rerolled all at one time; these cookies will be less tender. Rolled cookies are usually cut with cookie cutters, or patterns may be cut out of cardboard and traced on the dough with a sharp knife. Dip the cutter or knife into flour before cutting the dough. Use a spatula to transfer cutouts to the baking sheet.

REFRIGERATOR COOKIES

These cookies, like rolled cookies, are thin, tender and very crisp, but are often sweeter. The dough is usually shaped into long rolls, but may be molded into pinwheels, ribbons or checkerboards; it is always tightly wrapped in waxed paper or foil and kept for several hours in the refrigerator before baking. The dough is sliced with a sharp knife just before baking. If too firm to slice, let it stand at room temperature for a few minutes. The dough will keep for some time in the refrigerator, or it may be frozen.

DROP COOKIES

Almond-Lace Cookies
These delightful cookies are crisp and very tender.
MAKES ABOUT 4 DOZEN.

   1 cup finely chopped blanched almonds
½ cup butter or margarine, softened
½ cup sugar
   2 tablespoons all-purpose flour
   2 tablespoons milk

Cook and stir all ingredients in 2-quart saucepan over medium heat just until butter melts and all ingredients are well blended. Drop by level measuring-teaspoonfuls onto well-greased floured cookie sheets, leaving 3″ space between cookies. Bake in preheated 350°F. oven 5 to 6 minutes, or until lightly browned and glossy. Cool on sheets a few minutes until firm enough to remove to rack. Store airtight in cool place with plastic wrap between layers.

Old-Fashioned Apple Cookies
MAKES ABOUT 4 DOZEN.

   ½ cup butter, softened
1⅓ cups packed brown sugar
   1 egg
  ¼ cup apple juice
   1 cup finely chopped peeled cored apples
   2 cups whole-wheat pastry flour
  ½ teaspoon salt
   1 teaspoon baking soda
  ½ teaspoon ground cloves
   1 teaspoon cinnamon
   1 cup unsulfured raisins
   1 cup chopped walnuts or other nuts
      Glaze (optional) (see below)

Cream butter and sugar until blended. Add egg and beat well. Beat in juice. Add apples, flour, salt, soda, cloves and cinnamon, and mix well. Then fold in remaining ingredients, except Glaze. Drop by rounded teaspoonfuls about 2″ apart on greased baking sheets. Bake in preheated 375°F. oven about 13 minutes. Remove to racks and, if desired, brush with Glaze while still warm.

Glaze Mix well ½ cup confectioners' sugar, 1 tablespoon softened butter and 2 tablespoons apple juice (or enough to make a thin glaze).

Brandy Wafers
Delicate and surprisingly easy to manage.
MAKES ABOUT 90.

> 1 cup all-purpose flour
> ⅔ cup sugar
> 1 tablespoon ginger
> ¼ teaspoon salt
> ½ cup molasses
> ½ cup butter or margarine
> 3 tablespoons brandy

Stir together flour, sugar, ginger and salt; set aside. In saucepan bring molasses to boil. Stir in butter until melted. Gradually stir in flour mixture. Stir in brandy until well mixed. Drop by ½-teaspoonfuls 3″ apart on greased cookie sheets (one large sheet will accommodate 6 wafers). Bake in preheated 300°F. oven 10 minutes. Cool 1 minute, then remove with spatula and roll at once around handle of wooden spoon to form tube. (If removed too soon, wafer will shrink; if not soon enough, wafer will be too brittle to roll. If too brittle, return to oven 1 or 2 minutes to soften.) Repeat until all of dough is used, lightly greasing cookie sheet each time with paper towel, removing crumbs.

Choc-Oat-Wheat Drops
MAKES ABOUT 3 DOZEN.

    ½ cup butter or margarine, softened
    ½ cup packed light-brown sugar
    ¼ cup granulated sugar
    1 egg
    1 teaspoon vanilla extract
    ⅔ cup whole-wheat flour
    ¼ teaspoon salt
    ½ teaspoon baking soda
    1 cup quick-cooking rolled oats
    1 cup semisweet chocolate pieces
    ½ cup chopped nuts
    ½ cup raisins

Cream butter and sugars, add egg and vanilla and beat until fluffy. Mix flour with salt and soda. Stir into creamed mixture, blending well. Add remaining ingredients. Drop by teaspoonfuls onto greased cookie sheets. Bake in preheated 375°F. oven 10 to 12 minutes, or until golden. Remove at once from pan and cool on rack.

Cinnamon Drop Cookies
MAKES ABOUT 4 DOZEN LARGE COOKIES.

    1 cup butter or margarine, softened
    ½ teaspoon baking soda
    ½ teaspoon salt
    2 teaspoons cinnamon
  1½ cups packed light-brown sugar
    1 egg
    ½ cup dairy sour cream
  3½ cups unsifted all-purpose flour
      Pecan halves (optional)

Cream together butter, baking soda, salt and cinnamon. Gradually add sugar and beat until fluffy. Add egg and beat well. Add remaining ingredients and mix well. Drop by heaping teaspoonfuls 2″ apart onto cookie sheets (cookies do not spread). Bake in preheated hot oven (400°F.) 10 minutes, or until lightly browned. If desired, cookies can be topped with a pecan half before baking.

Coconut Cookies
MAKES 10 TO 11 DOZEN.

> ½ cup shortening
> 1 cup granulated sugar
> ½ cup packed brown sugar
> 2 eggs
> 1 teaspoon salt
> 1 teaspoon baking soda
> 1 teaspoon vanilla extract
> 2 cups all-purpose flour
> 1 cup shredded coconut
> 1 tablespoon water

With spoon stir shortening, sugars, eggs, salt, soda and vanilla until smooth; add remaining ingredients and mix well. Drop by rounded ½ teaspoonfuls about 1″ apart on lightly greased cookie sheets. Bake in preheated 375°F. oven 7 to 8 minutes, or until tops are firm and cookies are golden brown. Cool on racks. Cookies are crisp. Store in airtight container up to 3 weeks.

Date-Nut Drop Cookies
MAKES ABOUT 26 LARGE COOKIES.

    ½ cup butter or margarine, softened
    ⅓ cup packed light-brown sugar
    ⅓ cup granulated sugar
    1 egg
    ½ teaspoon vanilla extract
    1 teaspoon coffee or warm water
    1 cup, plus 2 tablespoons all-purpose flour
    ¼ teaspoon baking soda
    ¼ teaspoon salt
    ½ cup chopped pecans or walnuts
    ½ cup cut-up dates

Cream butter and sugars. Add egg and beat until light. Add vanilla and coffee. Gradually stir in flour mixed with soda and salt. Stir in nuts and dates. Drop by teaspoonfuls onto ungreased cookie sheets about 2″ apart. Bake in preheated 375°F. oven 10 minutes, or until edges are lightly browned. Cool on rack.

Lemon-Coconut Crisps
MAKES ABOUT 6 DOZEN.

    ½ cup butter or margarine, softened
    ½ cup sugar
    1 egg, separated
      Grated rind of 1 lemon and juice
    ⅓ cup flaked coconut
    1 cup all-purpose flour
    ½ teaspoon baking soda
    1 teaspoon cream of tartar
      Sugar
      Candied fruit, nut halves

Cream butter and ½ cup sugar. Beat in egg yolk and lemon rind and juice. Add coconut. Sift dry ingredients and add to creamed mixture. Using measuring teaspoonful of batter, drop small balls onto greased cookie sheet. Brush lightly with unbeaten egg white and sprinkle with small amount of sugar. Decorate tops with small piece of candied fruit or nut half and bake in preheated moderate oven (350°F.) 12 to 15 minutes.

Lizzies
MAKES ABOUT 10 DOZEN.

    1 package (15 ounces) seedless raisins
    ½ cup bourbon
    ¼ cup butter or margarine, softened
    ½ cup packed light-brown sugar
    2 eggs
    1½ cups regular all-purpose flour
    1½ teaspoons baking soda
    1½ teaspoons cinnamon
    ½ teaspoon nutmeg
    ½ teaspoon ground cloves
    1 pound (4 cups) pecan halves
    ½ pound diced citron
    1 pound candied cherries
    Confectioners' sugar (optional)

Stir raisins and bourbon together and let stand 1 hour. Preheat oven to slow (325°F.). Cream butter, then gradually beat in brown sugar. Add eggs one at a time, beating well after each. Mix next 5 ingredients and add, mixing well. Add raisins in bourbon and remaining ingredients, except last, and mix well. Drop by teaspoonfuls onto buttered cookie sheets. Bake about 15 minutes. Remove to cake racks and cool.

To Store Store airtight. Just before serving, sprinkle with confectioners' sugar, if desired. Can be frozen. Good keepers and shippers.

Spicy Oatmeal Cookies
MAKES ABOUT 6 DOZEN.

½ cup butter or margarine, softened
½ cup granulated sugar
½ cup packed dark-brown sugar
1 egg
¼ cup water
1 teaspoon vanilla extract
1 cup all-purpose flour
½ teaspoon baking powder
½ teaspoon baking soda
½ teaspoon salt
¾ teaspoon cinnamon
¼ teaspoon ground cloves
2 cups rolled oats

In large bowl of electric mixer cream butter and sugars until fluffy. Beat in egg, water and vanilla. Stir in flour, baking powder, soda, salt, spices and oats. Drop by heaping teaspoonfuls about 2½" apart on greased cookie sheets. Bake in preheated 350°F. oven 10 to 12 minutes, or until a slight dent remains when top is pressed lightly. Remove from pan and cool on wire rack. Store in airtight container.

Old-Fashioned Rocks
MAKES ABOUT 3 DOZEN.

½ cup butter, softened
1½ cups packed brown sugar
2 eggs
⅓ cup boiling water
2 cups seeded raisins
½ cup chopped walnuts
2½ cups sifted all-purpose flour
1 teaspoon baking powder
½ teaspoon salt
1 teaspoon cinnamon

Cream butter; add sugar and eggs, one at a time, beating until light. Pour boiling water on raisins; cool. Add nuts, sifted dry ingredients, and soaked raisins, including water; mix well. Drop by teaspoonfuls onto greased cookie sheets; bake in preheated moderate oven (350°F.) about 15 minutes.

Pine-Nut Cookies
MAKES ABOUT 5 DOZEN.

> 4 eggs
> 1½ cups granulated sugar
> ½ teaspoon grated lemon rind
>   Few drops of oil of anise
> 2½ cups sifted all-purpose flour
> ¼ teaspoon salt
>   Confectioners' sugar
>   Pine nuts

Put eggs and granulated sugar in top part of double boiler over hot water. Beat with rotary beater until mixture is lukewarm. Remove from water; beat until foaming and cool. Add flavorings and fold in flour and salt. Drop by teaspoonfuls onto greased and floured cookie sheets. Sprinkle with confectioners' sugar and nuts. Let stand for 10 minutes; bake in preheated moderate oven (375°F.) for about 10 minutes.

Orange Wafers
MAKES ABOUT 8 DOZEN.

> ½ cup butter, softened
> ¾ cup sugar
> 1 egg
> 1 teaspoon grated orange rind
> 1 tablespoon orange juice
> 1½ cups sifted all-purpose flour
> ½ teaspoon baking powder
> ¼ teaspoon salt

Cream butter; add sugar and egg; beat until light. Add remaining ingredients; mix well. Drop by level measuring-teaspoonfuls onto cookie sheets. Press flat with the bottom of a glass wrapped in cheesecloth wrung out of cold water. Bake in preheated moderate oven (375°F.) about 7 minutes.

Pineapple-Oatmeal Cookies
MAKES ABOUT 4 DOZEN.

    ½ cup butter or margarine, softened
    ½ cup granulated sugar
    ½ cup packed brown sugar
    1 egg
    1 can (about 9 ounces) crushed pineapple
  1½ cups quick-cooking rolled oats (not instant)
    1 cup sifted all-purpose flour
    ½ teaspoon baking soda
    ½ teaspoon salt
    ½ teaspoon cinnamon
      Dash nutmeg
    ½ cup chopped walnuts

Cream butter; add sugars and beat until light. Add egg and beat well. Add pineapple, oats, sifted dry ingredients and nuts; mix well. Drop by teaspoonfuls onto ungreased cookie sheets. Bake in preheated moderate oven (375°F.) about 15 minutes.

Sesame-Oat Cookies
MAKES ABOUT 4 DOZEN.

    ½ cup butter, softened
    1 cup packed light-brown sugar
    1 egg
    3 tablespoons milk
    ¾ cup sesame seed

1¼ cups quick-cooking rolled oats (not instant)
¾ cup dark unsulfured seedless raisins
1¼ cups all-purpose flour
½ teaspoon salt
½ teaspoon baking soda
½ teaspoon cinnamon

Cream butter and sugar until blended. Beat in egg and milk. Stir in sesame seed, oats and raisins. Mix together remaining ingredients, add and mix well. Drop rounded teaspoonfuls of dough on ungreased cookie sheets (cookies do not spread). Flatten slightly with hand and bake in preheated 375°F. oven 10 to 12 minutes, or until golden brown. Cool on racks.

BAR COOKIES

Applesauce-Raisin-Rye Bars
MAKES ABOUT 16.

¼ cup solid white vegetable shortening
⅔ cup sugar
1 egg
1 cup canned applesauce
1 cup rye flour
½ teaspoon salt
1 teaspoon baking soda
1 teaspoon cinnamon
¼ teaspoon nutmeg
⅛ teaspoon ground cloves
½ cup raisins
   Frosting (see below)
¼ cup chopped walnuts

Cream shortening and sugar together. Add egg and applesauce and mix well. Add remaining ingredients, except Frosting and walnuts, and mix well. Spread in greased 13″ x 9″ x 2″ baking pan and bake in preheated 350°F. oven 25 to 30 minutes. Cool in pan on wire rack. Spread with Frosting, then sprinkle with nuts. When firm, cut in bars.

Frosting Cream together 2 tablespoons softened margarine and 2 cups confectioners' sugar. Add 1 teaspoon vanilla extract and enough milk (about 3 tablespoons) to make frosting of spreading consistency.

Blond Brownies
Chewy with butterscotch flavor.
MAKES ABOUT 16.

> ¼ cup butter or margarine
> 1 cup packed light-brown sugar
> 1 egg
> ¾ cup all-purpose flour
> 1 teaspoon baking powder
> ½ teaspoon salt
> ½ teaspoon vanilla extract
> ½ cup coarsely chopped nuts

Melt butter over low heat. Remove from heat, add brown sugar and stir until well blended; cool. Add egg and mix well. Stir in dry ingredients, then add vanilla and nuts. Spread in well-greased 8″ square pan and bake in preheated moderate oven (350°F.) about 25 minutes. Cool in pan on wire rack. Then cut in 2″ squares.

Chewy Wheat-Germ Brownies
MAKES 24 TO 30.

> 4 squares (1 ounce each) unsweetened chocolate
> ¾ cup margarine
> 1¼ cups all-purpose flour
> 2 teaspoons baking powder

1 teaspoon salt
1 cup wheat germ
2 cups granulated sugar
3 eggs, well beaten
1 teaspoon vanilla extract
1 cup coarsely chopped walnuts

In small saucepan, melt chocolate and margarine and set aside. In large bowl, combine flour, baking powder, salt, wheat germ and sugar and mix well. Stir in melted chocolate mixture, eggs and vanilla and mix well. Fold in nuts and spread in greased 13″ x 9″ x 2″ pan. Bake in preheated 350°F. oven about 30 minutes. Cool and cut in squares. Keep well if stored airtight or frozen. Good for lunch boxes.

Chocolate-Date Petits Fours
MAKES 7 TO 8 DOZEN

1 package (8 ounces) pitted dates, chopped
¾ cup packed light-brown sugar
½ cup butter or margarine
1 package (6 ounces) semisweet chocolate pieces
2 eggs, slightly beaten
1¼ cups regular all-purpose flour
¾ teaspoon baking soda
½ teaspoon salt
½ cup orange juice
½ cup milk
1 cup chopped walnuts or pecans
Orange Glaze (see below)
Drained kumquats or candied orange peel

Preheat oven to moderate (350°F.). Grease well a 15″ x 10″ x 1″ baking pan. Combine first 3 ingredients and ½ cup water in 3-quart saucepan and cook over low heat, stirring, about 5 minutes, or until dates soften. Remove from heat, add chocolate pieces and stir until melted. Beat in eggs. Mix flour with baking soda and salt and add to chocolate mixture alternately with orange juice and milk, beating well with spoon after each addition. Stir in nuts. Spread in pan and bake 25 to 30 minutes, or until done. Cool on rack. Spread with glaze, cut in 1¼″ squares and decorate with strips of kumquat or candied orange peel.

To Store Store airtight in cool place. Can be frozen. Good keepers but poor shippers.

Orange Glaze Mix until smooth 1½ cups confectioners' sugar, 2 tablespoons softened butter, 1 tablespoon grated orange rind and 3 tablespoons light cream.

Coconut Brownies
MAKES ABOUT 16.

> 2 squares (1 ounce each) unsweetened chocolate
> ⅓ cup plus 2 teaspoons butter or margarine
> 2 eggs
> 1 cup plus 1 tablespoon sugar
> ⅔ cup all-purpose flour
> ½ teaspoon baking powder
> ¼ teaspoon salt
> 1 teaspoon vanilla extract
> 1 can (3½ ounces) flaked coconut

Melt chocolate and ⅓ cup butter in heavy saucepan over low heat, or melt over hot water. Beat eggs until foamy. Gradually add 1 cup sugar and beat until well blended. Add chocolate mixture and beat well. Stir in flour, baking powder, salt, vanilla and half the coconut (about ⅔ cup). Spread in greased 8″ square pan. Melt 2 teaspoons butter and add 1 tablespoon sugar and remaining coconut. Mix well and sprinkle evenly on batter in pan. Bake in preheated moderate oven (350°F.) 30 minutes, or until done. Cool in pan on rack and cut in squares.

Dark-Chocolate Brownies
Moist, cakelike, super-chocolate flavor.
MAKES ABOUT 24.

> 4 eggs
> 2 cups sugar
> ⅔ cup vegetable oil
> 4 squares (1 ounce each) unsweetened chocolate, melted and cooled, or 4 envelopes no-melt chocolate
> 2 teaspoons vanilla extract
> 1⅓ cups all-purpose flour
> 1 teaspoon baking powder
> ½ teaspoon salt
> 1 cup chopped nuts

Beat eggs until thick and lemon-colored. Gradually add sugar and beat until well blended. Stir in oil, chocolate and vanilla. Mix dry ingredients together and add to mixture, blending well. Stir in nuts and spread in greased 13″ x 9″ x 2″ pan; bake in preheated moderate oven (350°F.) 25 to 30 minutes. Cool in pan on wire rack. Then cut in 2″ (about) squares.

Double-Frosted Brownies
Brownies doubly rich and doubly good. Can be frozen.
MAKES ABOUT 20.

> 5 squares (1 ounce each) unsweetened chocolate, divided
> ½ cup butter or margarine
> 2 eggs
> 1 cup sugar
> 1 teaspoon vanilla extract
> ½ cup all-purpose flour mixed with ¼ teaspoon salt and ½ cup chopped nuts
> Frosting (see below)

Melt 2 squares chocolate with the butter; cool. Beat eggs; add sugar and mix well. Stir in chocolate mixture, vanilla and flour mixture. Spread in greased 11″ x 7″ x 1½″ baking pan. Bake in preheated 350°F. oven 20 to 25 minutes. Cool in pan on rack. Spread with Frosting. Melt remaining 3 squares chocolate and spread over Frosting. Chill several hours or until firm. Bring to room temperature, then cut in bars.

Frosting Mix 1½ cups sugar, ⅓ cup butter or margarine and ½ cup half-and-half in heavy 2½-quart saucepan. Bring to boil and cook over medium heat without stirring until small amount of mixture forms soft ball when dropped in ice water (236°F. on candy thermometer), about 6 minutes. Cool in pan of cold water until lukewarm. Add 1 teaspoon vanilla extract; beat until creamy, glossy and of spreading consistency.

Candied Orange Bars
They contain chopped nuts, too.
MAKES ABOUT 32.

> ½ cup butter or margarine, softened
> 1½ cups sugar
> 2 eggs
> 1 teaspoon vanilla extract
> 1 cup sifted all-purpose flour
> 2 teaspoons baking powder
> 1 teaspoon salt
> ¾ cup coarsely chopped nuts
> 1 cup finely chopped candied orange peel

Cream butter and sugar until light and fluffy. Add eggs one at a time, beating well after each addition. Add vanilla. Gradually add sifted dry ingredients, blending well. Stir in the nuts and peel. Spoon into well-greased 13″ x 9″ x 2″ pan. Bake in preheated moderate oven (350°F.) 30 to 35 minutes. Cool on rack in pan. Cut in bars about 2″ x 1½″.

Chewy Peanut Bars
MAKES ABOUT 36.

Crust:
>   1 cup flour
>   ½ cup packed brown sugar
>   ½ cup butter or margarine

Topping:
>   1 cup packed brown sugar
>   2 eggs
>   3 tablespoons all-purpose flour
>   1 teaspoon baking powder
>   1 teaspoon vanilla extract
>   2 cups salted blanched peanuts

Crust Measure flour and sugar into bowl. With pastry blender cut in butter until mixture resembles coarse crumbs. Spread evenly in a greased 13" x 9" x 2" baking pan. Bake in preheated 375°F. oven 8 to 10 minutes, or until crust appears slightly firm in center; cool.

Topping Mix sugar and eggs until smooth. Stir in flour, baking powder and vanilla until well mixed. Stir in peanuts. Pour over crust. Bake in preheated 375°F. oven 18 to 20 minutes, or until browned and edges are firm (center may be somewhat soft, but crusted over). Cool and cut in bars. Store airtight in cool place; will keep 1 week.

Chocolate Triangles
>   1 square unsweetened chocolate
>   ¼ cup butter
>   ½ cup sugar
>   1 egg, unbeaten
>   ¼ cup regular all-purpose flour
>   ⅛ teaspoon salt
>   ¼ teaspoon vanilla extract
>   ⅓ cup finely chopped walnuts or pecans

Preheat oven to hot (400°F.). In heavy saucepan, melt chocolate and butter over low heat (mixture should not be hot, simply melted). Remove from heat and stir in sugar. Add remaining ingredients, except nuts, and mix well. Spread in greased 13″ x 9″ x 2″ baking pan and sprinkle with nuts. Bake about 12 minutes. Cool slightly (must be cut while still quite hot); cut in 2″ squares, then in triangles. When cold, remove from pan to cake racks.

To Store Store airtight. Good keepers but poor shippers.

Cinnamon-Nut Crisps
MAKES ABOUT 48.

  1 cup butter or margarine, softened
  1 cup sugar
  1 egg, separated
  2 cups all-purpose flour, lightly spooned into cup
  1 tablespoon cinnamon
  ¼ teaspoon salt
  1 cup finely chopped pecans, filberts or unblanched almonds

Cream butter; gradually add sugar and continue creaming until light and fluffy. Add egg yolk, flour, cinnamon and salt and mix well. Spread in greased 15″ x 10″ x 1″ pan. Brush with lightly beaten egg white and sprinkle with nuts, then press nuts into surface. Bake in preheated slow oven (300°F.) about 50 minutes. Cut in squares while still hot. Store airtight in cool place. Good keepers and shippers.

Cinnamon-Nut Diamonds
MAKES ABOUT 5 DOZEN.

  1¾ cups regular all-purpose flour
  ½ teaspoon salt
  1 teaspoon ground cinnamon
  1 cup butter or margarine, softened

    1 cup packed light-brown sugar
    1 teaspoon vanilla extract
    1 egg yolk
    ½ cup ground walnuts or pecans
      (can be whirled in blender)
    1 egg
    ½ cup finely chopped walnuts or pecans

Preheat oven to moderate (350°F.). Mix first 3 ingredients and set aside. Put next 4 ingredients in large bowl of electric mixer and beat until light and fluffy. Add flour mixture and ground nuts and mix well. Spread in greased 15″ x 10″ x 2″ baking pan and pat down evenly with hands. Beat egg and brush on dough. Sprinkle evenly with chopped nuts, pressing into dough. Bake 25 to 30 minutes. Cut crosswise in 1½″ strips, then cut in diamond shapes. Remove to wire racks to cool.

To Store Store cookies airtight. Can be frozen. Good keepers and shippers.

Chocolate-Banana Bars
MAKES ABOUT 32.

    1 package (6 ounces) semisweet chocolate pieces
    1 cup minus 2 tablespoons all-purpose flour
    ¾ cup sugar
    ¼ teaspoon salt
    ¾ teaspoon cinnamon
    ½ teaspoon baking powder
    ¼ teaspoon baking soda
    1 cup mashed ripe bananas (about 2 medium)
    ¼ cup butter or margarine, softened
    1 egg
    2 tablespoons milk
    1 cup chopped nuts
    Brown-Velvet Frosting (see below)

Melt chocolate over hot water. Mix flour, sugar, salt, cinnamon, baking powder and soda and set aside. In large bowl, beat bananas and butter until blended. Beat in egg. Add flour mixture and milk and mix well. Stir in chocolate and nuts. Spread in greased and floured 13″ x 9″ x 2″ pan and bake in preheated 350°F. oven about 25 minutes. Cool in pan, then spread with frosting. Cut in bars about 2″ x 1½″.

Brown-Velvet Frosting

Melt 1 package (6 ounces) semisweet chocolate pieces and 2 tablespoons butter or margarine in heavy saucepan. Remove from heat and beat in 1½ cups confectioners' sugar, ¼ cup milk, ¼ teaspoon vanilla extract and ⅛ teaspoon salt.

Hermits
MAKES ABOUT 12.

> ½ cup butter or margarine
> ½ cup sugar
> ½ cup unsulfured molasses
> 2 eggs
> 2 cups sifted all-purpose flour
> ½ teaspoon salt
> ¼ teaspoon baking soda
> 2 teaspoons baking powder
> 1 teaspoon cinnamon
> ½ teaspoon ground cloves
> ¼ teaspoon mace
> ¼ teaspoon nutmeg
> ⅛ teaspoon allspice
> ¾ cup raisins
> ¼ cup chopped nuts
> Confectioners'-Sugar
> Frosting (optional, see below)

Cream together butter and sugar until light and fluffy. Add molasses and eggs and beat well. Sift together flour, salt, soda, baking powder and spices; stir in raisins and nuts. Add flour mixture to molasses mixture; blend well. Spread evenly in greased 12″ x 8″ baking pan. Bake in a preheated moderate oven (350°F.) 30 minutes. Frost with Confectioners'-Sugar Frosting while warm if desired. Cool and cut in squares.

Confectioners'-Sugar Frosting Mix confectioners' sugar with a little water (add 1 teaspoon at a time) until frosting is of spreading consistency.

Honey Date-Nut Bars
MAKES ABOUT 96.

> 3 eggs
> 1 cup honey
> Grated rind of 1 lemon (about 2 teaspoons)
> ¼ teaspoon salt
> 1 cup all-purpose flour
> 1 teaspoon double-acting baking powder
> 1 package (8 ounces) chopped dates
> 1 cup chopped pecans or walnuts
> Confectioners' sugar

Preheat oven to slow (325°F.). In mixing bowl, beat eggs until light and foamy. Add honey, lemon rind and salt, and mix well. Mix flour and baking powder and add with dates and nuts to first mixture. Mix well. Grease 13″ x 9″ x 2″ baking pan and line bottom with waxed paper. Spread batter in pan and bake about 40 minutes. Let stand a few minutes, then loosen around edges with small knife. Turn out on board and pull off paper; cool. Wrap in foil, seal and let ripen in cool place several days. Cut lengthwise in ½″ strips, then crosswise 4 times to form bars about 2″ x ½″.

Note Store in airtight container. Just before serving, roll in or sprinkle with confectioners' sugar. Good keepers and shippers. (Omit confectioners' sugar when shipping.)

Honey-Oatmeal Chews
MAKES ABOUT 36.

> ½ cup margarine
> ½ cup clover honey
> ½ cup granulated sugar
> 1 egg
> 1 teaspoon vanilla extract
> ¾ cup all-purpose flour
> ½ teaspoon baking soda
> ½ teaspoon baking powder
> ¼ teaspoon salt
> 1 cup quick-cooking rolled oats (not instant)
> 1 can (3½ ounces) flaked coconut
> ½ cup chopped almonds
>   Confectioners' sugar

Cream margarine, honey and granulated sugar until light and fluffy. Add egg and vanilla and beat well. Sift together flour, soda, baking powder and salt. Add to creamed mixture. Stir in remaining ingredients, except confectioners' sugar, and spread in greased 13″ x 9″ x 2″ baking pan. Bake in preheated moderate oven (350°F.) 25 to 30 minutes. When cool, sprinkle with confectioners' sugar and cut in bars or squares.

Lemon-Currant Squares
MAKES ABOUT 24.

> 1 cup butter or margarine, softened
> 1 cup sugar
> 1 egg, beaten
> 1 teaspoon vanilla extract
> 2 cups all-purpose flour
> 1 teaspoon grated lemon rind
> 1 cup dried currants, scalded and well drained
>   Confectioners' sugar

In large bowl or electric mixer cream butter and sugar until light and fluffy; beat in egg and vanilla; gradually beat in flour until well blended. With wooden spoon stir in lemon rind and currants. Pour into greased and floured 13″ x 9″ x 2″ pan and bake in preheated 325°F. oven 15 minutes. When cool, sprinkle generously with confectioners' sugar and cut in squares.

Maple-Nut Bars
MAKES ABOUT 18.

⅓ cup butter or margarine, softened
⅓ cup confectioners' sugar
1 egg
⅓ cup maple syrup
⅛ teaspoon salt
⅛ teaspoon baking soda
¾ cup all-purpose flour
1 cup broken nut meats
Confectioners' sugar

Cream butter. Add ⅓ cup confectioners' sugar and beat well. Beat in egg and syrup. Mix salt, soda and flour and add to mixture. beating only until smooth. Stir in nuts. Spread in greased 8″ square pan and bake in preheated 375°F. oven about 18 minutes. Cut at once in bars and roll in confectioners' sugar.

Oatmeal Apple Bars

Chopped apples between two layers of oatmeal pastry, topped with sugar and any nuts you prefer.
MAKES ABOUT 50.

> 2 cups unsifted all-purpose flour
> 1 teaspoon baking soda
> ¼ teaspoon salt
> 2 cups quick-cooking rolled oats (not instant)
> 1 cup packed light-brown sugar
> 1 cup, plus 3 tablespoons butter or margarine, softened
> 4 apples, peeled and chopped (about 3½ cups)
> 1 cup chopped nuts
> ½ cup granulated sugar

Sift flour, soda and salt. Add oats, brown sugar and 1 cup butter. Mix with pastry blender until grainy. Pat half into lightly greased 15″ x 10″ x 1″ pan. Cover mixture with the apples. Mix nuts and granulated sugar, sprinkle half on apples and dot with 3 tablespoons butter. Pat on remaining flour-oats mixture. Cover with remaining nuts and sugar. Bake in preheated slow oven (300°F.) about 1 hour and 15 minutes, or until done. While still warm, cut in bars about 3″ x 1″.

Glazed Orange-Shortbread Squares

MAKES ABOUT 48.

> 3 cups all-purpose flour, lightly spooned into cup
> ½ cup cornstarch
> 1 cup sugar
> Grated rind of 1 orange
> ¼ teaspoon salt
> 1 cup butter or margarine
> ⅓ cup orange juice
> Orange Glaze (see below)
> 2 squares (1 ounce each) unsweetened chocolate

Put flour, cornstarch, sugar, orange rind and salt in bowl and mix well. Cut in butter until particles are very fine. Add orange juice and toss to mix. Gather mixture together and work quickly with hands until crumbs form a dough. With lightly floured finger-tips, press evenly on bottom of lightly greased 15″ x 10″ x 1″ pan. Bake in preheated moderate oven (350°F.) 25 minutes, or until golden brown. Cool and spread with glaze. Let stand until set. Melt chocolate over hot water, cool and pour into small cone made from double waxed paper, leaving 1/16″ opening. Squeeze out onto glaze in desired pattern. Let stand until firm, then cut in squares. Store airtight in cool place. Fairly good keepers and shippers.

Orange Glaze Mix well 2 cups confectioners' sugar and ¼ cup orange juice.

Note If preferred, omit cone and drizzle chocolate over glaze with teaspoon.

Raspberry-Coconut Squares
MAKES ABOUT 48.

    1¾ cups all-purpose flour, lightly spooned into cup
    1½ cups sugar
    ¼ teaspoon salt
    ½ cup butter or margarine
    4 eggs
    ½ cup seedless red-raspberry jam
    ¼ cup butter or margarine, softened
    3 cans (4 ounces each) moist sweet shredded coconut

Put flour, ½ cup sugar and the salt in mixing bowl and blend well. Cut in butter until particles are very fine. Add 1 lightly beaten egg to crumb mixture and toss to mix. Gather mixture together and work quickly with hands until crumbs form a dough. With lightly floured fingertips, press evenly on bottom of lightly greased 15″ x 10″ x 1″ pan. Spread thin, even coat of raspberry jam on top. Cream butter and remaining sugar. Add remaining eggs one at a time and beat after each until light and creamy. Add coconut and mix well. Pour over top of jam and spread evenly. Bake in preheated moderate oven (350°F.) 20 to 25 minutes, or until golden brown. Cool on rack and cut in squares. Store airtight in cool place. Good keepers and shippers if well packed.

MOLDED COOKIES

Coconut Butterballs
MAKES ABOUT 3 DOZEN.

   ½ cup butter, softened
     Confectioners' sugar
   ½ teaspoon vanilla extract
   1 cup all-purpose flour
   ¾ cup flaked coconut, chopped slightly

Cream butter with 2 tablespoons sugar until blended. Add vanilla and flour and mix well, then stir in coconut. Shape in small balls and put on ungreased cookie sheet. Chill 15 minutes, then bake in preheated moderate oven (350°F.) 15 minutes, or until very lightly browned. Roll at once in confectioners' sugar.

Cherry Bonbons
MAKES ABOUT 8 DOZEN.

   1 cup butter or margarine, softened
   ½ cup confectioners' sugar
   1 teaspoon vanilla extract
   ½ cup finely minced nuts
  2¼ cups cake flour
   1 pound (about) red candied cherries
     Thin confectioners'-sugar frosting

Red food coloring (optional)
Additional red candied cherries

Cream butter and sugar until light. Add vanilla and nuts and mix well. Add flour and stir until well mixed. Wrap dough in waxed paper and chill well. Divide in 4 equal pieces. Shape each in roll about 1″ in diameter. Cut rolls in ½″ pieces, turn cut side up and in center of each put a cherry. With lightly floured hands, shape in balls, covering cherry completely with dough. Put on ungreased cookie sheets and chill 15 minutes. Preheat oven to moderate (350°F.). Bake cookies 15 to 20 minutes, remove to rack and cool. If desired, tint frosting a delicate pink with food coloring. To frost, set cookies, still on rack, on sheet of waxed paper. Spoon frosting over cookies, allowing it to run down and cover cookies completely. (Scrape up any frosting from waxed paper and reuse.) Decorate each cookie with a slice of candied cherry.

To Store Store airtight in cool place. Can be frozen. Good keepers and shippers.

Chocolate Nut Crackles

Balls of dough are rolled in nuts, sugar and cinnamon before baking.
Makes about 3 dozen.

½ cup butter, softened
1 cup packed light-brown sugar
1 egg
1 square (1 ounce) unsweetened chocolate, melted
1¼ cups sifted all-purpose flour
1 teaspoon cream of tartar
½ teaspoon baking soda
½ teaspoon salt
½ cup chopped toasted filberts or other nuts
2 tablespoons granulated sugar
2 teaspoons cinnamon

Cream butter, brown sugar and egg until light. Beat in cooled chocolate. Add sifted flour, cream of tartar, soda and salt; mix well. Chill. Then roll dough in 1″ balls. Mix nuts, granulated sugar and cinnamon. Roll balls in the mixture and put on lightly greased cookie sheets. Bake in preheated moderate oven (375°F.) 12 to 15 minutes.

Coconut Snowballs
A chewy delight of coconut and sour cream.
MAKES ABOUT 6 DOZEN.

> 1 cup butter or margarine, softened
> 2 cups granulated sugar
> 2 eggs
> 1 teaspoon vanilla extract
> 5 cups sifted all-purpose flour
> 1 teaspoon baking soda
> 2 teaspoons baking powder
> ½ teaspoon salt
> ¾ cup dairy sour cream
> 1 cup flaked coconut
>   Colored sugar

Cream butter and granulated sugar until light. Add eggs and vanilla and beat well. Add sifted dry ingredients, sour cream and coconut; mix well. Chill several hours. Shape in 1″ balls and sprinkle with colored sugar. Put on cookie sheets and bake in preheated moderate oven (375°F). about 10 minutes.

Cookie Men
Moist, spicy cookies.
MAKES ABOUT 2 DOZEN.

> 1 cup packed light-brown sugar
> ½ cup molasses

½ cup canned applesauce
¼ cup butter or margarine
1 egg
½ cup finely ground almonds (use blender)
3 cups all-purpose flour
1 teaspoon cinnamon
¼ teaspoon baking soda
¼ teaspoon ginger
¼ teaspoon ground cloves
Raisins

Combine brown sugar, molasses, applesauce and butter in medium saucepan. Bring to boil, simmer 5 minutes, then cool to lukewarm. Stir in egg and almonds. Add flour mixed with remaining ingredients, except raisins, and mix well. Cover and chill overnight. To shape, make 1″ balls for head, 2″ balls for body, 3″ strips for legs and 2″ strips for arms (about ½″ thick). Put on greased cookie sheets and press with finger in desired shape (dough is sticky, so wipe fingers with wet paper towel). Cut raisins for eyes and mouth and leave whole for buttons. Bake in preheated 325°F. oven 12 to 15 minutes (do not brown). Cool on racks.

Note Omit raisins and decorate cookies with cookie-decorating frosting, if desired.

Coriander Cookie Thins
MAKES ABOUT 7 TO 8 DOZEN.

2 cups all-purpose flour
1 cup sugar
2 tablespoons ground coriander
¾ cup butter or margarine
1 egg, slightly beaten
1 teaspoon vanilla extract
Colored or white sugar

Mix flour, sugar and coriander in bowl. Add butter and cut in with pastry blender. Blend egg and vanilla and work into mixture with hands to form a smooth dough. Roll in ½″ balls and put on un-greased cookie sheets. Flatten with moistened bottom of measuring cup dipped in colored or white sugar. Bake in preheated hot oven (400°F.) 6 to 8 minutes.

Crisp Chocolate-Chip Cookies
MAKES ABOUT 54.

>   2 cups all-purpose flour
>   1 teaspoon baking soda
>   1 teaspoon salt
>   1 cup butter or margarine, softened
>   1 cup packed brown sugar
>   ½ cup granulated sugar
>   1 egg
>   1 teaspoon vanilla extract
>   1 package (12 ounces) semisweet chocolate pieces
>   1 cup chopped nuts

Mix flour, soda and salt; set aside. In large bowl cream butter and sugars until light; beat in egg and vanilla until light and fluffy. With spoon stir in flour mixture, chocolate and nuts. Shape in 1″ balls and place about 2″ apart on cookie sheets. Bake in pre-heated 350°F. oven 15 minutes, or until flat and browned. (Cookies will have soft centers.) Cool completely on cookie sheets. Store in airtight container.

Fig Graham Cookies
MAKES ABOUT 84.

>   1 cup margarine, softened
>   1½ cups sugar
>   2 eggs
>   Grated rind of 1 lemon
>   2 cups unsifted all-purpose flour

1½ cups whole-wheat flour
1½ teaspoons cream of tartar
1½ teaspoons baking soda
½ teaspoon salt
16 (about 12 ounces) golden dried figs, chopped (2 cups)

Cream margarine and sugar. Add eggs and lemon rind and beat until fluffy. Stir in remaining ingredients. Shape mixture in 1″ mounds on cookie sheets and flatten by pressing crisscross with floured tines of fork. Bake in preheated 400°F. oven 8 to 10 minutes.

Note Recipe can be halved.

Ginger Crisps
MAKES ABOUT 4½ DOZEN.

¾ cup solid white vegetable shortening
¾ cup sugar
½ cup molasses
1 egg
2¼ cups all-purpose flour
1½ teaspoons baking soda
1 teaspoon cinnamon
½ teaspoon ginger
⅛ teaspoon ground cloves
¼ teaspoon salt
Granulated sugar

Cream shortening and ¾ cup sugar until light and fluffy. Add molasses and egg and beat well. Combine dry ingredients and mix with fork. Stir into creamed mixture, mixing well. Chill 2 hours. Shape in 1″ balls, then roll in granulated sugar. Put on greased cookie sheets and bake in preheated 375°F. oven about 12 minutes.

Lemon Snowflakes

Cornstarch cookies with a smooth, delicate texture.
MAKES ABOUT 4 DOZEN.

>   1 cup butter or margarine, softened
>   ½ cup confectioners' sugar
>   ¾ cup cornstarch
>   1½ cups all-purpose flour
>   2 teaspoons grated lemon rind
>   1 cup finely chopped nuts
>   Frosting (see below)

Cream butter; combine confectioners' sugar, cornstarch, flour and lemon rind and gradually beat into butter. Chill at least 1 hour. Shape dough in balls and drop into chopped nuts. Flatten with bottom of drinking glass dipped in flour. Put, nut side up, on greased cookie sheets. Bake in preheated 350°F. oven about 15 minutes. Cool on rack and spread with Frosting.

   Frosting Mix 1 cup confectioners' sugar, 2 tablespoons melted butter or margarine and about 1 tablespoon lemon juice.

Mexican Wedding Cookies

MAKES ABOUT 40.

>   1 cup butter or margarine, softened
>   1 cup confectioners' sugar
>   1 teaspoon vanilla extract
>   ¼ teaspoon salt
>   2 cups all-purpose flour
>   1 cup very finely chopped pecans
>   Confectioners' sugar (optional)

In large bowl of electric mixer cream butter and sugar until fluffy; blend in vanilla and salt. With wooden spoon gently stir in flour and nuts. Divide dough in 5 portions, shape each in a 12″ x 1″ roll, wrap in plastic wrap and chill thoroughly. When ready to bake, slice in 3″ lengths; cut in half lengthwise and place cut side down on ungreased baking sheet. Bake in preheated 375°F. oven 12 to 14 minutes, or until light brown. Cool on racks. Sprinkle with confectioners' sugar, if desired.

Maple Butter Thins
MAKES ABOUT 3 DOZEN.

   1 cup all-purpose flour
½ cup cornstarch
½ cup confectioners' sugar
   1 cup butter or margarine, softened
¼ cup maple syrup

Mix flour, cornstarch and confectioners' sugar. Add butter and syrup and mix with hands until smooth. Chill 1 hour, or until firm. With hands, shape in 1″ balls and put at least 3″ apart on ungreased baking sheets with sides (cookies become very thin when baked). Bake in preheated 300°F. oven about 20 minutes.

Molasses Crinkles
The water makes them crinkle.
MAKES ABOUT 48.

¾ cup butter, softened
   1 cup packed light-brown sugar
   1 egg
¼ cup molasses
2¼ cups sifted all-purpose flour
   2 teaspoons baking soda
   1 teaspoon cinnamon
   1 teaspoon ginger
½ teaspoon ground cloves
¼ teaspoon salt
    Granulated sugar

Cream butter, brown sugar, egg and molasses until light. Add sifted dry ingredients and mix well. Chill. Roll in 1″ balls and dip in granulated sugar. Put 3″ apart on lightly greased cookie sheets. Sprinkle each cookie with 2 or 3 drops water. Bake in preheated moderate oven (375°F.) 8 to 10 minutes.

Oatmeal Frosties
Crunchy cookies—the oats are a surprise ingredient.
MAKES ABOUT 3½ DOZEN.

> 1 cup butter or margarine, softened
> ¼ cup confectioners' sugar
> 1 teaspoon vanilla extract
> 2 cups all-purpose flour
> 1½ cups quick-cooking rolled oats (not instant)
> Confectioners' sugar

Cream butter and ¼ cup confectioners' sugar until light. Beat in vanilla. Add remaining ingredients, mixing until well blended. Shape in balls 1″ in diameter and put on ungreased cookie sheets. Bake in preheated 350°F. oven 13 to 15 minutes, or until browned on bottom. Roll in confectioners' sugar while still warm and repeat when cooled.

Old-Fashioned Peanut-Butter Cookies
MAKES ABOUT 3 DOZEN.

> 1 cup peanut butter
> ½ cup butter or margarine, softened
> ½ cup granulated sugar
> ½ cup packed brown sugar
> 1 egg
> ½ teaspoon vanilla extract
> 1½ cups all-purpose flour
> ¾ teaspoon baking soda
> ½ teaspoon baking powder

Cream peanut butter, butter, sugar, brown sugar, egg and vanilla until well blended. Stir in remaining ingredients, then chill several hours. Shape in logs about 1½″ long and ¾″ thick. Put on greased cookie sheets. Holding center of log with thumb and first finger, flatten with fork on each side, crisscrossing tine marks (cookie should resemble a large, flat peanut). Bake in preheated 375°F. oven about 10 minutes. Cool on wire racks.

Pecan Butterballs
MAKES ABOUT 4½ DOZEN.

    2 cups sifted all-purpose flour
    ¼ cup granulated sugar
    ½ teaspoon salt
    1 cup butter
    2 teaspoons vanilla extract
    3 cups finely chopped pecans

Sift flour, sugar, and salt; work in butter and vanilla. Add 2 cups nuts; mix well. Shape into 1″ balls. Roll in remaining 1 cup nuts. Bake on cookie sheets in preheated moderate oven (325°F.) for about 25 minutes.

Note Walnuts, almonds, or filberts can also be used. If desired, omit 1 cup of nuts, and roll cookies while warm in fine granulated sugar.

Raspberry Crescents
MAKES 24.

    1 cup all-purpose flour
    1 package (3 ounces) cream cheese, softened
    ½ cup butter or margarine, softened
    ¼ cup raspberry preserves
       Frosting (see below)

Combine flour, cheese and butter and knead with hands to form dough. Divide dough in half and shape each half in ball. Wrap and chill overnight. On lightly floured surface roll out each ball to about a 9″ circle. Cut each in 12 wedges. Put ½ teaspoon raspberry preserves on wide end of each wedge. Roll toward point and shape in crescent. Place point down on greased cookie sheet and bake in preheated 400°F. oven 10 to 15 minutes, or until golden brown. Cool on rack. Drizzle with Frosting. Store airtight in cool place about 10 days. Can be frozen up to 6 months.

Frosting Blend ½ cup confectioners' sugar with 2 teaspoons lemon juice, or enough to make a thin frosting.

Raspberry-Almond Cookies
MAKES 3 DOZEN.

>½ cup butter or margarine, softened
>⅓ cup sugar
>¼ teaspoon salt
>½ teaspoon vanilla extract
>1 egg, separated
>1 cup regular all-purpose flour
>¾ cup finely chopped blanched almonds
>Seedless raspberry jam
>Confectioners'-Sugar Frosting (optional; see p. 267)

Cream butter. Add next 3 ingredients and egg yolk and beat until light. Add flour and stir until well blended. Wrap dough in waxed paper and chill well. Preheat oven to slow (300°F.). Divide dough in 3 equal pieces. On lightly floured board, shape in rolls about 1″ in diameter. Cut rolls in ¾″ pieces and shape in balls. Dip balls first in slightly beaten egg white, then roll in almonds. Put on ungreased cookie sheets and press center of each cookie down with forefinger. Fill indentations with about ¼ teaspoon raspberry jam. Bake 20 minutes and remove to rack to cool. Decorate jam with a dab of frosting, if desired.

To Store Store airtight in cool place. Can be frozen. Good keepers and shippers.

Sesame-Seed Cookies
Easy cookies—crisp, with toasted sesame-seed flavor.
MAKES ABOUT 2½ TO 3 DOZEN 2″ COOKIES.

  ½ cup butter or margarine, softened
  ¾ cup sugar
  1 egg
  1 teaspoon vanilla extract
1⅓ cups all-purpose flour
1½ teaspoons baking powder
  ⅛ teaspoon salt
  3 tablespoons sesame seed

Cream butter and sugar. Add egg and vanilla and beat well. Add dry ingredients except sesame seed and mix well. Roll in balls the size of small walnuts and dip tops in sesame seed, flattening cookies slightly. Put 2″ apart on cookie sheets and bake in preheated 375°F. oven 8 to 10 minutes. Remove to racks to cool.

Little Butter S's
MAKES ABOUT 3 DOZEN.

  ½ cup butter, softened
  ⅓ cup sugar
  3 egg yolks, well beaten
  2 tablespoons milk
  ¼ teaspoon salt
1¾ cups regular all-purpose flour
  1 egg white, slightly beaten with
  1 tablespoon water
  2 tablespoons finely minced unblanched almonds mixed with
  1 tablespoon sugar

Cream butter. Add sugar and egg yolks and beat until light. Stir in milk, salt and flour until well blended. With lightly floured hands, gather dough into ball. Chill well. Preheat oven to slow (325°F.). Divide dough in 8 equal pieces and roll on lightly floured board into thin ropes less than ½″ thick. Cut in 3½″ pieces, tapes off ends and form in S shapes. While still on board, brush with egg-white mixture and press lightly into almond-sugar mixture. Put on lightly greased cookie sheets and bake 15 to 20 minutes. Remove to rack to cool.

Note Store airtight in cool place. Can be frozen. Good keepers but poor shippers.

Raisin Pfeffernuesse

MAKES ABOUT 8 DOZEN.

       1 box (15 ounces) raisins
       1 cup almonds
      ¼ cup cut-up citron
       2 cups all-purpose flour
       2 teaspoons cinnamon
       1 teaspoon ground cloves
      ½ teaspoon baking powder
      ½ teaspoon baking soda
      ½ teaspoon freshly ground pepper
      ½ teaspoon salt
       3 eggs
       2 cups packed light-brown sugar
          Confectioners' sugar

With fine blade of food grinder grind raisins, almonds and citron into bowl; set aside. Stir together flour, cinnamon, cloves, baking powder, soda, pepper and salt and mix into raisin mixture. In large bowl of electric mixer beat eggs and brown sugar until fluffy; stir into raisin-flour mixture and mix well with large spoon (dough will be stiff). Chill about 1 hour. With floured hands form 1″ balls and place 2″ apart on well-greased baking sheet. Bake in preheated 350°F. oven 10 minutes, or until cookies are brown on bottom but still soft on top. Remove to rack. While still warm, shake in bag with confectioners' sugar; cool. Store airtight at least 1 week before eating.

Spritz Cookies
MAKES ABOUT 6½ DOZEN.

2¼ cups regular all-purpose flour
¼ teaspoon salt
1 cup butter or margarine, softened
1¼ cups unsifted confectioners' sugar
2 egg yolks
½ teaspoon almond extract
1 teaspoon vanilla extract
1 egg white, slightly beaten
Colored sugar and Ornamental Frosting (see below)

Preheat oven to moderate (375°F.). Mix first 2 ingredients and set aside. Put butter in large bowl of electric mixer. Add confectioners' sugar and beat until light and fluffy. Beat in next 3 ingredients. Add flour mixture and beat just until blended. Fill cookie press with dough. Press dough in fancy shapes on ungreased cookie sheets. Bake 8 to 10 minutes. Remove to wire racks to cool. With egg white, brush areas to be sprinkled with colored sugar; sprinkle with the sugar. Decorate with tinted Ornamental Frosting.

To Store Store airtight. Can be frozen. Good keepers but poor shippers.

Ornamental Frosting In electric mixer, beat 1 egg white, 1 cup confectioners' sugar and ½ teaspoon cream of tartar until very thick but still capable of flowing easily through pastry tube. Add a little more sugar if necessary. Tint as desired.

Toasted-Almond Fingers
MAKES ABOUT 48.

    1 cup butter or margarine, softened
    ½ cup confectioners' sugar
    1 egg
    1 teaspoon vanilla extract
    2 cups sifted all-purpose flour
    ¼ teaspoon salt
    1 cup toasted almonds, finely chopped
    1 package (6 ounces) semisweet chocolate pieces
    1 tablespoon vegetable shortening
    Additional toasted almonds, finely chopped (optional)

Cream butter and sugar until fluffy. Add egg and beat well. Stir in vanilla. Add flour, salt and almonds and mix well. Wrap in waxed paper and chill until hard—about 30 minutes in freezer or several hours in refrigerator. Using measuring-tablespoonfuls of dough, shape in 2″ fingers and put on cookie sheet. Bake in preheated slow oven (325°F.) 17 minutes, or until done. Cool on wire rack. Melt chocolate and shortening over hot water. Carefully dip one end of each finger in chocolate and put on waxed paper to dry. Sprinkle with nuts, if desired. Store in cool dry place.

Vanilla Sesame-Seed Crescents
MAKES ABOUT 4 DOZEN.

    1 cup butter or margarine
    2 teaspoons vanilla extract
    ¼ teaspoon salt
    ⅔ cup sugar
    2¼ cups sifted all-purpose flour
    Toasted Sesame Seed (see below)

Blend together butter, vanilla, salt and sugar until light and fluffy. Stir in flour gradually to make a smooth dough. Chill dough until stiff enough to handle (about 1 hour). Shape into crescents. Roll in Toasted Sesame Seed. Place on cookie sheets about 1″ apart. Bake in a preheated moderate oven (350°F.) 12 to 15 minutes.

Toasted Sesame Seed Place seeds on a flat pan in a preheated moderate oven (350°F.) 20 to 22 minutes. Stir one or two times to toast uniformly.

Walnut Crescents
MAKES ABOUT 5 DOZEN.

> 1 cup butter or margarine, softened
> Confectioners' sugar
> 2 teaspoons vanilla extract
> ¼ teaspoon salt
> 1 cup chopped walnuts
> 1¾ cups regular all-purpose flour

Cream butter. Add ½ cup confectioners' sugar, the vanilla and the salt and beat until light. Stir in nuts and flour until well blended. Wrap dough in waxed paper and chill well. Preheat oven to slow (300°F.). Divide dough in 8 equal pieces. On lightly floured board, shape in thin rolls about ½″ in diameter. Cut in 2″ pieces, taper off ends and shape in crescents. Put on ungreased baking sheets and bake 18 to 20 minutes. Remove to rack to cool. Sift confectioners' sugar over tops.

To Store Store airtight in cool place. Can be frozen. Good keepers but poor shippers.

ROLLED COOKIES

Butter Thins
MAKES 50 TO 60.

  ½ cup butter, slightly softened
  ½ cup sugar
1½ cups unsifted all-purpose flour
  ½ teaspoon cream of tartar
  ¼ teaspoon baking soda
    Dash of nutmeg
  1 egg
  ½ teaspoon vanilla extract

Working with hands, cream butter and sugar until blended. Work in dry ingredients until smooth, then add egg and vanilla and mix well. Wrap in plastic wrap and chill 2 hours, or until firm enough to roll. Roll a small amount at a time on lightly floured surface until very thin. Cut in rounds with floured 2″ cutter and put on ungreased baking sheet. Bake in preheated slow oven (300°F.) 12 minutes, or until lightly browned. Remove to racks to cool.

Almond Butter Strips
MAKES ABOUT 6 DOZEN.

  ¾ cup butter
  ¼ cup, plus 2 tablespoons granulated sugar
  ½ teaspoon almond extract
  2 cups sifted all-purpose flour
  ⅛ teaspoon salt
  1 egg white, slightly beaten
  ⅛ teaspoon cinnamon
  ⅓ cup very finely chopped blanched almonds

Cream butter; add ¼ cup sugar and the almond extract; beat until light. Add sifted flour and salt. Chill for several hours, or until firm enough to roll. Roll to ⅛″ thickness. Cut in 1″ x 2″ strips with pastry wheel. Put on ungreased cookie sheets. Brush with egg white. Mix 2 tablespoons sugar, the cinnamon and almonds. Sprinkle on cookies. Bake in preheated moderate oven (350°F.) 8 minutes.

Apricot Foldovers
MAKES ABOUT 5 DOZEN.

> 2 cups regular all-purpose flour
> ¾ cup butter or margarine, softened
> 2 egg yolks
> 2 tablespoons sugar
> Apricot or other flavor preserves
> 1 egg, slightly beaten with 1 tablespoon milk
> Finely chopped nuts

Put flour in mixing bowl and make a well in center. Put thinly sliced butter, egg yolks and sugar in well. Work ingredients in well with fingertips until creamy. Gradually blend in flour. Sprinkle with 2 tablespoons very cold water, gather particles into a ball and flatten slightly. Wrap in waxed paper and chill well. Preheat oven to slow (325°F.). Cut dough in 2 equal pieces. Reserve one piece in refrigerator. Roll other piece on lightly floured surface (or use floured pastry cloth and stockinet) to about ⅛″ thickness and cut in 2½″ rounds. Repeat with second half of dough. Put rounds on lightly greased cookie sheets and, in center of each, put about level ½ teaspoon apricot preserves. Fold almost in half and pinch slightly around jam. Brush tops with egg mixture and sprinkle with nuts. Bake 18 to 20 minutes, or until golden brown. Remove to rack to cool.

To Store Store airtight in cool place. Can be frozen. Not very good keepers or shippers.

Filled Butter Rings

MAKES ABOUT 2 DOZEN.

    1 cup butter
    ½ cup granulated sugar
    3 cups sifted all-purpose flour
    ¼ teaspoon salt
      Apricot, raspberry or other preserves
      Confectioners' sugar (optional)

Cream butter; add granulated sugar; beat until light. Add flour
and salt. Roll to ⅛" thickness. Cut with floured, 3" cookie cutter.
Cut out centers of half of cookies with 2" cutter. Bake all cookies
on cookie sheets in preheated hot oven (400°F.) for 10 minutes, or
until lightly browned. Cool on wire racks. Spread whole 3" cookies
with preserves, piled higher at center. Top with cookie rings.
Sprinkle confectioners' sugar on rings, if desired.

Chocolate-Filled Almond Hearts

MAKES ABOUT 40.

    2¾ cups sifted all-purpose flour
    1 teaspoon baking powder
    ½ teaspoon salt
    ¾ cup butter or margarine, softened
    1 cup sugar
    3 eggs
    1 teaspoon vanilla extract, or ½ teaspoon each vanilla and
      almond extracts
      Blanched almonds
    ⅔ cup semisweet chocolate pieces, melted

Sift flour, baking powder and salt into bowl. Cream butter and
sugar until light and fluffy. Beat in 2 eggs and the flavoring. Add
sifted dry ingredients and beat until smooth. Chill 1 hour, or until
firm enough to roll. Roll a small amount of dough at a time on
floured board to ⅛" thickness. Keep remaining dough in the
refrigerator until ready to use. Cut in heart shapes, using a 2¼"

cutter. Beat remaining egg with fork and brush on half the cookies (about 20). Put a blanched almond in the center of each. Bake all cookies in preheated moderate oven (375°F.) 8 to 10 minutes. Remove to racks to cool. Spread cooled plain cookies with chocolate and top with almond-decorated cookies. Let stand until chocolate is firm. Store airtight.

Note Split almonds can be used, if preferred.

Christmas Tree Cookies
MAKES ABOUT 3 TO 4 DOZEN.

> ¾ cup butter
> 1¼ cups packed light-brown sugar
> 1½ teaspoons vanilla extract
> 1 teaspoon fresh lemon juice
> 2 eggs
> 3 cups sifted all-purpose flour
> 2 teaspoons baking powder
> ½ teaspoon salt
> Frosting (see below)

Cream butter, add sugar, and beat until light and fluffy. Add vanilla and lemon juice. Add eggs one at a time, beating well after each addition. Sift flour, baking powder and salt. Add to creamed mixture and mix well. Chill. Roll dough to about ⅛″ thickness. Cut into medium and small Christmas trees, using cookie cutter or paper pattern. Bake in preheated hot oven (425°F.) for 5 minutes, or until edges are lightly browned. Cool; cover with frosting; decorate.

Frosting

Heat and boil ½ cup butter in heavy saucepan until lightly browned; do not burn. Stir in 3 cups sifted confectioners' sugar and 1 teaspoon vanilla. Add a few drops of water until frosting is of spreading consistency. Frost cookies; then decorate with cake decorator, using colored frosting, and with colored sugar.

Note To stand, set each in large ring of bought jellied candies.

Cinnamon Cutouts
MAKES ABOUT 40.

>   2¼ cups all-purpose flour
>   ½ cup sugar
>   1 tablespoon cinnamon
>   1 cup butter or margarine, softened
>   1 egg, separated
>   Nut Topping (see below)

Combine flour, sugar and cinnamon in mixing bowl; with fork or
pastry blender cut in butter until particles are fine as cornmeal.
Stir in egg yolk just to moisten and quickly gather in ball; wrap
in waxed paper and chill 30 minutes. Divide dough in thirds and
roll each ⅛″ thick on lightly floured board. With cookie cutters
cut out desired shapes. Place on lightly greased cookie sheets, brush
tops with slightly beaten egg white and sprinkle with topping. Bake
in preheated 350°F. oven 10 minutes, or until lightly browned.
Cool on rack. Store airtight in cool place.

  Nut Topping Combine ¼ cup finely chopped nuts, 2 tablespoons sugar and ¼ teaspoon cinnamon.

Leckerli
MAKES ABOUT 6 DOZEN.

>   ½ cup honey
>   ½ cup sugar
>   ¼ teaspoon salt
>   2 teaspoons ground cloves
>   2 teaspoons cinnamon
>   ¼ cup finely diced candied orange
>   ¼ cup finely diced candied lemon peel
>   ¼ cup finely diced citron
>   1 egg
>   1 teaspoon baking soda
>   2 tablespoons brandy
>   1 teaspoon grated lemon rind

1 cup chopped blanched almonds
2¾ cups all-purpose flour
Glaze (see below)

Put honey and sugar in large heavy saucepan and bring to boil. Stir in salt, spices, peels and citron. Beat egg well and stir into mixture. Dissolve soda in the brandy and add to mixture with lemon rind, almonds and flour. Mix well, then knead in bowl or on board until well blended. Wrap in plastic wrap and chill 1 hour. Preheat oven to slow (325°F.). Cover cookie sheet with brown paper and grease. Roll dough on lightly floured board or cloth to a rectangle ½″ thick. Lift onto covered cookie sheet. Bake about 30 minutes. While still hot, brush with Glaze. Cut at once in 2½″ x 1″ strips and cool on wire rack.

Glaze In a small saucepan combine ½ cup sugar with ¼ cup water. Boil until syrup spins a thread when dropped from a spoon (234°F. on a candy thermometer).

To Store Pack in airtight container to ripen about 5 weeks before serving. Good keepers and shippers.

Molasses Ginger Cookies
MAKES ABOUT 9 DOZEN.

4 cups regular all-purpose flour
¼ teaspoon baking soda
½ teaspoon salt
1 teaspoon ground cinnamon
½ teaspoon ground cloves
½ teaspoon ground ginger
1 cup packed regular light-brown sugar
½ cup butter or margarine, softened
½ cup lard, softened
1½ cups light molasses
½ teaspoon cider vinegar
Ornamental Frosting (see below), colored sugar and tiny candies

In large bowl, mix first 6 ingredients. Add brown sugar and mix well. With pastry blender or 2 knives, cut in next 2 ingredients (or blend in with hands). Mix molasses and vinegar and gradually stir into mixture. Mix thoroughly, with hands if necessary; wrap in waxed paper or plastic and chill several hours or overnight (until firm enough to roll). Preheat oven to moderate (350°F.). Keeping remainder of dough refrigerated, roll a small amount at a time to 1/8" thickness, or less for very thin cookies. Cut with floured tree or other fancy cookie cutters. Bake on greased cookie sheets about 8 minutes (do not brown). Remove to cake racks to cool. Frost and decorate with sugar and candies.

To Store Store airtight. Can be frozen. Good keepers but poor shippers.

Ornamental Frosting In electric mixer, beat 1 egg white, 1 cup confectioners' sugar and 1/2 teaspoon cream of tartar until very thick but still capable of flowing easily through pastry tube. Add a little more sugar if necessary. Tint as desired.

Sugar Cookies
MAKES 9 TO 10 DOZEN.

      4 cups all-purpose flour
    1/2 teaspoon salt
      1 cup butter or margarine, softened
      1 cup sugar
      2 eggs, 1 separated
      1 teaspoon vanilla extract
      3 tablespoons lemon juice
         Ornamental Frosting, Tinted Coconut (see below), cinnamon drops

Mix first 2 ingredients and set aside. Cream butter and sugar until light and fluffy. Add whole egg and beat well. Add egg yolk and beat thoroughly. Beat in vanilla and lemon juice. Add flour mixture and mix thoroughly with wooden spoon. Divide dough in 4 parts and wrap each part in plastic. Chill several hours. Preheat oven to moderate (350°F.). On lightly floured board or cloth, roll one portion at a time to ⅛″ thickness. Cut with small floured doughnut or other fancy cutters and put on lightly greased cookie sheets. Slightly beat egg white and add 1 tablespoon water. Brush cookies with the mixture. Bake 8 to 10 minutes, or until very lightly browned. Remove to cake racks to cool. Decorate with frosting, Tinted Coconut, cinnamon drops, etc., as desired.

To Store Store airtight. Good keepers but poor shippers.

Ornamental Frosting In electric mixer, beat 1 egg white, 1 cup confectioners' sugar and ½ teaspoon cream of tartar until very thick but still capable of flowing easily through pastry tube. Add a little more sugar if necessary. Tint as desired.

Tinted Coconut Sprinkle 1 cup flaked coconut on waxed paper. Mix a few drops green or other food coloring with ¼ teaspoon cold water, sprinkle on coconut and mix with fingers until well tinted. Let stand until dry before using.

Crisp Honey Cookies
MAKES ABOUT 3 DOZEN.

> ½ cup butter or margarine
> ½ cup clover honey
> 1¾ cups all-purpose flour
> 1 teaspoon baking soda
> ½ teaspoon cinnamon
> ¼ teaspoon ground cloves
> ¼ teaspoon allspice
> ⅓ cup wheat germ
> Honey-Lemon Frosting (see below)

Cream butter and honey. Sift together flour, soda and spices and mix in wheat germ. Combine dry ingredients with creamed mixture. Chill about 1 hour. Roll on lightly floured board to about ⅛″ thickness. Cut with floured cookie cutter. Put on greased cookie sheets. Bake in preheated moderate oven (350°F.) 8 to 10 minutes. Cool on rack, then spread thinly with frosting.

Honey-Lemon Frosting

Mix ¾ cup confectioners' sugar, 1 tablespoon honey and about 1 tablespoon lemon juice or enough to make frosting of thin spreading consistency.

Assorted Decorated Lebkuchen
MAKES ABOUT 4 TO 5 DOZEN.

> ½ cup honey
> ½ cup molasses
> ¾ cup packed brown sugar
> 1 tablespoon grated lemon rind
> 1 tablespoon lemon juice
> 1 teaspoon cinnamon
> 1 teaspoon ginger
> 1 teaspoon nutmeg
> ¼ teaspoon allspice
> ¼ teaspoon ground cloves
> ¼ teaspoon salt
> ½ teaspoon baking soda
> 1 egg, well beaten
> 2½ cups all-purpose flour

In saucepan heat honey and molasses to just below boiling until bubbles appear at edges. Cool to lukewarm. In mixing bowl combine sugar, lemon rind, juice, spices, salt, baking soda and egg. Stir in honey-molasses mixture and mix well. Stir in flour until well mixed and smooth. Cover airtight and chill overnight. Pinch off a quarter of dough at a time, leaving remainder in refrigerator. On lightly floured surface roll out each quarter about ⅛" thick. Cut out desired shapes with cookie cutters dipped in flour. Place about 1" apart on well-greased cookie sheets. Press in desired decorations (see below). Bake in preheated 400°F. oven 10 to 12 minutes, or until light brown and just set. Remove at once to rack to cool. Store in airtight containers at least a week before serving.

Note Cookies can be used for Christmas ornaments. Make ¼" hole at top of each unbaked cookie. Run 6" colorfast cotton string through hole, tie ends, then bake.

ALMOND-CHERRY ROUNDS

Cut dough with 2¼" round cookie cutter. On each cookie press ½ candied red cherry in center and almond slivers in petal design.

CHRISTMAS WREATHS

Cut dough with 3" round cookie cutter, place on greased cookie sheet, then cut out center with 1" round cutter. Press in silver shots and cut-up mixed candied fruits.

CHRISTMAS TREES

Cut dough with Christmas-tree cookie cutter. Press in silver shots and cut-up candied fruits.

Fresh Orange Cookies
MAKES ABOUT 7 DOZEN.

    ½ cup shortening
    2 teaspoons grated orange rind
    ½ teaspoon ground mace
    1 cup sugar
    1 egg
    2 tablespoons fresh orange juice
    2 cups sifted all-purpose flour
    ½ teaspoon salt
    1 teaspoon double-acting baking powder

Cream together shortening, orange rind, mace and sugar until light and fluffy. Beat in egg. Add orange juice. Sift together flour, salt and baking powder. Stir into creamed mixture. Chill dough until stiff enough to handle. Roll out on a lightly floured board to ⅛″ thickness. Cut into fancy shapes with cookie cutters. Bake on ungreased cookie sheets in a preheated hot oven (400°F.) 8 minutes, or until lightly browned around the edges. Cool and frost with confectioners' sugar icing if desired.

Poppy-Seed Cookies
MAKES ABOUT 6 DOZEN.

        4 eggs
        ¾ cup sugar
        1 cup cooking oil
        ½ cup poppy seed
        4 cups sifted all-purpose flour
     1½ teaspoons baking powder
        1 teaspoon salt

Beat 3 of the eggs, the sugar and oil. Add seed and sifted dry ingredients; mix well. Roll thin on floured board; cut with desired cutters. Put on greased cookie sheets, brush with 1 beaten egg and bake in a preheated moderate oven (350°F.) 10 to 12 minutes.

Sand Tarts
MAKES ABOUT 2½ DOZEN.

        ½ cup butter, softened
        1 cup, plus 1 tablespoon sugar
        2 eggs, separated
        1 tablespoon milk
        ½ teaspoon vanilla extract
        ½ teaspoon salt
        1 teaspoon baking powder

1½ cups sifted all-purpose flour
15 unblanched almonds, split
¼ teaspoon cinnamon

Cream butter; add 1 cup sugar, the egg yolks, milk and flavoring; beat until light. Add sifted dry ingredients; mix well. Chill at least 3 hours. Roll dough very thin; cut with 3″ star cookie cutter. Put on greased cookie sheets; put a split almond on each cookie. Brush with unbeaten egg whites; sprinkle with 1 tablespoon sugar and the cinnamon. Bake in a preheated moderate oven (375°F.) about 8 minutes.

Spicy Molasses Cutouts
The dough must chill 24 hours before being rolled.
MAKES 8 TO 10 DOZEN.

1 cup butter or margarine, softened
1 cup sugar
1 cup light molasses
5 cups all-purpose flour
2 teaspoons baking soda
1 to 3 teaspoons ginger
½ teaspoon salt
½ cup cold strong tea
1 teaspoon vanilla extract
   Split almonds

Cream butter and sugar until light and fluffy. Beat in molasses. Add dry ingredients alternately with tea and mix well. Add vanilla. Chill at least 24 hours, then roll very thin on lightly floured board and cut in fancy shapes. Put on greased cookie sheets and decorate with almonds. Bake in preheated moderate oven (375°F.) 8 to 10 minutes.

Moravian Cookies
MAKES ABOUT 8 DOZEN.

    3¾ cups sifted all-purpose flour
    ¾ teaspoon baking soda
    ½ teaspoon salt
    ¾ teaspoon ginger
    ¾ teaspoon ground cloves
    ¾ teaspoon cinnamon
    ¼ teaspoon nutmeg
    ¼ teaspoon allspice
    1 cup molasses
    ½ cup butter
    ⅓ cup packed brown sugar

Sift flour, soda, salt and spices. Heat molasses and butter in large saucepan until butter is melted. Add sugar, and stir until dissolved. Add sifted ingredients; mix well. Chill several days. Roll out paper-thin on floured board, and cut into desired shapes. Bake in a preheated moderate oven (350°F.) about 6 minutes. Cookies improve on standing.

Springerle
MAKES ABOUT 2½ DOZEN.

    2 eggs
    ¼ teaspoon salt
    1 cup sugar
    2 cups all-purpose flour
    2 teaspoons crushed aniseed
    1 teaspoon grated lemon rind

Beat eggs and salt until light. Gradually beat in sugar, then continue beating until mixture is very thick and cream-colored. Add remaining ingredients, mix well and turn out on floured board. Knead a few turns, then roll or pat to ½″ thickness. To emboss designs, press floured springerle rolling pin or board firmly on dough. Cut around pictures and let stand overnight. Bake on greased cookie sheets in preheated 325°F. oven about 20 minutes (do not brown). Store in covered container at least 1 week before using. (An apple, quartered, in the container softens the cookies.) Can be frozen.

REFRIGERATOR COOKIES

Cardamom Cookies
MAKES ABOUT 10 DOZEN.

> 1 cup butter, softened
> 1 cup sugar
> 1 teaspoon ground cardamom
> ½ cup dairy sour cream
> 4 cups sifted all-purpose flour
> ¼ teaspoon baking soda
> ¼ teaspoon salt

Cream butter and sugar until light. Add remaining ingredients; mix well. Shape into two long rolls 2″ in diameter. Roll up in waxed paper, and chill overnight. Cut in ⅛″ slices; bake in preheated moderate oven (375°F.) 8 to 10 minutes.

Four-Leaf Clover Cookies

Refrigerator cookies flavored with chocolate and peanut butter.
MAKES ABOUT 12 DOZEN.

    ¾ cup butter or margarine, softened
    ½ cup smooth peanut butter
  1¼ cups sugar
    1 egg
    1 teaspoon vanilla extract
  2¼ cups all-purpose flour
  1¼ teaspoons baking powder
    1 square (1 ounce) unsweetened chocolate, melted and
        cooled
    ¼ cup finely chopped peanuts
    1 egg white, slightly beaten

Cream butter and peanut butter until light and fluffy. Gradually add sugar, beating well. Beat in egg and vanilla. Combine flour and baking powder and gradually add to first mixture. Turn out dough on lightly floured board and gather into ball. Divide dough in 2 equal parts. Work chocolate into 1 part until evenly mixed; work chopped peanuts into other. Divide each portion in 8 pieces, then shape in rolls ¾" in diameter, alternating chocolate and white rolls, brushing each with egg white and placing one on top of other to form logs of 4 rolls each. Roll logs in waxed paper and chill several hours, then cut in ¼" slices with thin, sharp-bladed knife (pinch rolls together if they separate while slicing). Put on lightly greased baking sheets and bake in preheated 350°F. oven about 10 minutes. Cool on racks.

Lemon Caraway Cookies

MAKES ABOUT 6 DOZEN.

    ½ cup butter, softened
    1 cup sugar
    1 egg
  1¼ teaspoons caraway seed

Grated rind of ½ lemon
2 tablespoons lemon juice
2½ cups sifted all-purpose flour
¼ teaspoon baking soda
½ teaspoon salt

Cream butter; add sugar and egg; beat until light. Add caraway seed, lemon rind, juice and sifted dry ingredients; mix well. Shape into a roll 2″ in diameter, wrap in waxed paper and chill for several hours. Cut in ⅛″ slices. Bake on greased cookie sheets in preheated hot oven (400°F.) about 10 minutes.

Butterscotch Maple Cookies

Good keepers and shippers. You brush them with maple syrup before baking.
MAKES ABOUT 40.

½ cup butter or margarine, softened
½ cup packed light-brown sugar
½ cup granulated sugar
1 egg
2½ cups sifted all-purpose flour
½ teaspoon salt
½ teaspoon baking soda
1 teaspoon cinnamon
Maple syrup
Almond halves

Cream butter and sugars until light. Beat in egg. Sift in flour with salt, soda and cinnamon. Stir until mixture forms a ball. Divide dough into 3 parts. Shape each on waxed paper in a roll about 2″ in diameter. Chill until firm. Cut in ¼″ slices. Put on greased cookie sheets. Brush with maple syrup. Place almond half on each cookie. Bake in preheated hot oven (400°F.) 10 minutes, or until golden brown.

Butterscotch Cookies
MAKES ABOUT 3 DOZEN.

 ½ cup butter or margarine, softened
 1 cup packed light-brown sugar
 1 egg
 1 teaspoon vanilla extract
 2 cups all-purpose flour
 ½ teaspoon baking soda
 ½ cup coarsely chopped walnuts

Cream butter and sugar well. Add egg and vanilla and beat until creamy. Stir in flour mixed with soda. Add nuts, mixing with hands if necessary. Pack in 9″ x 5″ x 3″ loaf pan lined with waxed paper. Chill overnight or longer. Slice about ¼″ thick and put on ungreased cookie sheets. Bake in preheated 400°F. oven about 8 minutes.

Crisp Almond Gingersnaps
MAKES ABOUT 6 DOZEN.

 1 cup butter or margarine, softened
 1 cup sugar
 ½ cup dark corn syrup
 2 teaspoons cinnamon
 2 teaspoons ground cloves
 2 teaspoons ginger
 1 teaspoon baking soda
 1 cup chopped blanched almonds
 3 cups all-purpose flour

Combine butter, sugar, syrup, spices and soda in large bowl of electric mixer. Beat until well blended and light. Stir in almonds and flour. On lightly floured surface shape dough in 2 logs about 10″ long. Wrap airtight and chill overnight. Cut in ⅜″ slices and bake on greased cookie sheets in preheated 325°F. oven until light brown (about 10 minutes). Remove to rack to cool. Store in airtight container in cool dry place.

Brown Sugar Wafers

These cookies should be large, round and thin. They are very crisp and almost melt in the mouth.

MAKES ABOUT 14 DOZEN.

    2 cups packed light-brown sugar
1½ cups butter, softened (not runny or whipped)
    3 eggs
    1 teaspoon vanilla extract
    6 cups all-purpose flour (instant type can be used)
  ½ teaspoon salt
  ½ teaspoon baking soda
  ½ teaspoon cinnamon

Cream sugar and butter, using electric mixer, if available. When blended, add eggs one at a time, beating well after each addition. Add vanilla. Mix remaining ingredients. Add the dry ingredients gradually to the creamed mixture. Do not overbeat; as soon as mixture is smooth, remove from electric mixer. Shape in 4 refrigerator rolls 2″ in diameter. Wrap in foil, chill and freeze. (If using the dough at once, chill and cut into ¼″ slices.) With the fingers, mash each slice thin and even it with palms. Or mash with the bottom of a glass tumbler. Cookies should be ⅛″ thick or less, Place 2″ apart on cookie sheets. Bake in preheated hot oven (400°F.) 3 to 5 minutes, or until cookies are done inside and lightly browned; break one open to test. Remove from oven, loosen cookies with a pancake turner and let cool to room temperature before serving or storing. After freezing, thaw dough until soft enough to slice and proceed as above. Store airtight.

VARIATION

You can also roll a small amount of dough at a time and cut with scalloped cutter. Bake as above and decorate with frosting, if desired.

Note To halve recipe use 1 whole egg and 1 yolk.

Index